The Whole Mind Book

A graduate of Manchester University, Denise Winn is a former editor of *Psychology Today* and also of *Mind Out*, a magazine about mental health published by MIND (the National Association for Mental Health). She is now a freelance journalist specializing in psychology and has contributed to the *Sunday Times, Observer, Guardian, World Medicine, Nursing Times* and *Spare Rib*. Her first book, *Prostitutes*, was published in 1974.

The
Whole Mind Book

An A–Z of Theories,
Therapies and Facts

DENISE WINN

FONTANA PAPERBACKS

First published by Fontana Paperbacks 1980
Copyright © Denise Winn 1980

A hardcover edition of this book is published by
Julian Friedmann Ltd in association with Fontana.

Made and printed in Great Britain by
Richard Clay (The Chaucer Press) Ltd, Bungay,
Suffolk.

Author's Note

It is with some trepidation that I offer up this book, as I'm already hearing in my mind's ear (if such a thing exists) howls of rage from parties with a vested interest in its subject matter. So, here is a coward's forenote, to offset some of the criticism before it hits home base.

The Whole Mind Book is designed to be an enjoyable canter from A–Z through all things psychological. So many psychiatric terms, psychological meanings and jargon words have found their way into our everyday speech that it seemed a good idea to try and de-mystify them all in one book. The aim is to explain simply and, I hope, interestingly, just what people mean when they talk about Oedipal complexes or primal therapy or acupuncture or paranoia; and to give a potted up-date on all we know about such mental phenomena as dreaming or hypnosis, memory or perception.

The canvas is necessarily extremely broad. If one is going to look at all things to do with the mind, that means delving not only into definitions of various mental disorders, but exploring paranormal phenomena, such as ESP and moving objects, explaining what goes on in the whole crop of fringe therapies that have sprung up since the sixties, looking at new learning systems that claim to open up new human potential and dabbling in the multi-faceted aspects of human emotions and behaviour.

No doubt specialists in particular areas will feel I have made certain omissions or misrepresentations, in my zeal to explain everything in 300 words or less; enthusiasts of particular systems or cults will accuse me of doing less than justice to their chosen hobby horse. I accept that they may both be right. Nor do I claim to be free from personal biases in what I have written. But this does not mean I have contorted facts to fit my own fancy. It means I have sometimes allowed myself the privilege of comment, which the reader can accept or reject as he or she wishes.

My aim has been to give a flavour of all the work and knowledge, all the beliefs and the baloney, that currently colour our understanding about how the human mind works. While the book aims to be comprehensive, anyone who finds their imagination fired by a particular item will have to search out detailed books on that subject to plumb the depths of its potential.

I should also like to point out that length of entry does not necessarily indicate importance that I have attributed to it. Some significant facts or theories are simple enough for me to explain them in few words. Other more obscure and perhaps more marginal items have demanded more space, in order to explain them at all. I have not given weight to my personal interests, tempting though it was. And if readers notice that certain topics crop up time and time again, that is because their impact has been wide-ranging in the psychological field.

Just as our minds are a mass of contradictions, so has been my experience of writing this book. It has been fun and frustrating; demanding and daunting; engrossing and enervating. But, most importantly of all, it has been completed and for that I am hugely indebted to the painstaking work of Andrew Jarvis, my editor at Julian Friedmann Publishers, who asked an awful lot of questions and made me think; and to Helen Fraser, my editor at Fontana, whose assistance and enthusiasm have been invaluable.

But this book only exists at all because of writer and musician Mick Farren, who came round one day and said, out of the blue, 'What about a whole mind catalogue?' So the idea was born. I hope you enjoy the results.

DENISE WINN

A

Abreaction

Abreaction is the sudden release of long pent-up emotions induced by some external force. The term was originally used by the early **psychoanalysts** to describe the emotional outpouring that sometimes resulted if they hypnotized a patient and then asked leading questions about certain events in his life that had caused him distress. In his relaxed, hypnotized state the patient would often let go of his defences and express freely for the first time the hurts, fears or anxieties that he had long ago repressed.

Later the term was adopted in mainstream psychiatry to describe a similar emotional reaction whereby recall of painful events was induced by drugs. It was particularly successful with shell-shocked soldiers during the Second World War as a cure for sudden, inexplicable paralysis or for complete loss of memory. Psychiatrists gave the soldiers a drug to induce a hypnotic (but not unconscious) state and then probed the patients about their experiences of war. With their resistance lowered by the drug, the soldiers eventually let go of their emotions and re-experienced the particular horrors of death or mutilation witnessed while fighting at the front which they had, till that time, tried to shut off from their conscious minds. Verbal expression of emotions was often accompanied by physical reactions, such as severe shaking, outbursts of violence and even fainting. Once all the painful, stored-up emotions had been expressed, the original paralysis or loss of memory disappeared.

Abreaction is only really useful in acute conditions such as these. It is not particularly effective with less dramatic long-term and deep-seated problems.

Acupuncture

Acupuncture is an ancient Chinese method of healing, an accepted form of medicine there for over 5000 years; but it has only recently begun to find serious acceptance in the West. There are now a number of British and American acupuncturists, and in France and Germany it is available on the national health service.

Although its exact origins are unclear, the Chinese discovered

7

that certain areas of the skin increased in sensitivity when there was something wrong with other parts of the body. By investigating these areas they found that a whole series of points (acupuncture points) could be linked with the malfunctioning organ. There are 800 acupuncture points on the body. These points form certain patterns and the line that links the points in any one series is called a meridian.

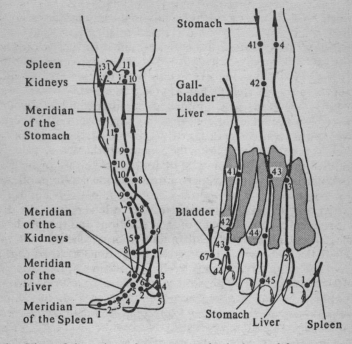

Fig 1.   View of the points of acupuncture in the leg and foot.

The meridians are seen as pathways through which energy flows – chi. In Chinese **Taoist** philosophy, **yin and yang**, the positive and negative life forces, make up the chi and if they are out of balance, illness occurs. To encourage the energy to flow easily again, long flexible needles made of copper, silver or gold, are inserted into the skin at specific points along the meridian. Needles inserted in parts of the feet, for instance, affect the condition of the liver. The result of the insertion is that specific nerves are stimulated to send electrical impulses to the brain and then to the diseased area. The needles are rotated to activate the points and are left there for up to twenty minutes, depending on the sensitivity of the patient.

Acupuncture has been particularly successful in the treatment of migraine, digestive troubles, ulcers, asthma, anxiety and depression. It claims some success too for helping heroin addicts kick the habit, for weight-loss and giving up smoking. In Chinese hospitals, it is commonly used as an anaesthetic agent: patients have actually sat up, wide awake, drinking tea, while having a lung removed!

It is not unknown as an anaesthetic in the West either and some doctors believe it could have a useful role to play during childbirth. It is not really known why acupuncture works in this way but a common view is that our bodies produce their own form of painkiller (see **pain**), and production is stimulated by the rotation of the needles. Another theory is that the rotation of the needles activates a part of the brainstem which is capable of blocking out pain signals and so eliminates the experience of pain completely. A patient's own belief in acupuncture as a reliable anaesthetic may well also help him to control the sensation of pain.

Addiction

A person is addicted to a drug if he is dependent on it in order to carry out his normal life. There used to be a distinction made between physically and psychologically addicting drugs but often it is impossible to draw a very clear line. Similarly, the word addiction was once used exclusively to describe a physical need for a drug – i.e., if the drug wasn't available, the individual would suffer physical withdrawal symptoms such as headaches, muscles cramps and vomiting; whereas *dependence* meant a psychological need for the drug. Someone who needs a drink in order to cope with social situations might have been described as dependent.

But the distinctions are not really meaningful because an addict will also have psychological need for a drug and the 'dependent' person will also suffer a little edginess if his lesser support is removed. So addiction and dependence now both refer to psychological/physical need for a drug.

When we talk of drug addicts, we tend to think of junkies, gasping for a fix. But the drugs which have the highest number of dependents are, of course, nicotine, alcohol and barbiturates (though these last are now less often prescribed as sedatives than they used to be). Tobacco and alcohol addiction cause definite physical damage to the body, barbiturates induce a heady, hazy state of mind and can lead to epileptic fits (and sometimes death) if withdrawn suddenly. A heroin addict, on the other hand, if forced to go cold turkey, would suffer physically but be extremely unlikely to die.

Heroin, morphine and opium are the so called 'hard drugs' which can, but don't always, create a physical dependence in the user and withdrawal symptoms when stopped. Psychedelic drugs, such as mescaline and LSD, often distort perceptions but don't cause withdrawal symptoms when stopped. Neither does the use of marijuana, although that doesn't mean that users won't become dependent.

Unfortunately, our bodies build up tolerance to drugs, so that larger and larger amounts become necessary to maintain the same effect. The one little drink before the guests arrive may become two or three, etc. Eventually, massive doses of a drug may only result in minimal changes of mood or physical state. This is what leads to serious addiction.

Various remedies for drug or drink addiction are available, including periods of assisted withdrawal in hospital, group therapy, **aversion therapy** (the addict learns to associate the addictive drug with electric shocks or nausea). But none of these treatments are totally effective. And treatment can never succeed if the addict doesn't want to be helped or doesn't believe he can be helped.

A negative attitude can be the most destructive factor. Research has shown that heroin addicts who positively decided that they did not want to be dependent on a drug all their lives could kick the habit without severe withdrawal symptoms at all. Whereas belief that the process will be painful and difficult will make it all the more so. So psychological elements play their part in defeating even physical symptoms.

People can also become addicted to activities, such as gambling and work (see **workaholic**).

Adler, Alfred
see **Neo-Freudians**

Adrenalin

A hormone produced by the adrenal glands to assist the body

in reacting to stress. It speeds up the heart rate and gears us for optimal physical and mental activity when we are under threat or facing some unpredictable situation. In short, it functions as a survival mechanism, triggering a reaction of fear or suspense. The adrenal glands also produce a hormone called *noradrenalin* which raises the blood pressure and also gears the body for action but this hormone triggers an aggressive, rather than a timid, response to danger and challenge (see **fight or flight reaction**). In colloquial usage we 'get the adrenalin going' when we are spurred into any sudden activity.

Ageing

We still know very little about the ageing process of the nervous system, the anatomical and biochemical changes that take place within it and affect the way our minds work as we grow old. For not every mental faculty seems to go into decline; our vocabulary store is much higher when we are older than when we are children but our reactions and the speed with which we process information seem to slow up. One theory is that the nervous system cannot extract information so quickly from the vast stores that are built up over a lifetime.

Regardless of our poor state of knowledge about the whys and wherefores of ageing, it seems to have been accepted up until recently that mental deterioration is inevitable and that it is a direct result of growing old. Now, new research challenges that view. Californian neuro-anatomist Marian Diamond says there is no convincing scientific evidence to show that we lose brain cells rapidly as we age. Her own experiments with rats show that the greatest decrease in cells occurs on reaching adulthood but from then on further decrease is negligible. The same might well be true of humans, she suggests.

Meanwhile, research carried out by the Russian Pyotr Anokhin, a leading student of Pavlov (see **conditioning**) indicates that our mental faculties could *increase* as we age. His work reveals the amazing potential of each individual neuron in our brains. Neurons, of which we each have ten billion, are complicated cells with branching prolongations which can connect with each other to transmit nerve impulses and information (see **nervous system**). Anokhin has shown that the more complicated activity we demand from our brains, the more connections the neurons are capable of making to deal with it.

Professor Mark Rosenzweig, at the University of California in Berkeley, has confirmed these findings by experiments on rats. Rats kept in large cages full of interesting objects to explore were found to have larger neuronal cell bodies and denser neuronal branching than other rats whose bodily needs only were met.

It is therefore possible that our brains deteriorate as we age because we come to expect less of them instead of more. People retire from work in their sixties, cease to play an important family role, become immobilized because of physical infirmities (thus reducing the amount of external environmental stimulus available to them) and generally come to feel that they have no further real contribution to make to life. Certainly old people's homes and hospital wards for the elderly offer little in the way of challenge or new experience. So it could be that, while we cannot prevent the ageing of our bodies, we are bringing psychological ageing upon ourselves.

Agoraphobia
see **Phobia**

Aggression

There is no doubt that humans are an aggressive species, but there is doubt about why. One of the most controversial questions in psychology is whether aggression in human beings is innate.

Sigmund **Freud** thought yes. He maintained that humans were governed by two basic instincts – one pushing us towards love, the other towards death – and that both were in perpetual conflict. When tension became too much, it was released through aggression. Freud said that unless aggression was channelled into acceptable outlets, such as sport or fantasy, it could express itself in war or turn inwards, resulting in suicide.

Konrad Lorenz, from his studies of animal behaviour, also maintains that aggression is instinctive. Most animals instinctively fight when their lives are threatened or their territory is attacked by other species but most do not fight to the death or kill other members of their own species. In most animals, according to Lorenz, there is some inbuilt inhibition against meaningless aggressive acts. Humans, however, have failed to develop it. The combination of this lack of inhibition and the development of sophisticated technological weapons of war make man the most dangerous of all species.

Behaviourists claim that aggression is not innate, but is learned. Parents who exhibit aggressive behaviour are likely to foster similar behaviour in their children. While it is by no means proven that this is the basis of human aggression, it is probably true that the degree to which we each control our aggression depends on our own experience and learning.

At one point, it became fashionable to link aggression with frustration; when we can't have what we want we vent our feelings violently. But this is, of course, only one possible *response* to frustration, so it cannot explain the basis of aggression.

Analyst Erich Fromm takes a totally different view. According to him, two completely different types of aggression operate in humans. Firstly, there is defensive aggression, as in animals, whereby we attack in order to defend ourselves. Secondly, we have what he terms 'malignant' aggression, known only to man. Humans have a need to love, to create, to be free and these needs are met in different ways in different cultures. But the more the species has evolved, the more we have come to understand about the universe, our minuscule role within it, our individual isolation and powerlessness. It is to fight this all-pervading alienation that we turn to aggression. For Fromm, contemporary so-called civilized society has increased alienation by reducing people to the status of small cogs in a large impersonal machine, where the only outlet for ensuing boredom and misery is aggression.

All of these theories leave questions unanswered and some researchers of both human and animal behaviour claim it is fruitless to look for one single cause for aggression, when it is so obviously a multi-dimensional response. But research, of course, continues.

Air Ions

Air ions are molecules of common atmospheric gases that have taken on a positive or negative charge. One cubic centimetre of air contains about ten million trillion uncharged particles and only a few thousand ions. But these ions are biologically active and affect all living matter, from bacteria to human beings.

Research has shown that air with a high ratio of negative to positive ions is beneficial for health while the reverse conditions cause considerable discomfort and even illness. Researchers at the Israel Institute of Technology, investigating the khamsin, a particular weather condition involving persistent wind and a fast rise in temperature, found that the positive ion concentration in the air increased before the khamsin's onset. The change coincided with reports of nervousness and physical discomfort. Investigation of the atmospheric conditions around health spas in France, Germany, Italy and the USSR, have revealed a high negative ion ratio.

Recent studies indicate that ions exert their influence on people through *serotonin*, a **hormone** that acts on the nervous system and is vital for maintaining our everyday awareness. Its level in the brain seems to fluctuate according to ion concentration in the air. If this is so, air ion generators may come to play a part in the treatment of anxiety. Negative ions reduce the amounts of serotonin in the brain and have a calming effect. Learning also appears to be affected by air ions; rats learn their way through a maze more quickly when the air is higher in negative ions.

Today, we are becoming all too accustomed to air unnaturally low in negative ions. Pollutants in the air combine with the ions and render them biologically inert. Even simple things such as dusting, cooking and the static electricity generated by synthetic fibres lower indoor levels of small air ions, according to American researchers Albert Krueger and Sheelagh Siegel. Investigators in Japan discovered that if they maintained workplace temperature, humidity and carbon dioxide at levels known to be comfortable but reduced ion levels, people soon started to complain of depression.

In the 1950s the first discoveries of air ion research led to the mass-marketing of air ion generators for which fantastic claims as cure-alls were made. Not surprisingly, they fell into disrepute. But Krueger and Siegel think the baby may have been thrown out with the bathwater. They say chronic ion deprivation does seem to cause lethargy, discomfort and a drop in general efficiency which correction of ion levels in the air may well be able to redress.

Alcoholism
see **Addiction**

Alexander Technique

Alexander is a technique for correcting destructive habits such as bad posture and bad breathing. Certain body actions, such as tensing the whole arm and shoulder, instead of just the wrist, when trying to open a bottle, can become so habitual that they end up as automatic reactions. We cease to be aware that there is any other way of going about things. The Alexander technique aims to make people conscious of bad body habits and regain control over them.

It has a curious history. At the end of the last century an Australian actor named F. M. Alexander developed trouble with his vocal cords that threatened his career. Because no doctor could come up with a cure, he had to help himself. He discovered, by means of endless investigations in the mirror, that when he recited he involuntarily jerked back his head, sucked in his breath and made a gasping sound. He found that ceasing to pull back his head had a good effect on his breathing and the functioning of his larynx. The result was the unlearning of a bad habit of which he previously had been totally unaware.

En route, he discovered that a correct head-neck-back relationship was vital for more than just his breathing; it affected the whole balance and poise of his body. Poor alignment caused tension in other parts of the body, leading to back ache, foot pain and even speech defects.

Alexander was so excited by the significance of his findings that he abandoned acting and devoted himself to teaching people how to unlearn bad body habits. He found that the best approach to the conscious inhibition of bad posture or behaviour patterns was not to strive to replace them with new patterns but to learn to relax and not strive at all.

Alexander coined the word 'end-gaining' to describe such zeal to achieve a chosen end that an individual will resort to means that, in fact, slow down his progress. Someone who tries so hard to see that he stares at an object instead of relaxing his eye muscles is an end-gainer. He ends up with strained eyes and the poorer vision for it. Another end-gainer is the over conscientious person who is so keen to complete all his work, and more, in record time that he puts himself under too much stress and in fact becomes less efficient.

Alexander pointed out that we don't often see our own restrictive body patterns and that exercise, which we blindly believe is good for us in itself, may just reinforce our physical defects if we don't re-educate our bodies. To change our habits we have to develop total awareness of our bodies; we have to change basics such as the way we sit, stand and walk.

Practitioners of the Alexander technique claim that it not only creates a better muscle-balance but a better mental balance too, as the two are inextricably linked. Increased tolerance, calmness, confidence and open-mindedness are amongst the benefits attributed to it.

Alpha Waves
see **Brain Waves**

Amnesia

A person suffering from amnesia suddenly forgets information about past events. This 'not remembering' is an unconscious attempt to stave off fear or anxiety about those events instead of facing them. A woman could forget, for instance, that she saw her small daughter run over by a car. The loss of memory could last for hours or it could last for months, depending on the person and the event he or she is repressing. But that same person might be quite capable of carrying out a normal job or daily routine. It is personal or emotional information that can't be recalled. In its severest form, people forget all information, including their name and address, and even wander off from home and take on a new identity. This extreme amnesia is known as the fugue state. The existence of such a state is a convenient aid to the scriptwriters of many TV thrillers, but it is not as common as they would have us believe.

Anal Phase
see **Psychosexual Stages**

Analytical Psychology
see **Jung**

Androgyny

Unpleasant though it may sound, it is no bad thing to be androgynous. It is a term coined by American psychologist Sandra Bem to describe a person who, instead of fitting the stereotype of a male or a female, has psychological characteristics of both.

Women have traditionally been stereotyped as the weaker, gentler sex – passive, vulnerable, emotional, timid, more suited to child-rearing than work in the 'real world'. Men, traditionally,

16

are meant to be tough, strong, ambitious, capable, dominant, protective – and they certainly mustn't cry.

With women increasingly taking on the traditional male roles as bread-winners and decision-makers, these stereotypes have become inhibiting and inaccurate – or they have perhaps always been. But traditions, alas, die hard. A great many people have set expectations about how men and women should behave, what work is 'men's' work and what characteristics are 'womanish'. And expectations are still generally lower for women. One experiment, in which psychologists and psychiatrists were asked to indicate the characteristics of a mentally healthy man, a mentally healthy woman and a mentally healthy adult of no specific sex, came up with alarming conclusions. Subjects of *both* sexes rated certain characteristics as healthy in a woman but unhealthy in an adult.

Sandra Bem's androgyny scale is an attempt to break away from stereotypes. She says that masculinity and femininity should not be regarded as being incompatible opposites. She treats them as separate characteristics found in both sexes, so that an individual can score high (or low) on both masculinity and femininity.

It has been found that people who are highly androgynous are likely to be well-adjusted, balanced and competent people. They seem to suffer fewer psychological problems, according to researchers such as British psychologist Jenny Williams and she suggests, therefore, that conforming to sex types may induce mental illnesses. Very feminine women, on the androgyny scale, are particularly prone to such problems. It also appears that, when meeting new people, androgynous types can communicate more easily than their less androgynous peers. Androgyny, says Bem, should be seen as the mark of psychological health; an androgynous man is not frightened to show his feelings; an androgynous woman can hold her own in the business world without losing any of her warmth.

Anorexia Nervosa

Anorexia is an enigmatic disorder that affects young women between the ages of fourteen and thirty. It is rare but not unknown in men. Superficially it involves resistance against eating, because of fears of putting on weight, and results in complete loss of appetite and severe weight-loss. But there are usually underlying emotional causes for the disorder. The sufferers become so obsessed with weight-loss, however, that their body image gets totally distorted: they see ugly excess fat whilst others see them as dangerously thin and under-nourished. Chronic anorexia in females can lead to cessation of periods.

There are many theories about the emotional causes of anorexia, the most popular being that the individual is using weight-loss as a way of resisting sexual maturity. By refusing to eat, the adolescent anorexic can prevent the development of the secondary sexual characteristics that start at puberty – the rounding of the breasts and thighs, for instance. However, whilst many young girls experience conflict about the onset of overt sexuality, far from all become anorexics. Some authorities believe that it is most common in homes where particular significance has been placed upon eating. Non-eating leads to parental concern and so it is a sure way to get attention or act out conflicts with parents in a way that is not openly hostile.

The refusal to eat may also be linked with non-sexual conflicts. One young girl worked hard at college but consistently obtained poor marks. She was also shy in social settings. By directing her attention to the avoidance of food, she was proving to herself that she could achieve certain goals she set herself, even if she couldn't meet those of her tutors. Her need to avoid food led her to avoid social arrangements which might involve eating, thus allowing herself to withdraw from company on that pretext instead of facing her shyness.

There are no easy ways to cure anorexia. But, because the condition can lead to severe starvation, it usually requires in-patient treatment, sympathetic encouragement to eat and the careful teasing out of underlying problems.

Anorexia nervosa is sometimes linked with the binge-diet syndrome. The sufferer doesn't eat for days, then suddenly cracks, raids the larder and eats a phenomenal amount of assorted foods. Self-revulsion after the event leads to forced vomiting and strict abstinence from all food for the next week or so.

This same syndrome is also evident in women who are *compulsive eaters*. Although they may never dwindle down to dangerously twig-like proportions, their obsession with not eating (in order to lose weight) and then over-eating is very akin to the behaviour of the anorexic. Compulsive-eaters go through the same routines of avoiding food, then eating everything in sight, being overcome with self-loathing and attempting to induce vomiting or taking high quotas of laxative pills. The over-eating is usually a secret activity and occurs when the individual is emotionally upset. And it is as hard to break the pattern as it is for the anorexic – harder, perhaps, because other people may never know the problem exists. It is quite possible to maintain a normal weight whilst spending one's life over-eating on a grand scale and then starving for days to compensate.

It is now felt that such a grossly disordered eating pattern warrants medical attention just as much as anorexia itself and represents a middle state between anorexia and the impulsive over-eating that leads to obesity.

Anti-Depressants
see **Psychotrophic Drugs**

Anti-Psychiatry

The anti-psychiatry (or radical psychology) movement expressed a reaction, particularly strong in the 1960s, against traditional methods of treating mental illness. During the fifties it had become more and more apparent that patients confined to mental hospitals didn't undergo miraculous changes, they developed other undesirable behaviour traits that were created by the hospitals themselves. The patients became institutionalized. They were left to sit around like vegetables, were treated as if they were idiots, were given no mental or visual stimulation and became extremely dependent, because they no longer needed to take any responsibility for themselves.

The views of two controversial psychiatrists very much sparked the anti-psychiatry movement into action. Scottish psychiatrist Ronald Laing claimed that schizophrenics, far from being mad, were seeking sanity in an insane society. Too sensitive to accept the conditioning and automatism that arises from conforming to societal standards, they experienced conflict that led to 'break-down'. Laing posited that what we call schizophrenia is really the attempt of certain people to 'break through the cracks in our all too closed minds'. Instead, therefore, of being herded into hospitals and regarded as insane, such people should be enabled to go through their crisis and emerge anew. Drugs, he said, suppressed the agony of conflict but prevented an individual from achieving growth and change.

Laing was particularly critical of the traditional psychiatric approach to 'ill' individuals. In his writings he graphically depicted

19

the case of a man who was placed before a hall of students as a case-study in a lecture. The psychiatrist pointed out his incoherent mumblings as signs of his confusion. But Laing realized that the mumblings were not incoherent. They were hostile, almost sarcastic, reactions from the patient at being treated like an inanimate object.

Laing followed up his ideas by setting up communes where people in severe stress and conflict could go through their suffering with the support of other people and therapists. Other psychiatrists, inspired by his methods, have adopted and refined his approach. A number of such crisis centres or long-term 'homes' still exist and flourish (see also **therapeutic community**). But many have criticized Laing's methods as being ineffective in the long run.

American psychiatrist Thomas Szasz, like Laing, rejects psychiatric labels and the humiliation of being hospitalized. He believes that mental hospitals are just a modern version of the old asylums, using chemical straitjackets instead of physical ones and applying words like schizophrenic or psychopath instead of witch. A person can be committed to a psychiatric hospital against his will; to be deemed sufficiently insane by certain other people is enough. Mental hospital staff are inquisitors, says Szasz, agents of the state, who help to correct the attitudes of those who don't conform to social norms.

Much sympathy with these views has been found with a vocal minority, ex-mental patients who have experienced the degradation of being pumped with drugs, treated as if they were too stupid to understand what was going on and fobbed off as 'hostile' or 'paranoid' if they tried to express themselves or complain. The rights of mental patients have at last become an important issue, fought for by patients themselves and voluntary organizations with them. Sentiments such as these, expressed by patients in a British mental health magazine, *Mind Out*, show how much there is still to be done:

> What upset me most was the difficulty in getting the staff to hold an intelligent conversation and answer questions and explain what was being done and why. They seemed to assume that one had neither the right nor the intelligence to be told what was happening. They tended to treat patients in a very impersonal way, as so many chemical specimens.

The whole institutionalising process was a humiliating experience stripping one of identity rather than equipping one for living.

Anxiety

Everyone experiences anxiety at some time or other since it is perfectly normal and natural to do so. Yet anxiety symptoms are often seen as a signal that something is 'wrong' with us. It is only when anxiety is experienced for no apparent or logical reason that it may warrant some kind of medical attention.

Anxiety is a feeling of uneasiness and inner tension, apprehension or even fear. In its severer forms it may be accompanied by any of a number of physical sensations such as sweating, weakness, nausea, palpitations of the heart, goose-pimples, diarrhoea, indigestion, feelings of constriction and draining of colour. Sometimes a very anxious person can experience severe and frightening muscular spasms but these can be alleviated quite easily by breathing in and out of a paper bag, to build up carbon dioxide levels.

None of these unpleasant sensations would be thought odd if you were confronted with a large bear rampaging round the front garden. It is said, in fact, that anxiety symptoms evolved as a way of getting the body on the alert for fight or flight, to deal with just such situations. Although nowadays such physical dangers are few, we still have the mechanism which is triggered by mental stresses instead of physical ones. When we are socially or emotionally threatened, we often experience exactly the same anxiety reaction that was once appropriate for facing dangers in the wild.

People vary enormously in the amount of anxiety they experience and the kinds of situations that provoke it. While a steeplejack will nonchalantly work hundreds of feet above the ground, most people feel a little uncomfortable about heights and some may be petrified to such an extreme that they won't even climb a ladder.

This last is an example of abnormal anxiety, i.e., anxiety that occurs in excess in situations that leave most others unmoved or just slightly tense. This is usually called phobic anxiety. People can be phobic about particular things, such as dirt, animals, knives or broken glass, or about places, such as confined or open space. Such **phobias** can usually be treated successfully by **behaviour therapy** and **biofeedback** techniques.

A second abnormal form of anxiety is *free-floating anxiety,* so called because there is no apparent reason for the feelings of panic experienced. Freudians maintain that this is simply the result of repression of anxiety-inducing feelings or experiences. The cause of the anxiety becomes successfully hidden from consciousness but the anxiety itself still exists.

We often try to defend ourselves against anxiety feelings instead of facing them. The man who is nervous about his sexual performance may brag instead that he is a great stud. The woman who feels inferior in her relationship with a man may try to avoid her discomfort by claiming that *he* is inferior (see **defence mechanisms**). Much therapy is geared towards encouraging a person to get in touch with the root cause of the anxiety and express it, instead of using these avoidance tactics and building up barriers.

We don't know for sure what causes abnormal anxiety. There are, of course many theories: painful early childhood experiences, conditioned anxiety (a child who gets burned by a fire may fear even a lighted match); guilt about sex; high expectations about personal performance; even a freak of biochemistry. However, only when our anxiety is a disabling experience is it a real problem and, even then, talking to a friend may be as valuable as any psychiatric treatment to reduce it.

Aphasia
see **Brain Damage**

Aptitude Test
see **Personality**

Archetypes
see **Jung**

Armouring
see **Reichian Therapy**

Artificial Intelligence

Over the past few years, advances in computer technology have opened up exciting new possibilities to researchers involved in **cognitive psychology**. It may seem strange that a computer can play a useful part in helping a psychologist find out how the mind works and what actually goes on when we see and recognize an object, memorize an experience or list, or think out solutions to problems. But programmes that enable computers to carry out complex tasks may in fact throw light on the processes we use to handle information in our brains.

Artificial intelligence refers specifically to the development of sophisticated programmes which enable a computer to act seemingly with an intelligence of its own; to play chess, to work out problems, even to hold interviews. A vast amount of varied information has to be fed into the computer to enable it to apply even the simplest concepts successfully. By finding out what information a computer needs to know in order to act intelligently, we may in fact be identifying the kinds of information we need to act likewise. We can actually isolate these processes from the rest of our sensory input and learning behaviour by testing them on a clean slate – the computer. This, say the psychologists, could take us leaps forward in understanding the mind.

Assagioli, Roberto
see Psychosynthesis

Assertiveness Training

Do you feel embarrassed about taking shoddy goods back to a shop? Do you see red if someone jumps ahead of you in a queue but say nothing? Do you think you have to put up with your neighbour's muddy footprints on the white carpet because it wouldn't be very nice to ask him to use the mat? So maybe you need some assertiveness training.

Assertiveness training (or, perhaps, The Art of Not Feeling Guilty) was developed by American Andrew Salter in 1949, but it is only in recent years that it has become really popular in America and Britain. It has been used for example by the women's movement in an attempt to teach women that they *do* have the right to say no, for, generally, women have been conditioned to be relatively passive, to deny their own feelings; men, on the other hand, have been conditioned to be more aggressive. Of course there are aggressive women and passive men. But the ideal goal for both sexes is to be *assertive*; taking account of their own and other people's feelings and, in the process, preserving self-esteem.

Assertiveness training takes people through the kinds of situations in which they find it difficult to assert themselves and helps them to do so.

Assertiveness training shows how often we allow ourselves to be manipulated into feeling guilty, giving in to unreasonable requests and then harbouring hostilities and resentments. It teaches people to change their expectations and their behaviour, but not by delving into their guilty pasts; it simply encourages a more assertive approach, first during therapy, then out in the 'real' world. Lack of assertiveness often comes from not wanting to upset people because it will result in our not being liked. Assertiveness training shows that, by being clear about ourselves, our needs and our expectations, people will like and respect us more.

Astrology

Astrology is concerned with the relationship between man and the planets, particularly the influence that the planets exert over man's character. Horoscopes in popular newspapers, with their bald predictions that all Scorpios will feel thwarted and anxious that day whilst everything is going right for Aquarians, are rough to say the least. Serious casting of horoscopes involves complex calculations of exact planetary positions at one's time of birth, infinitesimal differences which supposedly affect an individual's psyche.

For a horoscope, a circle is drawn, and divided into the twelve constellations that make up the signs of the zodiac – Aries, Taurus, Gemini, etc. These constellations, exactly thirty degrees apart and lying along the path of the sun, are the means by which the position of the sun, moon and other planets can be measured. The circle is also divided into twelve unequal 'houses' representing different departments of life. One may govern personality, another money and finance, others, parents, journeys, health, marriage, profession, etc. The planets which are present in these houses at one's birth determine our 'fate' in those departments. Each planet represents a force or characteristic: Jupiter represents cheerfulness, for instance, Saturn, pessimism, Mars, violence and Neptune, nervous agitation and catastrophe.

The constellation in which the sun appears to rise on the day of a person's birth determines his sign of the zodiac. The sun sign is most important in character formation, say the astrologists, but also highly important is the position of the moon and the

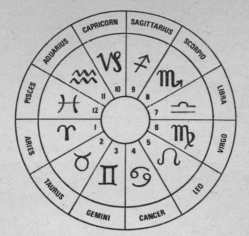

Fig 2. Astrology: the twelve houses and their signs.

rising sign: the sign that is against the eastern horizon at the moment of birth, as the earth rotates on its own axis.

Scientists have long looked askance at the workings of astrology and refuse to give it credence. But French psychologist Michel Gauquelin found, against his better judgement, that there's more to planetary influence than meets the eye. Although he rejects there being any significance in the signs of the zodiac themselves, he is intrigued by the power of planetary positions at birth. He and colleagues undertook rigorous analysis of the birth charts of people eminent in a particular field. They found that successful doctors, for instance, seemed remarkably prone to be born when Mars or Saturn had just about reached the horizon or reached its peak in the sky for that day. Amazed to say the least, they repeated their experiments with other groups and found similar pre-dominances of particular planets.

As there is a classic list of traits that are usually found in members of particular professions (tested by psychologists who have studied personality and career choice), Gauquelin supposes there might be some link between personality traits and particular planets. Relatively exhibitionist actors, for instance, were born twice as often as others when Jupiter had just risen; Saturn appeared more often at the birth of modest, self-absorbed scientists.

Gauquelin can't explain it, nor how the planet actually gets its influence into a child. And why is birth more important than the moment of conception? But as technical progress has made it possible, over the last couple of decades, to detect gravitational and magnetic variations emanating from the planets, it isn't so altogether ludicrous he says, to imagine invisible connections between biology and psyche.

Attention

The concept of attention-giving and attention-receiving is a fairly modern addition to the Western psychological vocabulary, although, it has long been a well known concept in the East. We are all now familiar with the attention needs of children, for instance, but some of the more subtle consequences of attention giving and getting still need investigation. In the late twenties, it took some American psychologists over a year before they realized that the marked increases in productivity in the workplace they were observing were due not to their introduction of rest-breaks or changed hours but to the attention that they themselves were paying the workers! (See **Hawthorne effect**.)

Attention theory has been most cogently formulated in the writings and university lectures of Idries Shah. He has shown how often all manner of business transactions, affiliations to causes, public gestures of generosity and adherence to belief systems are really disguised sources of attention getting.

If we seek attention consciously, it will enable us to be more efficient in our lives. Acknowledging and deriving attention from suitable sources frees us to fulfil other functions without a disguised attention-need factor confusing the issue.

Attention-getting, when it's appropriate, can have wondrous effects. The shy girl who suddenly comes to people's notice when she demonstrates a skill at chess may learn to develop a new self-confidence which she can carry over into other parts of her life. But the person who joins a group is in fact often really just seeking the attention that comes from being a part of it. Many people join cults and strange sects because they inherit an instant family, an immediate source of attention. They maintain their new belief system and defend it because it is their attention source and they can often, as a result, be persuaded to take actions which they would never have contemplated otherwise.

People who write to film stars, or youngsters who establish themselves as groupies, are seeking the attention that comes from reflected glory. They might be better nourished if they recognized that their basic need is for attention and derived it from a source where the exchange might be mutual.

The effects, therefore, of attention-getting on our behaviour and our learning processes can be extremely far-reaching.

Attraction

Why are we strongly attracted to some people and not to others? It is a question that has intrigued psychologists for years and such research that exists only shows that there is no simple answer.

One fairly obvious reason for attraction to particular individuals is similarity of interests. People like those who share their views or who enjoy doing the same things. It is a form of self-validation. But, on the other hand, the saying that 'opposites attract' is not without truth. Often complementary characteristics – one person being a talker, the other a listener, for example – lead to a fulfilling relationship. There is respect and mutual appreciation for the other person's abilities.

Mutual appreciation is a strong factor in attraction. We tend to like people who like us. Sometimes just the fact that we know someone likes us is what makes us start to like them. Such feelings become all the stronger when our own egos are bruised by some one or something else. An experiment with students illustrated this: a number of women, at separate times, were asked to sit in a waiting room until they were called in for some tests. As each one sat alone, she was approached by a good-looking male student who told her how attractive he found her and asked if they could go out together. Then the woman was called in for a personality test and was rated either positively or negatively. Afterwards she was asked, in her turn, to rate the personality of someone she had met in the waiting room – there had, of course, only been the young man. Those that had been given an ego-bashing in their own scores were particularly praising about the man's qualities! He after all had found them attractive.

We also tend to be attracted by, and admiring of, other people's talents. But while research shows we like men or women who have keen minds, are stimulating conversationalists, are good at practical things and fun to be around into the bargain, we are a bit wary of perfection – perhaps because, unconsciously, we are measuring ourselves up against them. Experiments demonstrate that we like super-able people better if they have some down-to-earth failing – e.g. occasional clumsiness. But we like people of average abilities *less* if they show the same weaknesses.

Some aspects of attraction have a very practical root. Proximity, for instance. Research shows that the vast majority of married couples lived within a mile of one another when single. And familiarity can also be an influential factor when it comes to finding someone attractive. American researcher Robert Zajonc showed a number of students a stack of photographs of young people. Some individuals' pictures cropped up five, ten, fifteen or twenty-five times in the same batch. When asked later whom they found most attractive, the students tended to plump for those whose faces they had seen most frequently.

But of all kinds of attraction, the physical variety is the most inexplicable. Why is it that some people feel an overwhelming sexual attraction for each other but often don't even like each other as people or can't be together for five minutes without arguing? The popular explanation at the moment is pheromones, substances we all produce and emit as an odour and which attract the opposite sex. We know that female monkeys produce pheromones called copulins and these are in highest concentration around the time of ovulation. But humans are unconscious of their own odours, although experiments show that we respond to them, even without knowing.

Researchers sprayed some theatre seats with male pheromones, some with female ones. Women gravitated to the former, the men to the latter. And, in some Mediterranean countries, men entice women to dance with them by dangling before them their handkerchiefs, having first impregnated them with their own smell by holding them under their armpits. They may not know about pheromones but the ploy must obviously work. However, most thinking about the power of pheromones is somewhat speculative at the moment, even if the experiments are fun.

Whatever the cause, physical attractiveness is a powerful quality and, unfair though it may be, most people are attracted to those they find physically extremely appealing. And, in new situations, physical appeal is more readily discernible than a shared interest in, say, Moroccan leather. However, despite initial attraction, research shows that we usually end up with partners who are fairly equal in attractiveness to ourselves.

Autism

Autistic children look quite normal and move without awkwardness. But their ability to communicate or relate to others is profoundly impaired. A large number cannot speak at all, few cry or coo as babies, they fail to imitate adults' gestures or facial expressions and make no move to reach out for affection. They seem to live in an inner world of their own, happy to spend hours watching a spot on the wall or simply staring into space. However, although they are totally disconnected from the larger world they live in, they do become upset if anything in their familiar environment is altered in any way.

Autistic children used to be thought mentally handicapped or schizophrenic, especially as some autistic children show violent behaviour such as inexplicably banging their heads repeatedly against a wall. Now few professionals believe that the causes are emotional and are instead looking for a neurological basis. About 4·5 in every 10,000 children are autistic.

It is easy to see how other-worldliness which prevents an autistic child from imitating actions and therefore learning simple tasks like how to tie a shoelace might well have been mistaken for mental retardation. The real irony is that very many autistic children are almost geniuses in some single area of expertise. Some compose music at a very early age, or have exceptional memories or an incredible grasp of mechanical workings. How can this be so?

Bernard Rimland, director of the Institute for Child Behaviour Research in San Diego, has a theory. He notes the autistic child's intense capacity for concentration in the chosen field and compares it with the absorption of recognized geniuses: Newton, for instance, once went down to his wine cellar during a dinner party to bring up a new bottle, and didn't return. Eventually, guests found him solving equations in the dust on a wine keg. He had been seized by an inspiration that he had to explore at once. Everything else was forgotten. Rimland believes autism too is connected with involuntary concentration, but with autistic children, it is permanent.

When we concentrate, we have to cut ourselves off from distracting elements in the environment around us. We can watch a film, taking in all the elements on the screen, rather than concentrating on the pupil of one actor's left eye. We cannot do both at the same time. The more specific the target of our concentration, the more we have to narrow our field of vision. Fortunately, we also have the survival mechanism of involuntary distraction. We can be deep in thought and suddenly come to our senses in time to realize that we're about to step off a cliff!

Autistic children, suggests Rimland, do not have these choices or distractions. They can only achieve intense concentration to detail and at the expense of a sense of background environment. There seems to be some disorder of the mechanism in the brain that controls attention span. For they can zero in on detail but they can't zero out. Rimland believes that if we can isolate the site of impairment in autistic children's brains, we will in the process learn much about our own.

Aversion Therapy

Aversion therapy is a form of **behaviour therapy**. It is a method of changing behaviour which is thought, by the person with the habit or by society, to be undesirable. The process works by forging unpleasant associations with the undesirable behaviour trait concerned and has come in for no little criticism because there is no attempt to replace those traits with acceptable ones. (In the film *Clockwork Orange*, a young thug was taught to find aggression distasteful and, as a result, lost the ability to defend himself in situations where it was actually warranted.)

Aversion therapy can only work at all if the patient has the motivation to *make* it work. It can't be effective if he is undergoing it against his will. Many so-called sexual deviants, such as fetishists, transvestites and paedophiles, have sought it as an aid to changing their proclivities and it has also been used, with less success, to combat excessive eating or drinking or smoking.

The aim of aversion therapy is to attach negative feelings to stimuli that are found inappropriately attractive. A fetishist, for example, may want to curb his attraction to women's underclothing. So the therapist (usually a psychologist) will show the patient pictures of panties or slips, or give him some to hold, and at the same time administer him an electric shock. The intensity of the shock is controlled by the patient. If the treatment is successful over a period of time, the fetishist will associate women's underwear with mild pain rather than pleasure.

Imagination can often be used to reduce attraction or addiction, instead of shocks. For example the alcoholic has to imagine himself taking a drink and force himself to feel nauseous at the same time. On seeing himself take a swig, he has to imagine being violently sick. By practising that his attraction to drink may after a while be reduced – but the motivation to succeed has to be very strong.

Success with aversion therapy is limited. As mentioned above, to say nothing of the ethical question of giving electric shocks for such a purpose, it does not replace undesirable behaviour with anything else. And many people, when back in the environment of drinkers of smokers, soon find new reinforcement for their old activities.

B

Barbiturates
see **Psychotropic Drugs**

Behaviour Therapy

Behaviour therapy is based on the view of psychologist John Watson that we can learn to change any behaviour if we are taught to respond in a new and different way to a situation that prompts it (see **behaviourism**). For instance, we can *learn* to pat alsations on the head even if, before, we trembled at the sight of one in the distance. The fault lies in our original conditioning and not in our stars. The behavioural therapist is therefore concerned to change actions and responses, not to locate and analyse underlying causes for those actions and responses.

There are a large number of treatments which fall under the general umbrella term of behaviour therapy, alternatively called behaviour modification (see **conditioning**, **aversion therapy**, **assertiveness training**). But all have one feature in common: they are based on learning. Three important elements here are *reinforcement*, *conditioning* and *extinction*. If a mother picks up a child every time it cries, the child will learn that this is the way to get attention. The mother is reinforcing the validity of this connection every time she picks him up. Consequently, every time he wants attention – at night, say, instead of going to sleep, the child will start crying and keep crying. The mother must change this negative reinforcement (crying always leads to attention) to positive reinforcement (attention comes if the child has been good at night

31

and didn't scream. The next morning he gets praised and cuddled). As the child learns that it is good behaviour rather than bad that leads to attention, he is being conditioned. The end result is that the child stops crying at night. The connection between that and attention has been extinguished.

Many such forms of behaviour modification are just plain commonsense. But they have been introduced systematically into psychiatric practice by psychologists and some psychiatrists to try, where necessary, to improve on these common-sense ideas. One such method is called *desensitisation* and it is the most popular and widely practised. It is commonly used with **phobias**. The patient is exposed in small, graduated doses to the activity that causes him anxiety so that it ceases to induce a panic reaction.

For example, the person who is frightened of going outside his home – an agoraphobic – is asked to provide a hierarchy of situations that alarm him. At the top might be shopping alone in town, at the bottom, walking down the front path. The therapist starts at the bottom of the list, and walks with the patient down his front path, after training him how to relax and cope with the anxiety if it arises. Gradually, and with home practice, the patient moves up through the list and slowly overcomes his phobia.

Sometimes imagination is enough. A person with a spider phobia is asked to imagine climbing a similar hierarchy of fears – first, one spider in the bath, finally a whole horde of them. In all such cases the patient is learning not to reinforce his fear by avoidance but to reinforce the realization that, if he goes out alone or sees a spider, nothing terrible happens. This approach can work for **obsessions** too.

Another method of behaviour therapy is *flooding*. Here, instead of working through a hierarchy, the patient opts to jump in at the deep end and, with the therapist's help, face his worst fears all at once. The traumatic experience is repeated until he overcomes his fear. This method is less pleasant and less often chosen by a patient, but its advantage is speed. It seems, however, that its effects are not as long-lasting.

All forms of behaviour therapy require the co-operation of the patient, say the behaviourists. This is their main defence against the not uncommon criticism that behaviour therapy is potentially manipulative; that it allows therapists to decide what is or what is not desirable behaviour and can be abused as a tool to instil conformist attitudes and responses.

Behaviourism

If psychology is now considered a science – and there are sceptics who still dispute that – it is largely because of the (behaviourist) ideas of American psychologist John Watson. In 1913 he reacted against the current vogue in psychology by declaring it ridiculous to try to get to grips with such intangibles as mental states and consciousness. It was impossible, he said, to put one's finger on emotions or ideas, but it *was* possible to identify the circumstances that induced certain emotions and ideas. Therefore, the only way to make psychology a useful science was to pay attention simply to that which could be observed, measured and recorded: in other words, behaviour. You can't 'measure' a thought, he said, but you can observe and draw conclusions from behaviour that results from a certain thought. Behaviourism was born.

Watson was particularly influenced by the work of Russian physiologist, Ivan Pavlov, who showed it was possible to condition behaviour (see **conditioning**). Pavlov noticed that dogs salivate when food is brought, and tried ringing a bell whenever he brought food. Eventually the dogs made the association and salivated at the sound of a bell alone. These discoveries led Watson to believe that all behaviour is a learned response to a stimulus and that if we could only discover which specific events triggered specific behaviour reactions, we could learn to make the world a better place.

Professor B. F. Skinner, the most influential of later behaviourists, does not, like Watson, ignore the existence of heredity and inner mental processes, but he does hold that all our thoughts, feelings and behaviour are effectively shaped by society and experience. Whether an action or an attitude becomes an established part of our individual 'repertoire' depends on whether that action or attitude brought pleasant or unpleasant consequences the first time round.

Behaviourism has been attacked because it presents such a limited cause-and-effect view of human behaviour. Its scope too is limited: if the answer is not obtainable by observation and measurement, the behaviourists don't ask the question! However, behaviourism is no longer a 'school' of psychology, as such. It refers simply to the scientific methods used; theories that underpin them and the kind of problems approached vary greatly amongst the psychologists who apply it.

Berne, Eric
see **Transactional Analysis**

Beta Waves
see **Brain Waves**

Bioenergetics

Bioenergetics is one of the **body therapies**. It was developed by American psychiatrist Alexander Lowen, who studied under psychoanalyst Wilhelm **Reich**, himself a pupil of **Freud**. Freudian analysts were quite content to deal with the problems of repressed sexuality from the safe distance of a chair set apart from their patient's couch. But Reich decided it had to be tackled directly through manipulation and massage. That was too much for the traditional analysts and Reich's methods fell into disrepute until they re-surfaced with the **growth movement** therapies.

Bioenergetics leans most heavily on Reichian thought: repressed anxiety or emotion expresses itself internally in muscle tension. Tension dulls feeling and we spend a great deal of time tensing up as a defence against uncomfortable or painful emotional experiences. Eventually the tension, which is unconscious, becomes chronic and a barrier against feeling anything at all. The chronically tense person is as incapable of surrendering himself to pleasure as he is to pain.

Reduction of feeling, says Lowen, leads to reduction of energy. According to him, we probably all live at a much lower energy level than we might but are totally unaware of it because we know no other norm.

Bioenergetics is concerned with helping people to re-experience their bodies and free their emotions. This includes learning how to experience one's own sexuality fully but also the basic functions of breathing, moving, feeling and self-expression, restrictions on all of which express themselves in body tension. It is here that Lowen parts company with Reich, for Lowen does not believe that *all* emotional problems have sexual repression as their root.

An important exercise, unique to bioenergetics, is *grounding*. This involves standing with knees bent in such a way that maximum stress is placed on the legs. The stress of holding the position will eventually induce leg vibrations which send strong feelings from the feet to the pelvis and creates a sense of their being fully connected. Many people do not normally feel a flow of energy that connects their limbs to the rest of the body. The energy is blocked by muscle tensions.

Bioenergetic exercises are designed to identify and reduce the muscle tension that prevents energy flow and therefore a feeling of wholeness (see also **orgasm**). Accordingly, the therapist will manipulate or suggest exercises to stretch muscles that have become tight and locked, restricting movement. The muscles in the neck may have shortened, for instance, because of a childhood tendency to raise the head to hold back tears and which has now become a habit, leaving the individual with a chronic upward tilt of the chin.

While body tensions are being worked on in therapy, the therapist also deals with verbal expressions of emotions and anxieties that are released along with the release of bodily defences. So standard psychotherapeutic methods are also involved in the process.

Lowen's years of practice have led him to devise a hierarchy of character types. Individual methods of dealing with pain, rejection, etc., in childhood lead to the development of particular muscle tensions that reveal themselves in people's body structures. Most of us are a mix of elements from each but the five basic character types are called *schizoid, oral, psychopathic, masochistic* and *rigid*.

In Lowen's terminology, the schizoid type is someone who avoids intimacy; the oral type wants to be close to others but only to get his own needs for warmth and support met; the psychopathic type needs to control a relationship, so he can only allow limited closeness; the masochistic type is capable of being close but he is so terrified of losing the other's affections that he is very dependent and submissive; the rigid character forms fairly close relationships but remains a little guarded. Each of these character structures contains conflict, for the individual wants intimacy but also wants to express himself freely and fears the two cannot co-exist. He adopts one or other of the above compromises and then becomes stuck with it. Resolution of the conflict means coming to an understanding that need and independence are not necessarily mutually exclusive.

Each type has not only different psychological characteristics but marked physiological characteristics too. The oral character, for instance, has a strong need to cling to others for support and suffers from suppression of intense feelings of longing. The

35

musculature is therefore under-developed, the legs seem too thin to support the body, the pelvis is often immature and breathing is shallow, because oral deprivation has reduced the individual's ability to suck. Good breathing relies on sucking in air.

Bioenergetic therapists can therefore 'see' a person's underlying problems from his body structure and work accordingly.

Biofeedback

Biofeedback is a method of learning to control what once were considered to be involuntary bodily processes, such as heart rate and breathing. Yogis have been doing such things for centuries but only recently have Western scientists been able to achieve the same results, with artificial aids in controlled laboratory experiments.

Biofeedback machines work by helping us become *aware* of processes to which previously we gave little thought to at all. Awareness has to precede control. If you unconsciously run your hands through your hair when thinking, you remain unconscious of the fact until someone points it out. Next time, you might think twice and stop yourself. In biofeedback, machines replace the need for someone else to tell you first. By amplifying bodily signals of which you were unconscious, you become aware of them for the first time and the way is open to learning how to control them.

Biofeedback machines come in various forms but most gauge tension levels: some monitor skin resistance (there are measurable changes in the skin when we become tense), others monitor muscle tension. A patient is linked up to one of these machines and, when tension rises, he is alerted to the fact by a bleep from the machine or a visual signal on a screen. Gradually the patient learns to control the bleep and then to control his own tension response.

The key to success of biofeedback in tension reduction is the alpha brain-wave, which is the predominant rhythm in our brains when we are relaxed. Patients learn to generate alpha, with the assistance of the machinery – the bleeping or flashing of the signals tells them that they are not relaxed and are not, therefore, generating alpha. Magnified sounds of the alpha rhythm or of breathing patterns help the individual learn to identify it and relax.

Although it is still in fairly infant stages, biofeedback has found its major usage – and claimed much success – in the alleviation of tension, migraine, phobias and general anxiety. But it can also be used to increase control over blood flow and heart rate. In laboratory experiments rats have even been taught to control urine excretion from the kidneys and to raise and lower blood flow to specific areas, such as the ears.

Biorhythms

We all experience 'up' days, 'down' days and sometimes 'off' days, but while most of us would put that down to a mood of the moment or particular events, biorhythm enthusiasts claim it is written into our body patterns.

Biorhythm theory has it that within the human body there are set cycles that affect and dictate how a person feels physically, emotionally and intellectually. These cycles start the day we are born and carry on till death. The physical cycles last 23 days, the emotional 28 and the intellectual 33. The first half of the cycle is supposedly positive – we are active and effective and functioning at peak, other circumstances permitting, while the second half is the negative or regenerative stage. The crucial days (or critical days, as they are called) occur whenever there is a changeover from active-to-passive or passive-to-active phase. On these days, the theory goes, we are likely to be at an intellectual low, unable to cope emotionally as well as we could or are physically clumsy.

No outside force is involved although people often confuse biorhythms with astrology, because of the 'predicting' of behaviour that is involved. There is no proved connection between biorhythms and other bodily rhythms such as the circadian (the twenty-four hour cycle that affects eating, sleeping and other daily functions), or menstrual rhythms. Biorhythms, however, can only predict how you are going to feel, in general terms, not what will happen to you on a specific day. So, on a critical physical day, you might slip on a kerb when any other day you would have been more careful.

Biorhythm cycles were first noted by the German Wilhelm Fliess and the work was followed up by, amongst others, Dr Hermann Sweboda, from Vienna and American Dr Rexford Hersey. But it is the Japanese who have eagerly adopted the findings and applied them at work. One transport company insisted that all employees' biorhythms were calculated so that they should know to take more care when driving on physical critical days. Their accident rate dropped by fifty per cent in one year, even though there was more traffic on the roads and the accident rate for Japan as a whole increased. Critics, however, claim that the very fact the employees were warned of possible carelessness made them conscious of their driving and more alert.

Despite such scepticism, biorhythms have become popular in America and England, with numerous companies producing computer printouts, dials, calculators and watches to eliminate the mathematics involved.

Bisexuality

A bisexual person is attracted to and capable of sexual and emotional relationships with both men and women. While this is a generally accepted definition there are, however, a large number of people who are similarly motivated but don't dare to act on their desires because of society's emphasis on heterosexuality as the acceptable norm. These people are bisexual in orientation if not in fact.

While a vast amount of attention has been directed towards the rightness, wrongness and roots of homosexuality, bisexuality has not been much studied in itself. German psychiatrist Charlotte Wolff, however, undertook a study in recent years. She claims that bisexuality is at the root of all human sexuality and of all physical and emotional reactions.

It is expressed firstly in gender identity, the awareness of the maleness and femaleness in each of us which, she believes, has generally been suppressed by education and upbringing. She gives as evidence of this duality the fact that, for the first three months of life, the foetus in the womb is potentially either male or female; and male and female sex hormones which exist in both the testes and the ovaries, are closely related biochemically.

Only secondly, she says, is bisexuality expressed in terms of psychosexual relationships and then only in those individuals who have escaped the 'brainwashing' of societal norms and are prepared to give full rein to their true sexuality, even in the face of societal disapproval.

Body Clocks

All over the natural world, there is evidence of cycles: day turns to night, seasons come and go, the tide ebbs and flows. We take all this for granted, but we are far less aware of our own internal cycles.

We do know, however, that some of us are most efficient first thing in the morning whilst others would rather burn the midnight oil; some weeks we are all go while other times we can't get down to a thing. This is because of our natural cycles and we have several of them.

The shortest known is the ultradian cycle (lasting an hour and a half). Research has shown that when we are asleep, we dream about once every ninety minutes, our stomachs contract every ninety minutes or so (indicating we want food, although we are conditioned to ignore the signal due to the convention of three square meals) and tests into daydreaming show we even have peaks of fantasy occurring at ninety minute intervals.

We have similar rhythms with a longer cycle. The circadian rhythm is the name for our daily cycle of waking and sleeping and the twenty-four hour day that we have adopted is a fair approximation of it. Some people have a twenty-five hour cycle whilst others may more normally be twenty-three. But most of us don't even know our own norm as we live by the conventional day.

Strength and vitality not only show daily but monthly (infradian) peaks and our body clocks are also affected by the seasons. One of the most powerful triggers is light, which affects our nervous systems and our glands, and stimulates growth.

We need the rhythms for our bodies to function efficiently, whether we are consciously aware of them or not. Cell division, production of enzymes and hormones, regulation of heart beat and monthly reproductive cycles are perpetuated by regular internal cycles. The delicate workings that determine these cycles are easily off-balanced by hallucinogenic drugs, the Pill or emotional crises, for example.

An obvious modern cause of disturbed body time is jetlag. The clash between internal time and the time shown on the clock at another end of the globe may give rise to upsets such as indigestion, irritability, depression, dehydration, blurred vision and reduced levels of concentration.

Body Language

Two couples are sitting at separate tables in a restaurant. Couple A are leaning back against their chairs. The man in talking, the woman is turned slightly sideways in her seat and her legs are crossed. The man has his arms folded. Couple B are also talking. They are both leaning towards each other and their eyes are locked. The man is leaning on his elbows, the woman is fingering the stem of the glass in front of her.

Without hearing a word, an onlooker would know that there is a closeness (at least at that moment) between couple B which is lacking between couple A. How? Their bodies tell him.

Over recent years, psychologists have become particularly interested in non-verbal communication: the clues we give to other people by the way we sit, smile, break or keep eye-contact and touch. We can see when someone is in a good mood because they give off 'good vibes', a now common slang expression that describes so well the feeling that emanates from a person. Vibes can be general: you feel good so you have a smile for the world, an easy walk, an aura of security and conviction. Or vibes can be directed specifically to one person – as in the case of sexual attraction.

Non-verbal communication is an important but underestimated element of our everyday relationships with other people. We raise an eyebrow to show we are being sarcastic; we fold our arms to say 'don't get close'. Most of the time, we are unconscious of doing it.

But body talk isn't given out and picked up with unconscious ease as one experiment clearly showed. Subjects were asked to act out various emotions and an audience interpreted them. One girl was thought to be consistently showing anger even when *she* thought she was demonstrating such varied feelings as seductiveness, fear, happiness and misery! Underlying but predominant emotions may prevent us from communicating what we mean or others' pre-conceptions may prevent them from picking up the correct cue. Non-verbal behaviour can, therefore, baffle people just as often as it can aid them.

Body Therapies

This is a general term used loosely to describe therapies that emphasise a physical approach to resolving deep-rooted emotional blocks or problems. Body therapists stress the importance of seeing and treating mind-and-body as a whole instead of, as in psychoanalytic or psychotherapeutic practice, isolating the mental problems and trying to deal with these verbally.

Body therapists believe that when emotions such as anger and fear are repressed instead of expressed, they have to be contained internally and this may result in physical constrictions such as

40

muscle tension, headaches, back pain or poor posture. Someone who is trying to hold back tears, for instance, might draw the stomach muscles in or tighten the chest. Unexpressed anger might find its outlet in back tension or a thickening of muscles in the neck. Over time this tension can get further and further locked in and actually affects body shape.

Body therapists say that they can tell a person's personality type from his body structure and claim that even elements of appearance which we usually consider an accident of birth may well be the result of early repressions: a woman with very narrow boyish hips may be shaped that way because she has denied her sexuality to herself.

To reach back to the emotional cause of the problem in the first place, the physical tension that is holding it in has to be recognized and released. Then the emotion may also be re-experienced and resolved and energy can flow freely again. Contact with sensitive areas of tension can cause much pain and a flood of equally painful memories.

Body therapies can take a variety of forms but the most common are **Reichian therapy, bioenergetics, primal therapy, Alexander, rolfing** and **postural integration.** Amongst techniques used are manipulation, massage and breathing exercises.

Brain

The capacities of the human brain are so vast and complex that the specific functions of over two-thirds of it still defy understanding.

Physically, it seems to be divided into three main areas, each with its own functions. The first part of the brain to evolve was the *hindbrain* and this is found in most species of animals. It is located on the *brainstem*, the stalk that links the spinal cord to the lower parts of the brain, and is responsible for basic bodily processes, such as control of heart rate and respiration (performed by the *medulla* and the *pons*, two structures within the hindbrain) and co-ordination of movement and balance (performed by the *cerebellum*). A very important structure that stretches from the lowest part of this section of the brain right up to the highest centres of the forebrain is the *reticular activating system* (RAS). The RAS acts as a kind of censor, selecting from all the sensory information that comes into the brain the messages which should be sent on to the higher centres. It plays a particularly important role in sleep, when it selects out vast amounts of incoming information instead of sending it on, so that the sleeper can rest undisturbed.

The *midbrain* lies above the hindbrain. It is concerned with the relaying of messages to higher brain centres and houses the middle part of the RAS.

The *forebrain* bulges out over the brainstem by which it is supported. It houses the *thalamus*, the *hypothalamus*, the *cerebrum* and the *corpus callosum*. The thalamus is in the centre and all sensory information from other parts of the body come here before being sent up higher into the brain. It is also thought to be involved in control of the autonomic nervous system (see **nervous system**). Below the thalamus lies the hypothalamus, an important structure that governs motivation and emotion as well as playing a part in functions such as eating, sleeping and sex. It is also in control of glands and hormones.

The thalamus and hypothalamus are part of a circle of structures that is called the *limbic system* or the old brain, because it evolved very early on and is found even in reptiles. The limbic system is just below the cerebrum, the highest and most recently evolved structure of the brain, and incorporates the *hippocampus*, which is concerned with memory and the *amygdala*, which is thought to be associated with aggression.

The cerebrum, at the top of the forebrain, is the part of the brain that makes man unique. Here are the centres for language, thought and creativity. The cerebrum is made up of two hemispheres, the left and the right. The *left hemisphere* controls the right side of the body, whilst the right governs the left side. If a shell is held up to the left ear, the sound of murmuring will be transmitted, by nervous impulses, to the *right hemisphere*. Both hemispheres are connected by a stout cord of nerves called the *corpus callosum*. So it is via the corpus callosum that the right hemisphere informs the left hemisphere about the murmuring sound coming from the shell. At one time it was believed that epilepsy could be cured without side-effects by severing the corpus callosum. The hunch was wrong but the experiment opened up a whole new field of exciting discoveries about the specialized functions of the left and the right hemispheres (see **split brain**).

The hemispheres are covered by a thick layer of nerve cells called the *cerebral cortex*, the famous wrinkled grey matter of the brain. Here are the centres concerned with memory, thinking, speech and creativity, all the processes that are uniquely human.

It also stores sensory information and controls movement. If opened out and unwrinkled, the cortex of an adult would be more than two square feet in size.

Also in the forebrain are the various lobes that are responsible for interpreting sensation. The *occipital lobes*, concerned with vision, have cells so sensitive that some will only respond to vertical slits of light whilst others only respond to horizontal ones. The *temporal lobes*, concerned with sound, show equally sophisticated specialization, some cells only responding to high tones, others to low ones. The *parietal lobes* deal with feelings of heat, cold, pain and pressure. The *frontal lobes* are mostly concerned with the processes of reasoning.

Although this potted excursion through the brain accentuates the separateness of particular structures and specialization in function, the brain of course works as an inter-dependent whole and particular functions are not necessarily limited to the structure that seems especially designed to deal with them. Work with brain-damaged patients has shown that undamaged parts of the brain can compensate for the losses sustained elsewhere. In the famous case of a Portuguese woman called Maria, the whole of the right hemisphere of her brain was removed because of severe damage. Despite the fact that the right hemisphere controls the movements of the left side of the body, instead of being paralysed, she was up and about and functioning as normal within a month. It is now believed that brain damaged patients who suffer apparent memory or speech impairment because of damage to specific centres of the brain, can be helped to 'train' the undamaged parts to take over those functions.

This view, that vast areas of the brain are involved in every thought process, although some are more involved than others, is borne out by the work of American **physiological psychologist** Roy John. He has noted that when nerve cells 'fire' (a chemical process by which nerve cells are alerted to transmit an impulse on to the next, see **nervous system**), specific chains of nerve cells fire in synchrony whereas others elsewhere in the brain also fire but at random. This seems to indicate that all of the brain is in some way involved in the process.

New exciting brain research is regularly bringing forth new discoveries. One such is the distinct relationship between brain function and our external environment. Rats kept in an 'interesting' environment, full of objects to explore, actually showed a growth in brain size. The cerebral cortex was thicker and the nerve cells were larger than those of rats kept in cages with adequate food and water but no external stimulation. This work has considerable implications (see **ageing**).

In their book *The Evolving Brain*, Tony Buzan and Terence Dixon wrote: 'To compare the brain with a galaxy is in fact a modest analogy ... Every normal brain is capable of making more patterned interconnections than there are atoms in the universe.'

Brain Damage

Brain damage can take many different forms and the effects will vary accordingly. Some babies are born mentally handicapped because of brain damage that occurs before, during or after birth. Their mental capacities are either mildly or severely retarded for life and sometimes they suffer accompanying physical disabilities (see **mental handicap**).

Brain damage is also suffered as a result of external head injuries. Sometimes the damage may be limited to *concussion*, a temporary loss of consciousness after a head injury but dealing no permanent damage. More serious is *contusion*, in which the actual brain tissue is bruised. A patient with brain contusion may go into a coma that can last for days and will be partially disorientated for a while afterwards. Most serious of the injuries that can be caused by some external force is *laceration* of the brain, where brain tissue is destroyed (e.g. by a bullet). Depending on which tissue gets destroyed, the person may be severely mentally impaired for the rest of his life, or, if lucky, escape with limited damage to the brain functions. It is now believed that other parts of the brain can sometimes compensate for the functions of the damaged area (see **brain**).

Damage to the brain can also be caused by internal malfunctions. *Cerebral thrombosis*, for instance, is caused by a clot that prevents flow of blood to the brain (a stroke) but the patient can often fully recover. Cerebral haemorrhaging occurs if a blood vessel in the brain bursts, spilling blood directly on to the brain tissue. If the patient survives, he will probably suffer severe mental impairment.

Aphasia is a speech disorder that can result from either external or internal injury to the brain. Sometimes an aphasic person cannot understand words properly, or else he can read but can't speak properly. He may also suffer distorted vision.

Brain damage is difficult to diagnose because impairment can

44

present itself in such varying forms (see **brain** for full explanation of brain functions) and sometimes a disability, such as memory loss, may have psychological rather than physical causes (see **amnesia**). However, study of the symptoms of brain damage has started to throw light on the separate functions of the brain hemispheres. It has been noted that in men whose left hemispheres were damaged, speech and analytical faculties were badly affected but their spatial abilities (e.g. for visualisation or drawing) were not. The reverse was found true when damage was done to the right hemisphere. This has led many researchers to claim that, in males at least, the left hemisphere controls our logical thinking abilities while the right is more concerned with practical, creative, intuitive thinking and tasks (see **split brain**).

Brainwashing

We are all familiar with the notion of brainwashing as the torture meted out to prisoners of war to encourage them to 'change sides'. But, according to a British doctor, the same force that is operating to break down the prisoners' resistance is also operating at pop concerts, football matches, political rallies and tribal rituals. What is common to all is physiological brain change induced by intense emotional arousal.

British psychiatrist Dr William Sargant has made an extensive study of the brain activity that results in collapse and sudden heightened suggestibility, as a result of his own discoveries in clinical practice (see **abreaction**). He has travelled extensively amongst primitive tribes, observing their various rituals, and it was he who, in the face of strong opposition, firmly declared that Patty Hearst had genuinely been brainwashed.

The phenomenon now known as brainwashing was first discovered by the Russian neuro-physiologist Pavlov. In experiments with dogs he found that if he pushed their stress levels to breaking point, they reacted in a set pattern of ways. Firstly, either a weak or strong stimulus would provoke the same intensity of response from the dogs. This, in human terms, might be equivalent to becoming as upset, while under stress, about a broken washer on a tap as about the loss of one's job. Next, the dogs started to react more strongly to weak than to strong stimuli. This is because the brain is inhibiting response in an effort to fight stress; so major stresses produce no reaction whilst trivia can still be responded to. In this state, an individual may be emotionless on

45

hearing that his mother has just died but be capable of sympathizing with his neighbour because his car has broken down.

As Pavlov continued to increase the stresses imposed on his dogs, they moved into a third phase of brain response which involved them in a complete reversal of familiar or conditioned behaviour patterns. They bit the hand of a feeder they had previously liked but responded to one that they had previously disliked. Further stress finally resulted in the dogs' collapse and a state of suggestibility which made them amenable to substituting completely new behaviour patterns for old ones. Each stage of response was marked by measurable brain change.

Pavlov found that the most stable of his dogs took the longest to collapse but, once they had reached breaking point, they adopted the new behaviour patterns so thoroughly that it was difficult to break these patterns later. Dogs with more neurotic personalities collapsed quicker but clung on to their newly conditioned behaviour less tenaciously.

Pavlov induced severe stress in his dogs by a number of methods: he not only subjected them to pain but gave them a variety of confusing signals (e.g. leading them to expect food, then not producing it) and also weakened them physically by tampering with their body chemistry. (Creating confusion is a common brainwashing technique.)

Sargant has observed that the same kind of stress build-up is created in highly emotionally charged atmospheres. In the religious conversion rituals of the old evangelists, congregations received a non-stop barrage of evocative verbiage about hell-fire. The sessions culminated in the hysterical collapse of most of the people present and sudden conversion to Christianity. Modern day religious cults use the same techniques and supplement them often with physical methods of bringing individuals to breaking point. At the People's Temple, for instance, cult members had to work extremely long hours and were given food that was lacking in nutrition, so that they became debilitated and less resistant. In tribal healing rituals, emotion is heightened by the monotonous rhythm of drum-beating and the system weakened by non-stop dancing. Result, collapse and miraculous recovery from depression or freedom from possession by the devil.

Sargant maintains that in all these cases, the effects are the results of an over-charged brain reacting to extremely severe stress. The build-up to collapse can be put to good use as a treatment method in psychiatry. A person who is encouraged to 'blow' (his defences having been lowered by a relaxant drug) can be relieved of a crippling build up of tension (see **abreaction**).

But the ability to induce systematic stress is also a powerful tool for those who know how to abuse it. Severe, prolonged stress must lead to collapse and suggestibility and, with manipulation, to sudden conversion to a previously alien belief system. No one, says Sargant, can be strong enough to withstand brainwashing techniques indefinitely. There is a frighteningly thin line between 'knowing' a truth and just accepting new ideas in an ultra-suggestible state of mind.

Brain Waves

A German scientist, Hans Berger, discovered the existence of brain waves shortly after the First World War. From experiments with electrodes attached to a person's head, he found two different kinds of electronic responses which he called alpha rhythms and beta rhythms. But we now know that there are four main types of brain rhythms, each of which accompany particular brain activity.

The normal waking rhythm of the brain is the beta rhythm, associated with talking, thinking and the carrying out of all our daily tasks. When the alpha rhythm takes over, the individual is relaxed, turning his attention inwards and concentrating on inner awareness. Theta is associated with drowsiness and usually appears just as a person is dropping off to sleep but it is also connected with sudden bursts of inspiration and creativity. Delta occurs during deep sleep.

The advent of **biofeedback** equipment has enabled people to tune in to their own mental states and learn to produce, say, alpha rhythms at will. The ability to get in touch with 'inner states' while producing alpha rhythms has led alpha production to be dubbed the quick road to enlightenment. But some researchers say that alpha experiences of a mystical nature are purely the product of the subject's expectations.

Others are more interested in the power of the theta brain wave. Thomas Budzynski, clinical director of the Biofeedback Institute of Denver, claims that in the period between waking and sleeping, when producing theta rhythms, we are open to new ideas and capable of learning more easily than when our logical and analytic faculties are in full control. Teaching people by biofeedback to identify and hold the theta state, he says, enables them to use that time to absorb difficult learning programmes or directions on how to eat or smoke less. It is this 'twilight state of theta', says Budzynski, which is akin to altered states of consciousness such as those experienced under hypnosis or whilst meditating.

Breastfeeding

Mother's milk is now being endowed with an ever-increasing range of life-enhancing properties, from protection for the baby against allergies and constipation through to emotional security and freedom of spirit. But the bonuses of breastfeeding should not be taken out of proportion.

What is vital for a very young child is the knowledge that food, warmth, comfort and physical contact will regularly and willingly be supplied. He is totally dependent on others for the fulfillment of these basic needs and the one place where he can be assured of receiving them all is at his mother's breast. Breastfeeding establishes an extremely strong bond between mother and child, with the opportunities it provides for the satisfying of both attention and nutritional needs.

It has been demonstrated that the closer the physical contact between mother and child from as early an age as possible, the more the likelihood of an ever-growing love and trust. Mothers who are allowed to fondle and suckle their newborn babies in the first fifteen minutes of their lives are more likely to experience a sense of bonding that communicates itself to the child. This bond is most easily and most naturally developed through regular breastfeeding.

But breastfeeding, despite its obvious virtues, is simply one means of supplying essential needs rather than an irreplaceable source. It is the *fulfilling* of the needs for food, warmth, comfort and contact, willingly and warmly given, that is vital. Mothers who cannot breastfeed can still provide a world in which these needs are met and mothers who breastfeed may not automatically use the experience to instil a sense of loving trust in a child. Their attention may be elsewhere or their own sexual insecurity may lead them to repress the natural sensuality of the breastfeeding experience, all of which may communicate itself to the child. It is an atmosphere of acceptance and love that helps a child develop trust and confidence, however it is provided.

C

Castration Anxiety
see Psychosexual Stages

Catatonic Schizophrenia
see Schizophrenia

Chemotherapy
see Psychotropic Drugs

Children of God
sec Cults

Chiropractic
see Manipulative Therapies

Christos Experience

This technique purports to take one back into a past life (or, failing that, to induce lucid dreaming) without the use of hypnosis or any artificial effects. Although not discovered by him, Australian novelist Gerry Glaskin has done most to publicize the phenomenon by writing three books about it. He claims he has, via its means, re-experienced previous carnations in Egypt and Africa.

Here is a simplified description of the method used: the would-be dreamer lies on the floor and has his ankles massaged by one helper whilst another massages the lower centre of his forehead with the edge of his curved hand. This massage is meant to be vigorous and continues until the subject's head buzzes. Then mental expansion exercises begin. The subject is asked to imagine growing two inches longer through his feet, then apply the same process to his head. This is repeated several times with him growing longer and longer and then returning to normal. Eventually, he has to imagine both ends extending twenty-four inches, stay there and visualize himself expanding like a balloon. At that stage, he is encouraged to start 'seeing' things.

The helper who is giving the directions asks him to visualize his own front door from the ground, then 'see' his neighbourhood from his roof, then from 500 yards above his roof. He has to turn around (mentally) and change day to night and night to day in his visualization. Then he is asked to come in to land and at this point is supposed to waft down towards some alien terrain and commence an action-replay of a scene from a former life.

Glaskin claims it works, as he has experienced coming down on unfamiliar territory, seeing himself as an Egyptian leader of old and watching that second self going through his day whilst never losing consciousness of his present self, lying in the here-and-now on his own living room floor. Later Glaskin travelled to Egypt and checked up on facts about the terrain, the houses and the clothes he 'saw'. He says they corresponded perfectly with a particular place and time in ancient Egypt.

Chromosomes
see Genes

Clairvoyance

Clairvoyance is a form of extra-sensory perception, the apparent ability that some people have to perceive something without using any of the five known senses. It refers particularly to the ability to visualize a distant object or event clearly in the mind. Clairvoyants may be able to 'see' the symbols on cards that are laid face down upon a table. Clairvoyant healers claim they can diagnose illness from far away, without needing to see the person who is suffering from the illness at all. (See also ESP.)

Claustrophobia
see Phobia

Client-Centred Therapy
see Rogerian Therapy

Clinical Psychologists

As their name implies, clinical psychologists work in a clinical setting, be it a hospital for the **mentally ill** or **handicapped** or in specialized units e.g. for **addiction**. A great many people confuse **psychologists** with **psychiatrists**, presuming anyone who has 'psych' at the beginning of their professional label must be in the business of trying to put people's heads straight. But there are many kinds of psychologists and it is in fact only clinical psychologists whose work specifically involves them with people suffering from mental problems or malfunctions.

A clinical psychologist is a psychologist who has taken special training in the treatment of people with mental disorders. His training may parallel that of a psychiatrist but he has no medical qualifications and his aim is not to treat illness by medical means. He is interested in how and why people behave the way they do and what, in particular, causes them to behave abnormally.

Some clinical psychologists spend their time exploring the causes of mental disorders. Others specialize in diagnostic techniques, using psychological tests, measuring **intelligence**, screening for **brain damage** or memory loss, etc. With the advent of **behaviour therapy**, a great many are responsible for trying these techniques with suitable patients such as phobics.

Co-Counselling

Co-counselling is perhaps the nearest thing to a do-it-yourself therapy. There are no experts or therapists. Instead, there are just two people who take it in turns, using co-counselling techniques, to help each other.

The key to co-counselling, developed by American Harvey Jackins in the fifties and much refined since, is the giving and receiving of free attention. Working in pairs, each individual takes a turn at being counsellor and then client, swapping roles with his or her partner after an hour. Dispensing with the traditional pattern of helper and helped, the method teaches that we all can – and do – fulfil both functions at different times.

The counsellor and the client of the moment sit comfortably together and, for an hour, the counsellor gives his total attention to the client as the latter works through whatever is on his mind – a relationship problem, perhaps, or an underlying hostility to the opposite sex, or difficulties with coping at work. The free attention creates a sense of supportive presence from another person while the client attempts to sort out his problems for himself.

Advising, sympathizing, criticizing and interpreting all interfere with the client's ability to get to grips with his own experience and so are strictly taboo. The counsellor will certainly listen and may even set the client gently back on track if he is meandering away from his subject, but he will not break in with responses like 'Oh, how awful, that's just what happened to another friend of mine. And you know what *she* did ... !' Although such a comment is common between friends and is intended to be supportive and consoling, it just takes attention away from the individual's problems and prevents any emotional release.

One of the aims of co-counselling is this emotional release, or 'discharge' as it is called. The client is encouraged to feel free to express tears, anger, laughter, whatever emotion comes out of his feelings. The thinking behind this is that these emotions have, at some time, been repressed and stored instead of expressed. This undischarged distress, according to Jackins, leads to repetitive and stereotyped patterns of behaviour whenever we are in similar circumstances. We can't break out of these patterns without expressing and resolving the original pain. According to co-counselling theory, a woman who makes unrealistic demands on friends and just can't help herself getting angry and hostile when they don't ring her every day (even though she knows it is unnecessary) may be repeating in new situations an old hurt felt about ceasing to be the sole centre of attention at home when, say, a younger sister was born. Only by getting in touch with this buried resentment will she be able to face it and stop injecting the same feelings on to current relationships. She may need to re-experience the original distress several times, until all the layers have been stripped away.

Other important co-counselling techniques besides free attention are *validation* – the client is not allowed to moan 'I feel a failure'; he must declare 'I am a success!', not in an effort to make him believe it out of the blue but to set him away from a negative and destructive tack. Similarly, he may be directed by the counsellor towards *repetition* – repeating what seem to be key phrases ('I hardly saw my mother as a child'), until breakdown and discharge is induced. These are the only kinds of direction a counsellor is allowed to make and, even then, only with client co-operation.

Co-counselling is not seen as appropriate for everyone. The criterion for participation is that each person must be able to give attention as well as receive it. So it is not for the deeply distressed person who is so low that he or she has no capacity left to give to anyone else. It is instead most useful for people who are 'coping' by ordinary standards with their lives but who want to overcome troubling rigidities in their attitudes and behaviour.

Cognitive Dissonance

This is a theory proposed by American psychologist Leon Festinger: people automatically try to avoid inconsistency in their thinking or behaviour by going to great lengths to rationalize it. So, if a woman is torn between buying a long blue dress or shorter black one, once she has made her difficult choice, she will probably start to emphasize the undesirable aspects of the unchosen item. She chooses the black: now the blue dress is undesirable because it would show more dirt, it would catch in escalators, its shoulder staps are too thin, etc.

If an individual is, say, asked to give a speech on the advantages of nationalized industries when really he doesn't think they work, his attitudes will change in inverse proportion to the amount of pressure that is put on him to give the speech. So, if he is told that his chance to develop a particular project depends upon his ability to give a good speech, his real attitudes towards nationalized industries won't change very much, despite his words, because the pressure put on him from above serves as a sufficient rationalization for doing it. If, however, he is just politely asked to give the speech and he knows it will look good if he does (but no one is forcing him) the conflict between his attitudes and his speech-content will be greater. So he will find himself looking for reasons to believe that nationalized industries are a good idea, to justify his actions to himself.

However, many people do seem capable of holding conflicting attitudes about each of which they are equally adamant. The man who is all in favour of sexual freedom may be firmly convinced that his teenage daughter should not indulge in it.

Collective Unconscious
see **Jung**

Colour Therapy

Research shows that different colours have differing effects on our nervous systems. How we come to see colour at all is a complex matter of optics and our perception of colour is a very subjective experience. But some generalizations can be made, from which there may be implications for therapy.

Colours are commonly divided into two temperature groups. Warm colours such as red, orange and yellow are seen as aggressive and advancing; cool colours – blue, green and violet – are thought of as receding and passive. So red walls *seem* much closer than blue ones and one researcher has demonstrated that the width of a parking space between two blue cars seems wider to motorists than it really is, resulting in more dented wings on blue cars!

It is thought that the use of reds and oranges makes people feel warmer too. Laboratory tests show that the colour red does stimulate the nervous system – blood pressure rises and respiration and heart rate speed up – while blue has the opposite effect.

Colour as a therapeutic aid has been introduced into some psychiatric hospital wards and furnishings, based on the thinking that manic patients need to be quietened down by the cool colours and depressive patients need to be cheered up by exciting ones. While the therapeutic use of colour in physical settings may still be the subject of controversy, some years ago psychologist Dr Max Luscher developed a personality test based on individuals' preferences for particular colours. He subscribes to the school of thought that colours have a particular, unchanging connotation based on associations with the natural environment – dark blue always signifies peace and quiet – but that attitudes to each colour and to that colour's meaning will vary according to personality traits. So he maintained that healthy balanced individuals would rate highly his colour cards for blue, green, yellow and red, as they represented the fundamental psychological needs for contentment and affection, self-assertion, success in actions and aspiration to higher things. On the other hand preferences for the auxiliary colours of violet, brown, black and grey indicated a negative attitude to life. Luscher devised a complex set of personality ratings based on all the permutations of choice available when one is asked to place these eight colours in order of preference.

Architects and psychologists alike are sceptical about the validity of such simple assumptions about colour. Some recent research has even been suggested that excitable people need the stimulating colours to help re-direct their tensions, while cool colours may help the introverted to come out of their shells. Other research claims that greens and blues are really no more calming than reds – it is the *strength* of the colour used that is important and so a strong blue may be as exciting as a strong red and considerably more exciting than a weak red.

Opinions about the comparative warmth of colours, say the critics, cannot be separated from expectations we hold about the coloured object itself. Red may be meant to be warmer than blue but which would seem warmer, a red plastic bag or a blue woollen sock?

Neurologists have suggested that the nervous system reacts not only to stimulation but to *changes* in stimulation. It may be that, rather than one colour being more exciting, subduing or warming than another, it is the variety of colour that is in itself psychologically beneficial.

Community Mental Health

This rather grand sounding title refers to the trend (albeit a slow-moving one) over the last couple of decades to move away from the treatment of mental or emotional disorders in big psychiatric hospitals. Most countries have very large **mental illness** hospitals, usually situated away from the centres of towns because they were built at a time when 'madness' was little understood and insane asylums were places in which the sufferers could be locked away, out of sight and out of harm's way.

Now it is realized that large packed wards, where someone with a minor depression and the chronic schizophrenic were lumped in together, do not create the best ambience for the treatment of mental disorders. Instead of learning to cope within their own environment and amongst the circumstances which perhaps caused a breakdown in the first place, mentally ill people were in effect put away in sterile surroundings, divorced from reality.

Today psychiatric hospitals are far less depressing, although in many cases they are still housed in the original, old-fashioned buildings. But the modern therapeutic approach is to help people, as far as possible, while still living in their own communities. As a result we have a growth of neighbourhood advice centres, out-patient clinics, centres specifically concerned with marital problems or addiction, and twenty-four hour crisis centres. A whole variety of staff may be involved, from doctors to community psychiatric nurses (who make home visits), social workers and psychologists. But, alas, there are far too few of such resources because of the finances needed for both premises and staff.

A growing trend in the community mental health movement is the halfway house. Patients who have been in hospitals for many years become institutionalized (incapable of making decisions for themselves or of coping with survival needs, such as shopping and cooking, because everything has always been provided for them). They are now being given the chance to make a graduated step back into society. Living in small houses in groups usually of four to eight with on-call help from a social worker and doctor, these patients re-experience what it is like to live in ordinary streets, with neighbours and local shops and parks. Half-way houses have also been successful in helping **mentally handicapped** patients learn to live outside of hospital. Mentally handicapped people are not ill but damage done to their brains makes their capacities limited. They used to be relegated to hospital for life but the half-way house (or group home) scheme has proved that many *can* learn to cope for themselves in the community.

Not only have the mentally handicapped and chronically mentally ill shown they *do* have a valid contribution to make to community life but people who live nearby (and who may have had negative feelings about 'idiots' or 'nutters') are also learning that people with some kind of mental disorder are not necessarily frightening or alien after all.

Complex

'He's got a complex about his height', we might say of someone who is so embarrassed about being tall that he deliberately stoops and rounds his shoulders.

In current usage, we think of a complex as something negative, the more so because we're all familiar with the term 'inferiority complex', a state of affairs where, for example, a man who feels dominated in his relationship with his wife may attempt to compensate by being a steely tyrant at work.

But the word 'complex' had very different beginnings in its psychoanalytic past. Carl **Jung** coined it to express the combination of the facets of a person's way of thinking and acting which together form a personality type. The two extreme forms of personality were, he said, the **introvert** and the **extravert**, but most people are a mix of the two. The elements that made up all the bits of each he called complexes (clusters of personality traits) and there were no negative connotations.

Later another psychoanalyst, Alfred Adler, developed the idea of the inferiority complex, meaning the particularly important set of ideas and reactions that centre around what someone considers to be his shortcomings. This particular complex of ideas, Adler said, is created by all adults to avoid the anxiety of feeling inferior. The result is compensation in another area, as with the work tyrant.

Compulsive Eating
see **Anorexia Nervosa**

Conditional Positive Regard
see **Rogerian Therapy**

Conditioning

If we are conditioned, it means we have learned to make an association between two particular things which consequently affects our actions. Although the word conditioning smacks of brainwashing, it in fact refers to a process that goes on throughout all our lives. Depending upon the effects of our actions, we learn to repeat or eschew them.

The conditioned response was discovered by Russian physiologist Ivan Pavlov at the beginning of the twentieth century. Realizing that the dogs in his laboratory salivated when given their evening meal, he tried an experiment in which a bell was rung at the same time that the food was brought. After a while, he started ringing the bell but not bringing food. The dogs still salivated. What Pavlov had discovered was that he had conditioned his dogs to associate bells with food. He had taken an *unconditioned* response (an involuntary reaction such as salivating over food) and had produced a *conditioned response* (an unnatural but now equally automatic association between salivating and bells).

This is called *classical conditioning*. An animal or a human simply reacts to something that happens to it and makes an association. A woman is watching a programme on TV when fire breaks out in her home. Next time she sees that programme she may unconsciously link it with fire and feel anxious. The role that conditioning plays in forming human behaviour patterns was taken further by John Watson (see **behaviourism**) and, more particularly, by Professor B. F. Skinner, who concentrated on the effects of actions rather than reactions.

Skinner maintained that we learn by *reinforcement*. If a child puts a jigsaw together correctly and then receives a cuddle from his mother, the pleasantness of the consequences of his action will encourage him to repeat it. His behaviour has been positively reinforced. If he does the jigsaw and says, 'Look!' but his mother is too busy to pay him attention, he may well lose interest in jigsaws. This is negative reinforcement. It is a useful way to discourage undesired behaviour whereas punishment, says Skinner, is not (see **learning**).

He introduced the idea of *operant conditioning*, the shaping of behaviour through rewards. He showed that it could even work to shape behaviour that is unusual. Pigeons, by being given food every time they approached a marble and butted it with their beaks, were taught to bowl – not a natural pigeon activity.

A particular therapy, based on operant conditioning and called the *token economy* system, became popular in mental hospitals some years ago. The idea was to give rewards every time desired behaviour was exhibited. A patient who usually refused to comb his hair was allowed the privilege of making a phone call or being at the head of the meal queue every time he did consent to put a brush through it. But this system was criticized on the grounds of being cruel, since the giving of rewards necessarily entailed the withholding of rewards and some of the 'rewards' were thought to be a patient's basic right, any denial of which, for whatever purpose, was inhumane.

Skinner does not deny the part that heredity and cognitive processes such as reasoning and memory play in behaviour. But he believes our actions, thoughts and feelings are overwhelmingly conditioned by society and that free will or grand concepts such as altruism and goodness are illusions. Different things act as reinforcers for different people. Some people will become humanitarian, upright individuals because their behaviour gets reinforcement from the approval of society or the feeling of having done something effective. Others will be selfish and greedy because, for them, money and the comforts it brings is a stronger reinforcer than respect.

The 'rewards' of an action may well encourage us to repeat actions we choose to take but they don't always effectively condition us to incorporate into our behaviour actions we wouldn't normally wish to take. In one experiment, some children were given a reward if they ate their greens whilst others were just told to eat up and not given anything for doing so. When the rewards for the first group stopped coming, the children also ceased to eat their greens, whereas the authoritarian approach with the second group led to their continued consumption! (See also **learning, behaviourism** and **behaviour therapy**.)

Conjoint Therapy
see **Sex therapy**

Consciousness

To most of us in the West, the word consciousness means simply our normal waking state, when we are thinking, working, eating, relaxing – doing virtually anything but sleeping. When we are conscious, we are aware of what's going on.

However, exciting research that has taken place over the last years shows that we are in fact aware of very little that goes on. Our brains have to filter out a great deal of available sensory information or else the overload would lead to breakdown of the system and eventual extinction. But, in the West, we have made the mistake of thinking that what we perceive is all there is to perceive.

Tales have long reached us from the East of Yogis who can control what we have always considered involuntary processes – heart rate, blood flow, temperature, etc. And, even in the West, there are thousands of individuals who claim some kind of extra-sensory perception (ESP), can inexplicably read the future or move objects by power of the mind. All too often such phenomena have been dismissed out of hand as the hallucinations of diseased brains or complex pieces of fraud.

However, the feeling that there is more to man than matter has pervaded the ideas of many distinguished thinkers. 'Higher consciousness' is the goal of **psychosynthesis**, developed by an analyst contemporary of Freud; Abraham Maslow created the school of **transpersonal psychology** to pay attention to intangibles such as higher awareness and ESP, and even Freud, in his later life, came to believe that higher centres did exist and admitted that, if he had his life over again, he would have chosen to explore the paranormal.

59

Till recently, these have just been isolated cries in the midst of a scientific community convinced by nothing except scientific proofs. Now we are starting to receive that proof. The development of **biofeedback** equipment enables us to tune into and control our own internal processes, just as Yogis do; distinct changes in awareness have been monitored in people undergoing drug experiences or meditating; work on biological rhythms (see **body clocks**) has shown that we are affected by seasonal cycles as much as animals and our growth relates to light and dark; but, perhaps most importantly, experimentation on the brain has shown that our left and right hemispheres have different functions. The left side, its functions emphasized in the West, controls analytical, logical, linear thinking whereas the over-shadowed right is the creative, intuitive, holistic centre of our brains. It rarely is allowed to gain dominance, because we lay so much stress on practical, sequential thinking, but it comes into its own at that hazy time between waking and sleeping and probably in dreams. (See **split brain** and **brain waves**.)

These findings led American psychologist Robert Ornstein to write his book *The Psychology of Consciousness*, in which he proposes that man has two major modes of consciousness, one analytic (left brain), the other holistic (right brain). He believes that, to develop further as human beings – and to develop further in psychology as a science, we must now learn to take account of that other, mysterious, darker side of ourselves – right brain consciousness. We must learn to give as much weight to the activity of that side of the brain because this is our link with a wider cosmic consciousness.

He demonstrates 'right brain' concepts that are unfamiliar, even difficult for us in the West but which are natural to people in the East and elsewhere. Time is one such concept. We think in hours, minutes and seconds and one moment follows the next in a logical, automatic sequence. We distinguish between past, present and future; and, in our thinking, we try to move forward, take sequential steps in problem-solving, instead of incorporating all information – allowing ourselves to think 'sideways' (see **lateral thinking**). In the East, time is experienced as ever-present, all-encompassing, holistic. Time is non-linear, infinite. (People during a drug-experience often experience this new concept of time.)

Practitioners of **Zen-Buddhism** and **Yoga** are taught special exercises which aid them to tune out ordinary, daytime sensory awareness and concentrate on inner senses and a resultant feeling of being one with the universe. Even this idea of some energy force uniting us and the universe is no longer so alien to Western thought. Many thinkers have posited the idea of a vital force; physicists are now expanding their ideas on the nature of energy. Chinese TAO philosophy has the life energy *ch'i* which runs through everything, including man; in Japanese **martial arts** it is *ki*. Scientist and astronaut Edgar Mitchell has said, 'Consciousness exists and our brain is a terminal which enables us to tap into it'.

Robert Ornstein has written that we have 'automized' consciousness for the sake of survival. But in so doing we have lost richness of experience. If we can deautomize our senses, as 'mystics' do, scientists will be able to perceive and study a whole variety of subtle influences on man, from sources such as the rotation of the earth, the atmosphere and the gravitational field.

It is not ludicrous. As mentioned, we have only recently discovered the effects on our own pituitary hormones of light and dark. Light affects ovulation. And the atmosphere is now known to influence psychological changes. Charged electrical particles called **air ions** actually act on the production of the **hormone** serotonin in our brains. Serotonin is linked with **anxiety** levels and **depression.** So man *can* be acted upon by external forces.

Western researchers who have turned their attention to the previously untapped areas of our consciousness often enthuse about the outcome of acknowledging and experiencing a life energy that unites us and everything; we will connect not with communities and nations and continents but with humanity as a whole, they say.

Everything in the universe changes, revolves, ebbs or flows. To make sense of the world, man has created his own stance, stability, from which to view it. But we are part of that moving landscape and our link is that powerhouse of infinite potential: the brain.

Control Groups

When experiments are carried out to test reactions to particular stimuli, the experimenter has to be sure that the reaction he is looking for is genuinely caused by the stimulus he is providing and not by something else. So two sets of subjects need to be used. One set receives the stimulus, the other does not. The set that doesn't is called the control group.

Suppose a psychologist decides to test the hypothesis that a person will readily reveal intimate details about himself if he receives positive expressions of interest and concern from the person he is talking to. The psychologist will arrange to have two different sets of talkers and listeners. The listeners in the group which is to receive the stimulus (i.e. positive expressions of interest) are told to be attentive and show concern. The listeners in the control group are told to look bored while their partners are talking, look around the room, scratch their earlobes and generally appear uninterested in what they are hearing. The talkers do not know of these instructions. They are just told to talk about their lives.

If the result is that members of the first group reveal their life histories in five minutes to a total stranger while members of the second group end up talking about the weather or mowing the lawn, the psychologist can be fairly sure that an interested ear leads to breaking down reserve. If, on the other hand, both groups talk equally readily about their lives or some in each group do and some don't, then the psychologist will realize that a supportive listening ear does not provide the essential ingredient for self-revelations. In that case, the hypothesis will not have been supported.

This is, of course, a simple example. In complex experiments the formation of control groups will also be more complex. There may in fact be several, in an attempt to account for all the possible variables that may have an effect upon behaviour. Only if the experiment subjects react significantly differently from the control groups in whatever task or reaction is being tested can conclusions then be drawn.

Crisis Intervention

A crisis is, literally, a turning point – usually a moment of danger or suspense. We talk about 'getting over a crisis' when somebody has ceased to be in a turmoil about whatever circumstances precipitated it. But that person may simply have suppressed the emotions which momentarily came to the fore, instead of experiencing them as a turning point at all.

Instead of saying 'There, there, it will all go away, have a pill and don't think about it' therapists involved in crisis intervention are concerned to help the sufferer see his crisis through because it is an expression of a desire to change his life situation in some way. But, because it is frightening – involving perhaps a sense of disorientation, inability to cope with daily life, or despair – the sufferer may want to stop the bad feelings as soon as possible instead of experiencing and coming to terms with them fully. Dedicated support is therefore essential.

Live-in crisis intervention centres now exist (although all too few) for people who need sudden, immediate aid and support but who don't want to escape into non-feeling under the stupor of drugs. A range of therapists, including psychiatrists, psychiatric nurses and social workers act as a team to help counsel the person in crisis. Different centres of course take different approaches but, in many, the support of other people who are recovering from similar types of breakdown is an important part of the process.

Some psychiatric hospitals now provide crisis intervention teams who can be called out to help in a crisis that has broken out in a home – where, say, an adolescent child has suddenly gone berserk and the parents don't know what to do. The team works with the family, establishing perhaps, that the parents are making unrealistic demands on the child and helps the family as a whole to gain a new insight into the affair. Instead of the child being removed to a mental hospital and given treatment, crisis intervention of this nature may well prevent hospital admission altogether. Therapists, by directing their attention towards the family as a whole, are often able to show that the problems which manifested themselves in the breakdown of a child, are in fact created by all of them. (See also **Family Therapy**.)

Critical Days
see **Biorhythms**

Cults

Religious cults that smack of the old evangelical crusades have proliferated throughout America and Europe over the last decade. Thousands and thousands of young people have, for a time at least, flocked to join such movements as Hare Krishna, Sun Myung Moon's Unification Church, The Children of God, The Divine Light Mission, The Jesus People and other lesser known off-shoots. Young people, lost and searching for meaning in life, or who rejected their drug experiences of the sixties as escapism, have ended up finding purpose and salvation as part of some tight-knit religious group.

What unites most of these cults is the presence of a charismatic leader, whose doctrine is sacred and whose orders must be obeyed. Support and love is provided in abundance and so is relief from responsibility and self-determination. Fears about the sinister effects of such cults have run rampant, especially from parents whose children have severed all ties to join one. The mass suicide that occurred at the Guyana base of The People's Temple cult, on the instructions of its leader, threw horrific light on the power that cult leaders hold.

The best known and the richest religious group is 'Reverend' Sun Myung Moon's Unification Church, which has thousands of followers called Moonies. The Moonies accept Moon's doctrine that God intended Adam and Eve to have perfect children and that they themselves must help rectify the fall by producing perfect people to unite the world in a new age of faith. Crusaders at street corners invite people to attend introductory workshops in which support, friendship and acceptance are freely offered. If the newcomer is persuaded to go on further, serious indoctrination begins. He is worn down by lack of sleep, long lectures, constant activity and then is asked to commit himself full time.

Full time commitment means contributing a great deal of money or property and moving into a Moonie commune, where disciples pray, sing and work hard to raise more money to spread the word by making and selling things. The religious fervour generated is strong. Members absorb Moon's thinking and live by his wishes. He is puritanical about sexual contact and often arranges marriages himself between Moonies who have never met. Moon is accused of brainwashing and conning his way into a massive income, which allows him a very luxurious lifestyle somewhat unlike that of his followers.

The Children of God, a more underground cult that is little known of now, also raised fears of brainwashing by its authoritarian practices. Here, converts were taken away to 'Babes Colonies' where, cut off from contact with anyone but members, they were taught discipline and obedience and memorized the writings of leader Mo, who was believed to be the direct link with God. The Children of God regarded all non-members as the enemy, so great kudos arose from taking advantage of the system outside. Members lived in squats and begged for or stole their food.

Hysteria from parents of cult-bound children has led to the emergence of 'de-programmers', individuals who try to catch cult members alone and then brainwash them out of their brainwashing. Others believe that the cults do no real harm, giving lost, lonely people a sense of purpose and a ready-made loving family. But such views may have been blighted by The People's Temple suicides.

One person who is sure that all such cults are dangerous is the American author Dusty Sklar. She traces Hitler's power to occult societies in Germany which required blind obedience to the leader, performance of horrific deeds if necessary for 'mankind' and total faith (*God and Beasts: The Nazis and the Occult*). She sees in cults, including **scientology**, and systems such as **transcendental meditation** and **EST** the tell-tale signs of blind obedience to a leader, blind devotion to a particular package of truth, unquestioning acceptance of irrational doctrines, secrecy and belief in 'special powers'. She fears that any of these systems could, with time, lead to another Hitler-type takeover, with all its horrific atrocities performed in the name of purifying mankind.

D

Defence Mechanisms

When we are anxious about something we don't want to face, we often employ a variety of cover-ups – what Freud called defence mechanisms.

Defence mechanisms can take several forms. Perhaps the most common is *rationalization*. We invent very reasonable-sounding excuses for our behaviour because we can't face our real motives. So the man who misses an important business meeting tells himself it would have been a waste of time, instead of facing the fact that he was too lazy to go.

Another mechanism is *repression*. Here a feeling is so troubling (be it sexual guilt or mother-hate for example) that it is pushed right back into the unconscious. As a result, the repressed individual is literally not aware of the cause of his anxiety, although he may still *experience* anxiety which he consequently finds inexplicable.

Regression, on the other hand, involves responding to the cause of anxiety, but in an infantile way. According to Freud, an adult who regresses has got stuck in some earlier childhood reaction to a particularly traumatic problem. So a cool, understanding boss may suddenly burst into a temper tantrum in a crisis because that was how he got his way as a child.

Denial is a defence mechanism that is similar to repression, but it is a conscious ploy. Here a person just refuses to see an unpleasant fact or situation although he knows that is what he is doing. Parents who are brilliant intellectually, for instance, may refuse to acknowledge that their child is not so gifted and insist on treating him – and driving him – as if he were.

Displacement involves directing anxiety feelings away from their real source and on to something else, less threatening. A man who is too frightened to stand up to his boss may take his unexpressed anger out on his wife.

Projection occurs when the individual lays his own hang-ups on others. The woman who is too frightened to stand up to her husband is convinced it is her neighbour, not herself, who has this problem. The secretary who has a secret hankering for her boss tells her colleague that she should take care not to become too besotted with him. She believes it is her friend, not herself, who is in danger of letting the situation get emotionally out of hand.

Finally, there is what Freud called *reaction formation* which means going overboard in an opposite direction in order to mask guilt and anxiety. An example is a woman who dislikes her neighbour's children, but goes out of her way to give them sweets and pat them on the head, to convince herself that she is not a child-hater at all.

Delta Rhythms
see **Brain Waves**

Delusions

A delusion is a false and unshakable belief which to an observer quite obviously has no basis in reality. It is often an accompaniment of certain **psychotic** disorders, such as **schizophrenia**, **paranoia** and **manic-depression**, where the sufferer seems to lose complete touch with external reality and operates in a world of his own.

A delusion can be of two main types. It can seem to spring

from nowhere, as in the case of the manic-depressive who, in his high phase, decides that he can buy the world or take over an opera-house for an impromptu performance of his own; or the schizophrenic who may firmly believe that he is Jesus Christ or a member of a secret sect of karate experts.

On the other hand, the delusion may be the result of an individual's attempt to explain some real but inexplicable phenomenon he is experiencing. So the person who is suffering from a persistent buzzing in the head may come to believe that he is the vehicle for the transmission of secret messages from Russian agents.

As, in the absence of proof, the only criterion by which a belief is usually judged a delusion is if it is unfeasible to other people or society in general, it is important to be sure that there really is no grounding in fact before labelling someone as deluded. Old people, for instance, may complain that their relatives are trying to get rid of them – and sometimes they are right! Fortunately for psychiatrists who make the diagnosis, delusions are usually bizarre enough for mistakes to be unlikely.

Dependence
see Addiction

Depression

To the non-professional, depression means feeling sad. And there can be many good reasons for feeling sad, such as grief or bereavement. Depression only needs treatment if there are certain severe symptoms. Psychiatrists call this clinical depression.

Clinical depression can take two main forms: *endogenous* and *reactive* (or neurotic). The endogenous variety is the more severe. The word itself means 'coming from within' and that is an extremely good description of the kind of depression it is. There seem to be no clear causes, no external circumstances, which explain the deep misery into which the sufferer descends. He experiences not only misery but a sense of worthlessness and utter dread of the future and this affects his whole life. Often sleep will be disturbed; the common pattern is to wake up early in the morning and be unable to get back to sleep again.

The mornings are the worst for the sufferer of endogenous depression. He loses all interest in work and relationships and may be unable to do anything but sit and brood. He may wander around restlessly, playing at things and fidgeting, but nothing productive will be achieved. The depression may also be accompanied by loss of appetite and sexual interest.

The reactive depression can be just as intolerable for the sufferer, but the symptoms are different and at least he has the cold comfort of knowing that his feelings are a reaction to some circumstances of his life, such as the loss of a loved one, a marriage break-up, failure to be promoted at work. But, because of his make-up, his reaction is more extreme than that of others. In reactive depression, a person often finds it hard to get to sleep but, once having done so, doesn't suffer early morning waking. He feels happiest in the morning and then gradually goes down as the day goes on. Sometimes he can be taken out of himself by a little cheerful company – a ploy that never works with endogenous depression. But he spends a great deal of time in self pity and blaming others.

It is often difficult for people who have never experienced such a low of either kind to understand that it is impossible for the sufferer to 'snap out of it'. That takes motivation of some kind – a positive decision to read a book, go for a walk, make a nice meal, ring an old friend – and motivation is exactly what the depressed person lacks. Sufferers of severe depression find it impossible to give that necessary lift to themselves and have to be taken out of the self-perpetuating mire of misery before they can start to make their own contribution to recovery. For this reason, anti-depressant drugs can be very useful as an initial means of alleviating the inner turmoil and freeing the individual to start doing something constructive about changing his circumstances (if it is reactive depression) or enjoying life again.

For reactive depression, drugs can only ever be a starting point. The person may well need to be removed from his troubling environment for a while, so that he can get things back into perspective, and perhaps undertake a course of psychotherapy to help him cope with his situation. The more severe endogenous depression calls for drug treatment or even electro-convulsive therapy (ECT), a controversial form of therapy which has sometimes been found to be effective. Interestingly, ECT has no positive effect in cases of reactive depression, although we don't know why.

Depression is, fortunately, the most easily treatable form of mental illness and symptoms lift quite quickly once treatment starts. However endogenous depression, as it seems to arise without cause, may recur at any time during a person's life, even after an interval of years. Both forms are extremely incapacitating while they last and they should never be dismissed lightly, for such depths of despair can be reached that a person may even attempt suicide.

Developmental Psychology

Developmental psychologists are interested in the stages that all humans pass through from infancy to old age. Every individual varies, of course, but for all of us there are basic patterns to our development from which we deviate little. Developmental psychologists tend to concentrate their attention on childhood, for this is the time when the most rapid and exciting changes take place. But also of interest to this group of psychologists are the stages we go through in adult life, in forming relationships, finding fulfilment at work, retirement, old age and eventually death.

Some noted developmental psychologists have proposed specific schemata for the various stages of human development. One such is the theory of *intellectual development* devised by Swiss psychologist Jean Piaget. His books on the subject, written over a span of twenty years reaching up to the late 1940s, have revolutionized our views about child development, and his theories remain substantially unaltered to this day.

Piaget, as a result of his own extensive study of children, concluded that there are four major stages to a child's intellectual development. First, from birth until the age of two, children go through the *sensorimotor stage*: initially a baby is only capable of making circular type of movements, touching itself or sucking its thumb. After a few months, it extends its interest to objects outside of itself – making simple shaking movements with rattles and so forth. It starts to appreciate sounds, such as those made by the rattle, and to be aware of independent movement – children enjoy dropping objects on the floor to watch them fall. By the age of two, a child has learned that objects are separate from itself and that they continue to exist, even when hidden. If a building block is hidden under a cushion, the child now knows that, if it lifts the cushion, it will find it there.

Next comes what Piaget terms the *preoperational stage*. Children now manipulate objects and, with the development of language, can ask questions about their world. But at this age, between two and four, they are totally egocentric. They think they

69

are the centre of the world and expect everyone else to have the same perspective on it as they do. They are surprised that their mother, who is a distance away, cannot see the same object that they are seeing or that mother can see objects up high which they themselves cannot. At this stage, they also start to name and categorise things.

The *concrete operations* stage lasts from age seven through to eleven. Children now start to deal with abstracts and reasoning. Particularly important is their new ability to understand what is called the *conservation* of objects. They learn to appreciate that the amount of water in a flat dish can still be equivalent to the amount of water in a tall thin glass, even though the latter looks more. They appreciate that the number of counters in one row is still the same as the number in another row that are more widely spaced, therefore making the row look longer. They can distinguish quantity from appearance.

Finally comes the stage of *formal operations*, which develops over the ages of twelve to fifteen and carries on into the rest of an individual's life. Children now learn to deal with relationships between things, to understand forms and to involve themselves in abstract problem-solving. They question and test images and concepts and formulate their own views about the world.

This scheme of things stresses innate intellectual programming, but Piaget was also aware of the role environment plays in learning. Stimulation that is provided by parents and teachers has a considerable effect on the speed and degree of intellectual development achieved by each child.

However, in recent years, Margaret Donaldson, professor of psychology at the University of Edinburgh, has completed research which now questions the whole foundations on which Piaget's theories are based. She maintains that we have underestimated children's competence as thinkers and over-estimated their ability to understand language. She no longer agrees with Piaget that, till age seven, children are extremely limited thinkers and believes that this misconception may explain why children so often become bored and unhappy at school.

From her own research, she has found that children often give the wrong answer to problems, not because they do not yet have the intellectual ability to understand what's going on, but because they have a different understanding of the question. In one experiment she showed children a model of garages, each of which had a car in it, plus one car that was outside the garages. When asked if all the cars were in the garages, the children all said yes. It turned out that the children were understanding the question to mean, did all the garages have cars in them? And their answer was right. The mistake was due to a misunderstanding of the word 'all' and not an inability to see what was in front of them.

Professor Donaldson says we are asking the wrong questions and, by presuming sophisticated language knowledge, teachers fail to understand a child's point of view.

American psychoanalyst Eric Erikson has plotted a Piaget-type ladder to account for normal *psychosocial development* in humans. He suggests eight stages. If the problems confronted in each fail to be satisfactorily resolved, they carry over into the next stage. As each stage involves the firming up of an individual's identity, people who move through to adulthood without resolving most of their earlier conflicts end up with an identity crisis (see **identity**).

Stage 1, at age one, is *trust versus mistrust*. According to whether a mother meets a child's needs for attention, affection and food, the child will learn to trust the outside environment, i.e., things or people outside of himself. Stage 2 is *autonomy versus shame and doubt*. By the age of three, the child is busy exploring his world and acting independently. If his parents encourage him, he learns to trust himself and his actions; if not, he starts to doubt his abilities. Stage 3 is a further step in learning independence. Between four and five, children are questioning and doing, making up their own games, coming up with their own ideas. This is *initiative versus guilt*. Encouragement and patience from parents leads to confidence in the child, whilst a negative response generates guilt and an unwillingness to initiate activity for himself. In adulthood, he is likely to be dependent. Stage 4, *industry versus inferiority*, particularly involves school. If a child performs well and receives approval, he will increase his efforts to learn and achieve. If he feels he is failing to meet others' standards, he may well learn a sense of inferiority.

At twelve, children enter the important Stage 5, *identity versus role confusion*. Now, with the onset of puberty, each child has to accept that he or she is approaching maturity. If earlier stages of development have all been resolved, he will be strong enough to trust in himself and weather the turbulence of adolescence. If not, it is a time of frightening identity crisis and uncertainty about the future.

By eighteen, young people are starting to form close relationships with the opposite sex (usually) and must be secure in themselves if they are to allow themselves to be vulnerable to others (*intimacy versus isolation*), i.e., a close relationship demands sharing and the closeness is too threatening if the individual has not developed his own secure identity. He pulls away and keeps others at arm's length in order to protect himself.

The next marked stage in human psychosocial development, Stage 7, falls around middle age. By this time goals have either been met or abandoned, and the approach to the future has to be realistic, not idealistic. It is a time of *generativity versus stagnation*, when we either choose to do something for the world by involving ourselves in causes or groups or else focus on ourselves alone.

Finally comes Stage 8, *integrity versus despair*, when old age has set in. Those who have led fulfilling lives can now accept themselves for what they are; those who are filled with regrets for missed opportunities eat their hearts out in the last sad years.

Lawrence Kohlberg has devised a system to explain *moral development.* Unfortunately, progression is not automatic and we may stick forever at any one stage along the way. First comes decision making (e.g., to steal or not to steal) based on whether we are likely to get caught. Second is conventional morality, such decision-making being based on avoiding disapproval from others. Third is the moral decision determined by awareness of the needs of one's community. Not many of us achieve this, says Kohlberg, and even fewer reach stage four; morality based on individual conscience, a sense of universal rights and wrongs and the willingness to stick one's neck out for it.

Dissociative Reactions

Dissociative reactions are methods of avoiding intense anxiety feelings. They differ from **defence mechanisms** because, although the root of the anxiety is successfully hidden from the conscious mind, the anxiety expresses itself through the emergence of some kind of separate personality. This unconscious split enables a person to hold conflicting attitudes at the same time, without experiencing any anxiety that would require him to resolve them.

There are three main kinds of dissociative reaction. One is *somnambulism*, or sleepwalking. Whilst in a sleeplike state, the sleepwalker may perform automatic physical tasks, such as running a bath or winding a clock, and remember nothing about it on waking up. Or he may do something which has some deep psychological significance, such as smashing a picture of his ex-wife, and still, of course, not remember having done it next day.

Extreme **amnesia**, the fugue state, is also a dissociative reaction as it involves the abandonment of parts of one's personality by means of 'forgetting' essential information such as name and address, and perhaps the taking on of a completely new identity.

The third form of dissociation is the **multiple personality** where the conflicts created by long-term unresolved stress lead to the emergence of a separate, or several separate, personalities embodying the behaviour traits that the person has unconsciously been trying to repress.

Divine Light
see **Cults**

Doman-Delacato

Doman-Delacato is a method for trying to increase mentally handicapped children's physical and mental potential. It was pioneered over fifteen years ago at the Philadelphia Institutes for the Achievement of Human Potential and involves a rigorous routine that has to be carried out for several hours every day. The routine is called 'patterning' and to apply it, a number of adults have to work together to coax the child to perform normal (to other children) activities such as crawling, rolling and grasping as well as less normal activities such as hanging upside down and somersaulting. The adults actually manipulate the child's limbs in an effort to stimulate his own muscles and, it is hoped, to stir the brain to stimulate those muscles for itself. Another technique involved is 'masking', a breathing technique aimed at increasing the blood flow to the brain, so that the brain will be less sluggish.

The whole process requires an immense amount of energy and dedication on the part of the adults, as patterning needs to be sustained over a period of years, and often the difficulties of finding neighbours, friends or relatives who are willing or able to help out on such a regular basis are insurmountable. But many who have persevered claim dramatic increases in their children's abilities.

Certain Yale psychologists are not so sure. They studied three groups of brain damaged children for a year, only one group of which received the Doman-Delacato treatment, the second receiving other 'motivational' treatment and the third conventional institutional care. The researchers found no significant advancement in the Doman-Delacato group but as this group and the second group both progressed more than those given just institutional care, the researchers credited the development to the fact that they received **attention**.

Down's Syndrome

Down's Syndrome is the correct name for mongolism, a form of mental retardation that has a genetic base. It is caused by a chromosome abnormality (see **genes**) and was discovered by an English doctor, John Down, in 1886. Whereas the norm is for a human being to have forty-six chromosomes in a cell, mongoloid children have forty-seven.

The result is that a mongoloid child has considerably lower than average mental ability, poor physical co-ordination, is short in height and has a particular slant of the eyes. Mongols do not usually have a very long lifespan. Some do live into adulthood but always remain relatively childlike. It is perhaps this 'childishness' that often makes them very warm, loving and trusting, traits for which mongols are well known.

They are capable of enjoying a relatively normal life, despite their reduced abilities and intellect, but many of them have had to live out their lives in hospitals for the mentally handicapped because of the constant, sometimes crippling, demands their early care makes on their parents. Although it used to be thought that mongols could not be taught to look after themselves, handle money and jobs, etc., nowadays many can achieve some degree of independence, if given the aid of an understanding community and sheltered work environments.

Dreaming

Shakespeare wrote '... to sleep, perchance to dream.' Modern knowledge tells us that there's no perchance about it. About every ninety minutes throughout the night we go into a state of dreaming. But why we dream and what exactly is going on is still a matter of controversy.

Freud thought that dreams were a tool of the unconscious mind. During sleep, when our minds are relaxed and daytime defences are dropped, the unconscious, according to Freud, can bring

74

deeply suppressed memories and experiences into awareness, in the form of symbols in dreams: typical symbols are relatives' deaths, being naked in public, flying and falling. (See **Freud**).

Ann Faraday, author of *Dream Power*, also believes that all dreams should be taken seriously. According to her, all the material is relevant to our lives but is not necessarily linked to the deep unconscious. She maintains that it is degree of interest that determines whether we recall our dreams or not. Cool, matter-of-fact people who are not very concerned with their emotions tend to recall little whereas those with an open approach to life remember their dreams more.

Ann Faraday believes that each recalled dream should be looked at on its merits rather than interpreted automatically as an expression of the deep unconscious. So if you dream of falling, she says, look first to see if there is any practical reason for it. Maybe some important piece of information has failed to register properly. She herself had a dream of falling off her balcony. Next day she examined the rails and found them extremely rickety. She assumes she half-noticed the fact the previous day but had been too pre-occupied to take conscious note.

If, on examination, however, there seems to be no threat of a real-life fall, the dream is metaphorical. Her own dream collection reveals several such examples; a colleague who dreamed of falling down the stairs at work at a time when he was fearful of demotion; a schoolboy who dreamed of falling down stairs at school after he had received a poor term report card; a woman who dreamed regularly of falling after her husband had been promoted, because of her fear that she would no longer be able to keep up with him.

Dreams, says Ms Faraday, reflect how particular feelings or experiences are affecting us at the moment in time that we dream them, regardless of whether the problem is a deep-seated repressed one or has simple, more superficial causes. Dreams are the 'thoughts of the heart' which can reveal themselves when the busy, practical pressures of our waking lives are removed.

American psychiatrist and sleep researcher Robert McCarley has an interesting new theory for the familiar symbols and patterns of dreams. Whilst not denying the power of the unconscious and the likelihood that our minds work through problems whilst we are asleep, he believes that the actual form the dreams take is linked with neuronal activity in the brain. He has concentrated on the dreams of REM sleep, light sleep characterized by rapid eyeball movement (see **sleep**) and says sudden scene shifts, changes of character, flashes of colour, and sensations of falling or paralysis are all linked with physiological activity. The memories, drives and personality of the particular dreamer will then be the factors that determine the actual 'story-line' of the dream and the role that the physiological sensations play in it.

The *brainstem*, which is at the lowest part of the brain, is critical for sleep. It controls functions such as heartrate, respiration and temperature as well as sleeping and waking. The middle of the brainstem, an area called the *pons*, is particularly concerned with the sleep cycle. The pons contains very large cells, called *giant cells*, the electrical activity of which can be monitored by microelectrodes inserted in the brain. These giant cells have been found to increase their activity just before and during REM sleep. The giant cells are connected with eye movement and also with the spinal cord neurons, so the rapid movement of the eyes and the muscular twitches noted in sleep might be a result of giant cell activity.

When our eyes move, we don't perceive the environment as being on the move as well. This subjective stability is created because certain higher parts of the brain receive the message that the eyes are to move and make compensations that alter our perception. But when the higher centres are not involved, the world does appear to move. This happens, for instance, when the brainstem has been strongly stimulated involuntarily as a result of a spin on a fairground ride. When we stop, everything seems to be spinning. McCarley suggests that eye movement in dreams is set in motion by the brainstem alone, the higher centres being uninvolved, and this gives rise to the spinning sensations in dreaming. The giant cells also play a part in giving us our sense of balance. If cell activity is highly stimulated during REM sleep, this could explain sensations of floating.

Another interesting connection between physiological activity and dream images comes from the giant cells' role in co-ordinating motor activities such as running and walking. The commands to move are being given but, because of muscle paralysis in sleep, are not carried out. (This was borne out by experiments on cats where the part of the brain that inhibits muscle movement was cut away and, as a result, the cats went through an amazing array of movements during REM sleep.) So, though movement in sleep is normally inhibited by muscles, other parts of the brain receive the motor commands and they become incorporated into our

76

dreams. Also, a sense of the muscular paralysis experienced during REM sleep sometimes expresses itself in a dream as an inability to move or slow motion running.

The research is still new but it may well help us understand the distinct but interrelated roles that both physical and mental processes play in our dream life.

Meanwhile, other research has concentrated on the role that dreams play in helping us resolve the problems that beset us during the day. Studies have indicated that in cases where an individual's mood improved after sleep, it was directly related to the content of his dreams. People whose dreams had taken the form of a 'sorting out' of problems or pressures awoke far more refreshed and with higher self esteem. Another experiment involved sixteen students who were about to undertake a course of psychotherapy and who were considered to be poor prospects for analysis because of their limited insight into themselves. These students agreed to be woken up every time they went into REM sleep and report their dreams. The idea was to see if they would stand a better chance in therapy if they had access to their concerns as expressed in their dreams. Sure enough, they all opened up rapidly in therapy, more rapidly than sixteen other students who had been deemed to have high insight but who didn't undergo the dream experiment.

On the strength of this sort of research, efforts have been made to 'programme' individuals to dream about specific things, by giving them a target topic before going to sleep. Although some dreams reported seem to indicate a disguised connection with the target topic, so far there is no concrete evidence that we can dream to order. Or rather, that's the case in the West. The Senoi tribe in Malaysia teach their children to control their dreams and dream-control is also a feature of certain esoteric systems. Don Juan, the Yacqui sorcerer that Carlos Castaneda made famous, supposedly taught Carlos to manipulate the substance of his dreams. So Western researchers are hopeful that, once we establish exactly what kind of and how much mental repair work goes on in our dreams, we too may be able to find ways to help it along.

Dream Telepathy
see **Telepathy**

Dyslexia

It has become very fashionable to say that an intelligent child is dyslexic if he or she has reading problems as if it were a new discovery and the condition could now be easily treated. Unfortunately, the word alone is new; the problem is an old one.

Dyslexia has been defined as follows: a disorder of children who, despite conventional classroom experience, fail to attain the language skills of reading, writing and spelling commensurate with their intellectual abilities.

Dyslexia may take the form of inability to recognize or name individual letters in a word, but easy reading of whole words; or inability to read words but easy recognition of letters. Some children who cannot identify individual letters have no difficulty in recognizing numbers or compound numbers.

Causes are unclear, though most experts would suggest that some neurological impairment is at its root. Because dyslexia is so little understood it takes its toll not only on the child but the family, who cannot understand their child's poor progress at school.

Of all dyslexic children, eighty per cent are boys and only twenty girls. American psychologist Diane McGuinness has a theory to explain this, and it relates to the specialized functions of the left and right hemispheres of the brain (see split brain) and the different rates at which they mature in girls and boys (see **sex differences**). A study of four-year-olds revealed that, when left alone to play, girls worked longer at any one project than boys and chose activities like painting and stringing beads. Boys were more keen on three-dimensional constructions, more efficient at them than girls and more noisy and disruptive than girls generally, while at play.

Boys, McGuinness says, learn by watching, manipulating and doing. They develop spatial skills first, whereas girls develop verbal skills and fine motor skills, which help them to draw and write. No wonder boys are often disruptive and unco-operative in class, if they are forced to sit quietly and listen, instead of testing things out for themselves. This is why, according to McGuinness, boys become labelled dyslexic and hyperactive far more often than girls. They are forced too soon into a form of learning that is alien to them, requiring skills which they develop later than girls. If they were left to develop at their own speed, they would learn these skills in due course. But once they are labelled dyslexic, of course, and put in remedial classes, they are well on the way to becoming dyslexic for real.

Dyspareunia
see **Sex Disorders**

E

ECT

Electro-convulsive therapy is a physical psychiatric treatment about which there has always been much controversy. It involves the application of electrodes to the head and the passing of a mild electric current through the brain, though, of course, the actual mechanics of the process are more highly sophisticated than that sounds. The aim is to induce a convulsion which is thought, by those psychiatrists who advocate it, to have a beneficial effect in the treatment of certain mental disorders.

It has long been known that electricity can stun. John Wesley, the Evangelist, was one of a few people who used primitive apparatus to shock the system back in the eighteenth century and claimed it did 'unspeakable good'. But ECT's real beginnings were in the 1930s when a Hungarian psychiatrist named Laszlo Meduna posited the theory (erroneous) that no one could suffer from epilepsy and schizophrenia at the same time and therefore, by inducing a fit of the former, patients could be cured of the latter. He used drugs but an Italian researcher, Ugo Cerlatti, who was at the time investigating changes in animal brain tissue caused by electrically-induced convulsions, suggested Meduna and he use this 'more precise' method for his patients. This was in 1938 and it didn't cure schizophrenia but it did have some positive effects on certain types of depressives.

However, early practitioners, in their zeal, sometimes gave patients multiple electric treatments in a single day, leading to confusion, incontinence and general inability to do anything. Nowadays a course of electric shock treatments is usually spread over eight weeks, muscle relaxants prevent a major and dangerous muscle spasm from occurring simultaneously with the convulsion (a spasm, if strong enough, could even fracture a spine) and a short-acting anaesthetic generally reduces discomfort. The electric shock itself only lasts a couple of seconds.

But the **brain** is an extremely delicate and complex organ which we do not yet fully understand. So is it really advisable to send a high-voltage electric current through it at all? Critics, of whom there are an ever-growing number, both within the psychiatric profession and without, think not. And while some patients are convinced that it has changed their lives for the better, others complain that, as a result, their memory has been impaired, they can no longer concentrate and their daily lives have been adversely affected. Researchers have claimed that the memory loss is only short-term, but that seems to be contradicted by some patients' testimonials that they have had to leave their jobs and settle for minor responsibilities because they could no longer function at their normal capacity.

Even most ECT enthusiasts would now agree that ECT seems to work only for certain illnesses and is relatively ineffective for others. As a treatment of depression for which there is no obvious cause ECT seems fairly successful, while for so-called reactive depression (a severe low caused by a particular event such as death in the family, dismissal from a job or lack of luck in love) it does not.

Some psychiatrists who are firmly oriented towards physical rather than psychotherapeutic (talking) treatments believe that ECT should always be tried because it doesn't do any damage. The anti-lobby say it *does* do damage and many believe it should be banned altogether, believing it to be a barbaric piece of butchery. Mental patients' rights groups still currently campaign for the right to *refuse* ECT, believing that any physically irreversible treatment should never be given to a patient against his will. (Patients who are compulsorily detained in hospitals, although nowadays relatively few in number, have no legal right to refuse treatment of any kind.)

Is there a middle way? Open-minded psychiatrists consider that ECT does have its place in psychiatry, but that it has been abused by being resorted to inappropriately as a quick, time-saving (but, in the long run, ineffective) method of treatment for patients who really required the chance to talk out their problems.

Educational Psychology

Educational psychologists are interested in the ways people learn, so much of their work is centred around schools. They study what motivates children to learn and compare the effects of various teaching methods, class size, the mixing of abilities, personality of both teachers and children, etc., on learning. Children who manifest some learning difficulty may be referred individually to an educational psychologist who will try to elicit the cause.

The teacher-child relationship is a particularly fruitful one for study by educational psychologists, as it is now clear that learning is not purely the result of ability. It has been discovered, for instance, that a teacher's expectations of particular children will very much mould their performance. In one experiment, teachers were told that certain children were extremely bright whilst others were not (although this wasn't really the case). As a result, the teachers' expectations communicated themselves to the children and so those designated 'bright' did do better than their apparently less fortunate peers. (See **primacy effect**.)

Ego
see **Freud**

Ego Psychologists

Ego psychologist is a general name given to those analysts who, after Sigmund Freud's death, broke away from strict adherence to his ideas and laid an emphasis on the *ego* rather than the *id* (see **Freud**). This group, led by Anna Freud (Sigmund's daughter) and Erik Erikson, believe that the ego, the realistic part of ourselves, develops independently from the id, the unconscious, baser part of ourselves. The ego, therefore, has its own store of energy which enables it to satisfy developing personal, social and creative needs without constant conflict with the id. Anna Freud and Erik Erikson have concentrated their attentions on children, as did fellow analyst Melanie Klein. But she believed that a primitive sense of good and evil is developed in the first few months of life, as a result of a baby's learning at the breast that needs can be thwarted as well as satisfied.

Electra Complex
see **Psychosexual Stages**

Emotion

Emotion literally means arousal, the word coming from the Latin verb *emovere*, meaning to stir up or excite. Our range of emotions is vast, spanning all the positive feelings such as **love**, pleasure and joy as well as the negative ones, such as **guilt**, **anger**, **jealousy**, **depression** and **fear**. Why and how we experience emotions has intrigued psychologists and philosophers for centuries and we still don't know all the answers.

The experience of emotion is very personal. The same situation may elicit fear from one person and excitement from another. Or, if the emotion experienced is the same, the intensity may vary. It seems that both physiological and psychological factors govern the experience of emotion.

All animals express emotion. Dogs wag their tails to show pleasure, cats flick their tails to indicate unease, while humans have a range of emotional behaviours that far exceed any other animal's. Charles Darwin believed that emotions are a means of communicating with others and are therefore important for well-being and survival. And we certainly have innate emotional needs, such as the need for warmth and love. Animals, deprived of love when young, grow up fearful and anti-social. And the same is true of humans. People who experienced little warmth and attention as children have great difficulty forming relationships and adjusting to their environment as adults.

In their search to find the triggers for various emotions, many psychologists have studied the physiological responses that accompany them. When we experience fear, for instance, our bodies are speeding up the rate they pump out blood and increase the production of adrenalin. The effect is to gird us into action to deal with the threat, whatever it is. But which comes first, the experience of fear or the bodily changes which, in turn, induce the feeling of fear? It is now known that the body changes in themselves are not sufficient to induce fear. In an experiment where subjects were injected with adrenalin, they reported feeling the physical sensations of heart palpitations, etc., but they didn't experience any real emotion. So it would seem there has to be an external trigger.

Research on the brain has revealed that a part called the hypothalamus is involved with the experience of emotions. Sensory impulses pass through this area and are directed on to higher areas of the brain, where the emotion is then 'experienced'. In the 1950s, it was discovered that the hypothalamus actually has pleasure-sites and, by stimulating these areas with electrodes, a person can be made to feel pleasant sensations. Later, it was discovered that similar sites for the feeling of aggression and fear could also be pinpointed the same way.

But, just because it seems that our brains have special centres primed for the experience of emotion, that does not make us virtual automatons who duly cry or smile when the necessary signals are triggered. Brain activity varies from individual to individual and the intensity of the experience of emotion will vary according to the degree to which the brain is activated. Some people need strong stimulation of the brain before they feel emotion, others respond to impulses of much lesser intensity.

Monte Buchsbaum, of the National Institute for Mental Health in America, found just such a difference in different individuals when he electrically stimulated their brains. Out-going extravert people needed strong and continuous stimuli, whereas more withdrawn, introvert people needed less stimulation and soon reached a 'cut-off' point after which they allowed themselves to experience no more. He also found, by measuring central nervous system signals, that women, in general, experience all emotions more strongly than men, and children experience them more strongly than adults. So there may well be a physiological difference between men and women, when it comes to the experience of emotions.

But the effects of learning cannot be ignored when talking about emotional reactions. As children we soon learn whether it is 'right' in our parents' eyes to be warm and affectionate or to cry openly or to express anger. In order to win parental approval and keep their love, we learn to suppress those emotions that they frown upon. Men have usually learned to suppress tears because it's 'unmanly', while there is an equally strong taboo against the expression of anger by females. This may explain why the experience of the same emotion may lead to very different behaviours by different people. A man who feels anger may let out his hostility by kicking the table leg. A woman, experiencing anger, may instead withdraw into herself or act out her anger in fantasy.

Because our emotions are so complex, we often misinterpret those of others, expecting them to react in the same way as ourselves. Someone who is direct and open and who spontaneously expresses love or anger when he feels it may not realize that someone else, who does not verbalize those feelings, is also feeling those things. One way that we can tell what people are feeling is by looking at what their bodies say about them. Someone who is sitting with arms folded and legs crossed tightly at the ankle is obviously trying to shut himself off, even if he is engaged in telling someone else that he loves and wants them. Our bodies can reveal emotions that are even a surprise to ourselves (see **body language**).

Encounter Groups

The early nineteen seventies saw the mushrooming of the **growth movement** (or what American journalist Tom Woolf satirized as the Me-Decade). Developing out of the work of Carl **Rogers**, groups started up in America and then elsewhere, devoted to helping people to strip off the layers of social conformism and discover their 'real, deeper selves'. The encounter group was one of the first, and still most popular, forms of this voyage to self discovery. (See also **T-groups**.)

Encounter groups dispense with experts, although there is usually a leader who will hold things together. Groups vary in length from a 'drop-in' evening encounter session lasting just a few hours, to a two-day session. There are even marathons, lasting for 48 uninterrupted hours, without sleep. They really get the defences down!

When people come for the first time to an encounter group, they probably know no one and perhaps have no idea what to expect. Often the leader will break the ice by suggesting they do some warming-up exercises – walking around the room, touching everyone's hand, making eye contact or just doing breathing exercises. Beyond that there may be no instructions at all. Participants just have to start in, saying whatever they want to say. 'I've got this hang-up about my breasts.' 'I feel such hostility towards my boss.' 'Sometimes I really want to cry but I just can't let go.'

It takes time for people to relax enough to open up and they may be greeted by hostility from other participants, especially if the problem being voiced is one someone else is unconsciously trying to suppress. Other groups may lead new members in more gently, by providing points for focussing attention. Everyone, for instance, may be asked to say what they like or dislike about their bodies or what they feel about each person in the room. The leader encourages participants not to skate over the surface of feelings. If they feel negative, they should express it. Someone might say: 'I dislike Bob because he reminds me of my father.' On the basis that such feelings should be expressed instead of

84

suppressed, the leader will probably provide a cushion and suggest the father-hater pound it and scream and shout and, in fact, express everything he or she had really always wanted to say to the father. With the whole of the group paying attention and giving emotional support, the result can be quite electrifying. Someone else might be frightened of being touched. With her cooperation, the leader may suggest that she lie on the floor while the rest of the group strokes her. In such a supportive environment she may allow herself to relax and accept that it is not 'bad' to enjoy being touched after all.

Usually encounter groups combine a whole mixture of therapeutic techniques, from verbal sharing to physical exercises, gearing each to every individual's particular needs.

Some people declare that encounter groups have changed their whole perspective on life. For others, if the group is not properly run, it can be frightening and forbidding. The critics of encounter groups dismiss them as self-indulgent.

Certainly there are pros and cons to such a group experience. The extremely personal nature of the emotions participants experience usually leads to a strong group identification and feelings of warmth and closeness, despite the fact that they were probably all strangers a few hours previously. But feelings of letdown may well ensue once the session is over and everyone goes back to their own lives. Encounter groups provide a rather sheltered environment in which permission is given, as it were, for the expression of any feeling at all, however rude and cruel. So how far an individual is capable of taking back his new assertiveness or understanding into his daily home and work relationships is presumably some measure of the group's success. Then again, some would claim that any new insight into one's motives and behaviour is of value in itself.

Epilepsy

Although it is no longer believed, as of old, that an epileptic seizure is a sign of being possessed by the devil, many people still do believe that epilepsy is a form of mental illness. In fact it is an organic disease and most sufferers show no psychological disturbance at all. If they do, then the illness is unrelated to the epilepsy (unless the years of social stigma and embarrassment take their toll as stress factors).

Epilepsy can be caused by brain tumours, brain injuries or

haemorrhages but in most cases has no discernible cause. It can, however, usually be controlled by medication. The two most common varieties are called *petit mal* and *grand mal*, and both can be precipitated by fatigue, over-excitement, too much alcohol or certain frequencies of sound or light – strobe lighting in a discotheque may be dangerous for the epileptic.

Petit mal, as its name (small illness) implies, is not very serious unless seizures are extremely frequent. It is more often experienced by children than adults and the seizures, which may last only a few seconds, can occur as often as thirty times a day. Because the episodes are so brief, there is only a very short loss of consciousness and the sufferer may even be unaware he has had a fit. Grand mal, however, is a seizure of the whole brain which can be dangerous. A sufferer may first experience a warning sign of the impending attacks, such as awareness of a particular smell or dizziness. There are intense muscular contractions, during which the body grows rigid, perhaps with one arm outstretched. This phase is followed by violent jerking, as the muscles relax, and then the sufferer loses consciousness. On regaining it, he feels intensely drained and confused.

Eric Erikson
see **Developmental Psychology**

Erogenous Zones
see **Psychosexual Stages**

ESP

ESP is a shorthand term for extra-sensory perception or, as it's often described, our sixth sense. It is the ability to receive and transmit information mentally and can take various forms: **psychokinesis** – the ability to move objects by mental powers; precognition – ESP of future events; **telepathy** – ESP between people; and **clairvoyance** – ESP of something that is out of sight or of some event elsewhere in the world.

Dramatic cases of ESP are frequently reported but scientists have traditionally been very sceptical about their validity. J. B. Rhine, an American, developed special cards to try and test ESP. One person would stare at a card showing a strong black triangle or a circle or some similar simple shape and the subject being

86

Fig 3. Cards used in laboratory-controlled ESP experiments.

tested would try to 'pick up' from him which card was being looked at. But, although Rhine found a number of people who scored well above statistical chance, he could not repeat the experiments with consistent success.

Some ESP researchers now claim that they do have a repeatable experiment and, that they have isolated the factors that increase the likelihood of ESP: relaxation and lack of external distractions. They point out that people who experience ESP are usually daydreaming, meditating, sleeping or dreaming. So perhaps ESP *is* a sixth sense, but a weak one, often masked by the stronger signals coming in from our other senses.

Recent research over the last few years has therefore concentrated on testing the ESP potential of relaxed subjects and comparing them with the abilities of unrelaxed subjects. Results seem to confirm the case. The relaxed subjects do 'receive' more images. Other experiments have attempted to simulate sensory isolation, blocking out all other input so that the experimentee can concentrate on ESP signals. This is done with what is called Ganzfelds. White noise, a repetitive, soothing sound (like the breaking of waves) made up of all audible frequencies is played through headphones, and halved pingpong balls are placed over the eyes to reduce light. In 26 recent such trials, as many as fourteen subjects reported strong ESP. Experiments with people under hypnosis have produced similar results. Again, there is relaxation and awareness of internal sensations.

The researchers are currently interested in the ways that personality factors, moods and even rapport with the experimenters themselves affect the experience of ESP. They, if not their more sceptical colleagues, are convinced that ESP is not such a rare ability after all.

est

est (always spelt in the lower case because that is unpretentious and so, say its supporters, is est) stands for Erhard Seminars Training. It is not a therapy or a religion but claims to be a technique to change people's lives. It was developed by American business man Werner Erhard and its sessions aim to show people that they live according to expectations and beliefs about what they think *should* be happening instead of accepting that they are what they are. What happens to them is usually of their own making and there is really nothing special to strive to 'be' anyway.

This may not sound like much of an insight but Erhard claims that it has to be experienced, not just acknowledged. The fact that participants are urged not to divulge the specifics of what actually goes on may do much to heighten curiosity value and consequent attendance.

The experience comes during sixty hours of 'training' spread over two weekends. During this time, 250 trainees, all of whom undergo the experience together, sit and listen to a barrage of unpalatable truths about themselves, their problems, hopes and aspirations in a deliberate attempt to shock them out of their complacency. The idea is to teach the trainees to take full responsibility for their own lives instead of blaming their failings on other people or seemingly unavoidable circumstances.

est has been endearingly described as the 'no-piss training', not because it's a straight-to-the-point and no-rubbish-sort-of technique, but because there are very few breaks for calls of nature – or even for food. The idea is not to create a cosy conference atmosphere but to batter the trainee so hard and consistently with the truth about himself that he is open to receiving the insight – or, in est jargon, 'getting it'. For this reason it has been criticized as using brainwashing techniques.

By all accounts it is strong stuff. As people's intricate cocoons of carefully constructed rationalizations and pleasing self-images are stripped from them, physical reactions are intense. Backaches, headaches and other ailments often develop and vomit bags (much used) are also provided.

People who 'get it' may go home freed from what were previously troubling goals and self-expectations – for a marriage to work out, or for promotion to come, or to save for a new deep-freeze. Instead they can put themselves whole-heartedly into what *is* instead of what they think should be and make decisions accordingly. There are, however, follow-up est sessions available, presumably to 'get' even more. And what about those who fail to 'get it' at all? Well, that, says Erhard, is what *they* got.

Ethology

Ethology is the study of animals in their natural environment with a view to discovering what kind of behaviour is genetically inherited and what kind of behaviour is learned. Ethologists are therefore interested in fixed patterns of behaviour, actions that are always carried out in the same way by all members of a particular species. Many modern ethologists are now interested in relating their findings to human behaviour: discoveries about young animals' needs for affection and warmth may throw light on our own, for instance. Konrad Lorenz has developed a theory about human aggressive instincts based on his studies of animals (see **aggression**).

Eugenics

Eugenics is 'the science which deals with all the influences that improve the inborn qualities of a race; also, with those that develop them to the utmost advantage', according to its innovator, Sir Francis Galton (a brilliant philosopher, physician, mathematician and geographer and cousin of Charles Darwin).

In other words, he was interested in selective breeding. He had decided, after studying men of greatness in various spheres, that their genius was owed to their genes. And if greatness could be inherited, it could be bred, which meant that a species could be 'improved' by breeding together members who were thought to have the desired genetic traits.

The words 'selective breeding' tend to bring to mind Nazi hopes of producing a 'pure' Aryan race. But less distasteful forms – indeed, positively useful ones – are common in medicine today. Most large hospitals have units where any genetic defects in unborn children can be detected well before birth. This is particularly valuable when there is a high chance of a child being born handicapped, because of the mother's age, or where one parent is known to have an inheritable disease for example. Parents are then given the option of abortion.

Exhibitionism

An exhibitionist likes to show him or herself off, whether it's by hogging the limelight at a party or wearing skintight clothing. But, while there is probably a little of the exhibitionist somewhere in all of us, the word also has a narrower, purely sexual, definition. Here the exhibitionist is the person who likes to expose his (and it usually is his) genitals in public. From the shock, awe or admiration he supposes will ensue he derives sexual excitement and even ejaculation.

Exhibitionists usually install themselves in quiet, out-of-the-way spots, such as alleys or heathland, and wait for a woman to pass. The fact that she can't escape a sudden confrontation with his genitals contributes to much of his pleasure.

Although the sudden ripping open of a raincoat or an unexpected leap into view from the bushes may seem to constitute an aggressive act, the exhibitionist is usually excessively timid and has great difficulty in forming relationships, particularly with the opposite sex. It is often because he is too frightened to approach girls that he jumps at them – the shock tactics make him feel in control of the situation. But the exhibitionist is usually harmless.

A support group started for teenage boys in England, who had been put on probation for offences of indecent exposure, found that all the boys had similar backgrounds. They had come from strict homes, usually with over-protective mothers, where sex was never discussed. They were introverted, had no real friends and tended to stay at home rather than go out in groups or to dances. They failed to meet girls and failed to understand the development of their sex drive during adolescence. Few knew anything at all about sex, let alone about the possibilities of its expression in an emotional relationship.

De-sensitization techniques (i.e. gradual doses of female company) have been found effective for many sex-offenders, not only exhibitionists, where the underlying problem seems to be an inability to form relationships.

The desire to·exhibit sexual parts is not wholly restricted to men but women are more easily able to 'disguise' their behaviour as accidental – the one button too many undone on a blouse or the seemingly unwitting display of black nylon pants under a short skirt.

Exorcism

Exorcism, the casting out of devils from those who believe themselves to be possessed by them, is as old as man's belief that the universe is made up of powerful opposing forces, struggling for the upper hand and prepared to use man as a means of achieving it. In Christian cultures, the struggle is between God and the Devil; in primitive societies, it is between good and bad spirits or forces of dark and light.

Many primitive tribes have regular exorcism ceremonies where people maddened by their host spirit are led into a frenzy by a healer, whilst drums sound all around to a rhythmic, monotonous, beat. Eventually the sufferers fall to the ground in a fit and come to their senses 'cured'.

Priests, in Western Christian religions, are ordained with the authority to try and exorcise devils, by invoking powers greater than the devil itself. Incense, bells and purified water may be used to dismay the spirit, as well as threats and violent behaviour. While this is going on, the possessed person feels as if he is the battleground of warring forces, and finally collapses. Other major religions, such as Judaism, Buddhism and Islam, also have their methods of casting out devils.

British psychiatrist William Sargant, who has studied possession in primitive cultures all over the world, says that the symptoms of possession are similar to those of extreme hysteria; contortions of the body, swollen features, wild staring eyes, involuntary howling. He believes that exorcism 'works' because of the physiology of the brain. The exorcist works the sufferer up into an emotional frenzy, either through his repeated invocations or by the accompanying rhythmic beating of drums and non-stop dancing. A point comes when the brain can take no more, which is when the individual suffers convulsions or collapses. At this time, as Pavlov's experiments on **conditioning** with his dogs indicated, the brain is in a highly suggestible state, and the individual is ready to believe anything he is told. He is freed from his devils because he now believes he is.

Whatever the thinking behind it, exorcism can be an effective way of bringing relief to a mentally ill person, who is convinced he has been taken over by devils. But, as Sargant himself warns, this method only works with people whose illness is acute rather than chronic. Intensely depressed or obsessional people, who cannot release emotion under any circumstances at all, may be harmed rather than helped by the process. This is recognized even in primitive cultures, where healers concentrate their attentions on the less seriously ill. (See also **brainwashing**).

Extinction
see **Behaviour Therapy**

Extravert

An extravert is someone who turns to his environment for stimulation, whereas an introvert relies more heavily on his inner resources. These two terms were coined by psychoanalyst Carl **Jung** as part of his personality theory. People can have elements of both, or appear to be one while really being the other but generally we tend towards either extraversion or introversion. The extravert enjoys being around other people, thrives on a variety of experiences and usually seeks attention, especially when under stress. The introvert prefers quieter pursuits and withdraws into himself when he is anxious.

Current research suggests that it may not be social learning that decides which one we are – instead our behaviour could be governed by biological processes. Research into sensation-seeking seems to show that high sensation-seekers (people who enjoy risk, new experiences, partying) are physiologically capable of responding to ever increasing intensities of stimulation, whereas low sensation-seekers reach a cut-off point after which they can't take any more. Their brains actually show a diminishing response to high intensities of stimulation.

It is thought that the differences may be due to fluctuations in the levels of chemical neurotransmitters in the brain (which affect the brain centres that govern mood and motivation). Sex hormones also seem to play a role. Male and female sex hormones are *both* found in both sexes but high sensation-seekers seem to have higher levels of each than low sensation-seekers.

This research is still at an early stage but if extraversion and introversion really are the effects of biology, it will be a blow to the Freudian view that people are driven towards sensation-seeking in order to mask anxiety.

F

Faith Healing

A man was suffering from a major prolapsed disc. He was in agony night and day and the only hope held out to him was an intricate operation on the spine that had less than a fifty per cent chance of success. He was recommended by a friend to go and see someone who had no medical qualifications but who just might be able to help. In desperation he went. In an ordinary living room in an ordinary house, the healer passed his hand up and down the afflicted man's spine. In a matter of minutes two years' pain was gone. That is a true story about the recovery of a man who later became a healer himself. How was it done?. Not by magic, not even by faith.

Though we generally refer to such inexplicable cures as faith healing, there is no *faith* as such involved. Not only does the patient not need religious faith, he doesn't even need to have faith in the abilities of the healer himself. Children and animals have even been treated this way. So those in the profession prefer to be called healers or spiritual healers. Such healing has never been looked on kindly by the medical profession. Whilst in Britain some doctors may now refer patients to healers, if they think it might help, in some other countries faith-healing is actually illegal.

It is the impressive dossier of successes that has lessened medical hostility towards the claims of healers, at least in Britain. But we are no nearer knowing exactly how it works. Healers themselves usually believe that there is some divine force involved, some power that is channelled through themselves.

Healers work in different ways but most sit quietly, relax, maybe let the mind wander, and pass their hands over the patient's body. If the pain is centred on a particular part of the body, they will concentrate on that spot. Instantaneous total cures are rare but immediate alleviation of pain and discomfort is common. The patient comes back over a period of weeks for more healing, until the condition is completely cured.

To most people, there is something slightly 'spooky' about faith healing and most turn to healers only as a last resort, when the resources of orthodox medicine have finally failed. But healers do also work on less crippling conditions, such as hay fever. Some healers even perform absent healing, if a patient cannot come to see them in person (see also **psychic surgery**).

Some experiments have been run in America and Britain in an attempt to pin down the healing force or at least to try to identify what is actually happening. Researchers have attempted to detect changes in the properties of the phials of water or salts that healers often hold in their hands when at work. And they have also tried to measure temperature changes, but without success. However, measurement of the healers' and the patients' brainwaves have yielded some interesting results: it would appear that the healers generate some unusual brain patterns which the patients pick up. Skin-response meters have also been used in an attempt to measure levels of emotional arousal, discernible only in the skin. (When tense there is low skin resistance and when relaxed, there is high resistance). Patients appear to drop quickly from tension to relaxation under the healer's hands.

Miraculous though it all seems, healers (who are often very ordinary people doing ordinary jobs and offering their healing powers for free in their own time) say they are only catalysts in the process. Patients must be prepared to change any habits which may have a bearing on their illness. Otherwise, the cure will only be temporary.

Family Therapy

Family therapy grew out of the realization that, often, when one member of the family was persuaded to see a psychiatrist because of strange or disturbed behaviour, the problem didn't actually rest with him alone. He may have been the one to manifest symptoms of disturbance but he was merely reacting to a situation that was, in fact, generated within the family as a whole. Family therapy, therefore, opts to work with the whole family and not just the individual manifesting the problem.

For instance, a couple may call in the doctor because their son is withdrawn, sulky and baulks their authority. They think he is deliberately trying to thwart them and bring them misery, despite all that they have done for him. His behaviour is so inexplicable to them that they presume he must be ill. If the doctor suggests family therapy, either one or two (male and female) therapists will be assigned to work with the family. While talking with the family together, encouraging them to open up freely about their feelings towards each other, the therapists may uncover a very different story from the one they were first given. It may be that the parents are not very happy in their relationship and each has unconsciously tried to make their son their own ally against each other. The son may, as a result, feel pulled both ways and distrustful of both. He becomes sulky and withdrawn and difficult to handle as a result.

The aim of the therapy is to help the family see this true state of affairs and improve their communication with each other, so that the son is no longer used as a weapon in a private fight between the parents.

Family therapy is now practised in a growing number of child guidance clinics, child psychiatric units and social service departments. Many of the therapists are social workers who have taken special training in its techniques. One of these is *sculpting* where family members are asked to create a tableau that to them represents their family relationships. The aim of such dramatic representation is to bring home to the family the ways in which their individual feelings and actions enmesh.

This idea is at the core of family therapy; that a family is not just a random group of people all acting independently, but a highly interdependent body in which the behaviour and needs of each member influences and is influenced by all of the others.

Fantasy

Fantasies are mental images, and can take many forms: day-dreaming, sleep-imagery and hallucinations are all forms of fantasy. Our ability to fantasize a life as we would like it may help us to cope with our actual lot. (Freud saw fantasy as an acceptable and necessary outlet for unacceptable aggression.) But whereas a little imagination may enrich our inner lives, too much can be dangerous. The person who allows his fantasy world to take over is dangerously out of touch with reality.

American psychologist Leonard Giambra used 1200 men and women in his research to discover that women daydream, at all ages, more and with greater intensity than men. Sexual fantasies are, however, more common to men, except between the ages of 30–34 when women have as many sexy daydreams.

Freud said that sexual fantasy and sexual 'perversion' were the outcome of a person's struggle to find sexual fulfilment in the face of taboos created by family and society. As no one can fail to reach adulthood without some kind of sexual scarring, according to Freud, we all end up as in some way 'perverted'.

Somewhat in line with this view, many of the newer sex therapists believe that no one should be ashamed of sexual tastes and couples should share their fantasies, however way-out.

Whereas we might well wish that our daydreams about promotion or winning a holiday to the Caribbean could be realized. many sexual fantasies take a form which the fantasizer has no wish to fulfil in real life. Some women fantasize about rape and submission not because they want to be raped but because it is a way of dealing with deep-rooted sexual guilt – sex should not be enjoyed. While it might be more desirable to eliminate the guilt, at least the fantasy enables the women to enjoy a functional sex life.

Complicated measurement procedures, including the use of clitoroplethysmographs (ingenious devices complete with photocells to measure blood volume changes in the clitoris) have enabled interested researchers to discover just what does and doesn't turn people on.

In general, women still fantasize about idyllic moonlit encounters with a loved one while men are more into sensuous strangers and group sex. English psychologist Glenn Wilson recently investigated the erotic effects of pornography on fantasy. It would appear that while sexual activity, particularly masturbation, increases on the day of viewing erotic material, satiation is rapid and behaviour quickly returns to normal. Sex dreaming at night decreases after viewing. He also studied sex offenders and discovered that all the deviant groups reported seeing less pornographic material as adolescents and adults and having less of a fantasy life than non-offenders. He concluded that, if anything, exposure to erotica inoculates people against risk of perversion – but not, of course, in the Freudian sense.

Fear

All very young children and young animals share one important aspect of growing up. In the same way that every youngster learns to recognize certain people, things and places as familiar, there develops a corresponding fear of the unfamiliar. So babies show definite signs of fear if left alone in a new, alien room in someone else's house. Animals show signs of fear if suddenly confronted with a peculiar object, like a tent, in their territory.

Sight of the strange object will set certain physiological changes in motion. The adrenal glands start pumping out **adrenalin** which helps the other organs get into gear to fight the 'emergency' (see **fight** or **flight reaction**), the salivary glands slow down and the digestive muscles contract.

These changes, safety measures linked with survival, give us our physical feeling of fear. But the psychological experience of fear is not necessarily in direct proportion to the physiological experience. A study of experienced parachutists revealed that the physical response (sweating skin, increased blood pressure and breathing rate, etc.) increased slowly until plane take-off but was falling steadily by the time the parachutes had opened, whereas their emotional experience of the fear was high before the flight, went down whilst they were on the plane and then rose sharply as they jumped. In first-time parachutists, the psychological experience of fear mirrored the physiological one.

This seems to show that, while experienced parachutists never lose their fear, their bodies actually adapt to it and reduce their response. Both reactions are important in survival. Lack of fear leads to complacency and error. But too much unnecessary physical upheaval, caused by physiological reactions, leads to undue stress and a breaking down of the system.

Behaviourist John Watson believed that all fear is a simple matter of response to a stimulus and that individuals can be **conditioned** to become frightened of anything. To prove the point he conditioned a young boy called Albert to become terrified of white rats. Everytime he gave Albert a nice little rat to play with, Watson struck a steel bar with a hammer. The loud noise startled the child and, as it occurred every time he touched the rat, he started to associate white rats with frightening noises. The association also extended to include fear of white fur coats, white rabbits and suchlike.

Behaviourists believe that most **phobias** are the product of such

97

faulty conditioning, an incorrect association between some frightening experience and a usually innocuous object. Sometimes a genuine alarm caused by an unpleasant experience (e.g. touching a boiling kettle) can become associated with the object rather than the experience. So a child fails to appreciate that it is the heat of the boiling kettle which causes a burn and becomes nervous of kettles generally, hot or cold.

Fear isn't only activated by physical danger. Several psychologists have found that *fear of failure*, for instance, is a strong motivating force in some people's actions. Children who come from authoritarian homes where they are pushed to succeed in school and to be obedient and tidy are actually motivated not to fail instead of to succeed. Their fear of failure allows them only to undertake easy projects that are assured of success or to attempt such incredibly difficult ones that their failure is automatically excusable.

Fear of Success
see **Sex Differences**

Fetishism

Fetishism means conferring on some object such sexual significance that orgasm can't take place without it. The object itself may have nothing to do with sex – it could be a handkerchief or a photo. But more likely there will be some sexual connection – e.g., panties, bra, a shoe or stockings. The fetishist will get aroused by kissing, fondling, smelling and tasting the fetish object. Most fetishists use the chosen object as an aid to masturbation but some actually use it for arousal as a preliminary to intercourse.

Boot and shoe fetishism and rubber and leather fetishism are so common that a number of magazines are produced as an aid to titillation and a forum for the sale of such wares. Why these particular fetishes should be so popular is unclear except, perhaps that rubber harks back to childhood rubber sheets and pleasant feelings of protection, while shoes seem to be symbolic of the vulva.

Fetishism seems to be restricted to men and they can often cross with the law when their zeal for new panties or bras, or whatever their fetish object is, leads them to raid women's washing lines or houses. For those who want to kick their fetish, **aversion**

98

therapy has claimed some success in breaking the link between object and sexual arousal.

Fight or Flight Reaction

Built into our body systems is a reaction known as the 'fight-or-flight' response, which swings into gear if we are under threat of attack. It is an important survival mechanism in animals and no doubt had a crucial role to play in man's own survival, when he was battling against wild animals for territory and for food.

In effect, when threatened with attack, a number of changes automatically take place in the body to prepare it to cope. The heart rate goes up and blood-flow to the muscles escalates, while blood flow to the skin decreases (to minimize bleeding if there is to be a wound); blood pressure and muscle tension increase, with the result that the body is ready for action – for fight, if there's a chance of victory or for headlong flight, if not.

The choice of fight or flight also seems to be dictated by bodily processes. It has been found that high levels of the hormone adrenalin are present when an organism experiences fear while high levels of noradrenalin, also produced by the adrenal glands, accompany strong feelings of anger. Rabbits, which turn tail and run, tend to show a predominance of adrenalin whilst fighters, such as lions, secrete more nor-adrenalin.

In humans, the same mechanism still functions but, now that there is no call for the basic survival needs of the wilds, the response has different triggers. Our bodies go into the fight-or-flight syndrome when we are presented with threats of an emotional nature as well as physical ones. So an unexpected summons to the boss or a fracas in the bus queue are the kinds of modern-day threats that our bodies gear themselves to respond to, although survival, as such, is hardly at stake. In unpredictable situations, such as the interview with the boss, the 'fear' reaction may be high, with increased secretion of adrenalin and resultant anxiety. And, as with animals, when our anger is roused and we are preparing to wade in and defend our rights, noradrenalin is on the up.

Some recent research on violent patients in maximum security hospitals seems to indicate that certain people have an abnormality of the adrenal glands whereby noradrenalin fails to be converted to adrenalin at the appropriate time. The result is that such people don't feel anxious or moved in circumstances that

99

bother most people, and tend to act aggressively in circumstances that don't warrant it. The patients who suffered this adrenal abnormality made up a high proportion of those who had committed seemingly senseless murder, usually of strangers.

Fight-or-flight reactions, when functioning correctly, have a vital role to play in animal survival. For humans the effects can be rather damaging instead. Unlike animals, the circumstances that elicit this reaction in us often don't provide the opportunity for fight or flight at all (we don't run out of the room when being given a dressing down by the boss, nor do we roll up our sleeves); the result is that the body is all geared up for action but has no way to let it go. It carries on pumping up the blood pressure, speeding the heart rate and tensing the muscles to no avail and this can be physiologically, as well as psychologically damaging (leading, perhaps, to furred arteries and muscle spasm). The only antidote to the build-up of stress is **relaxation**.

Fixation

A Freudian term which has crept into popular usage in a somewhat altered guise. We tend to say people have a fixation on something if they talk about it a lot or are excessively interested in it. In **psychoanalysis**, however, it refers to an arrested state of sexual development. The libido, the driving sexual force, passes through various phases as it grows to maturity: oral, anal, phallic and finally, genital (see **psychosexual stages**). If, at any one stage, the growing child does not have the needs of the libido met, he becomes fixated at that point. So, if the child doesn't get enough attention during the oral phase, he may carry on through life trying to meet his oral needs – by smoking, drinking, over-eating or being excessively dependent. Most of us are supposedly fixated at one stage or another but that doesn't mean that we never reach any of the rest. The individual who has an oral fixation may also have traits that go with the anal or genital stages.

Flooding
see **Behaviour Therapy**

Food Allergies

Can an allergic reaction to coffee, chocolate, eggs or any other food manifest itself, over time, in symptoms similar to those associated with severe mental disturbance? Orthodox psychiatrists tend to think not but there is a growing 'food for mental illness' lobby both in Britain and America.

An American allergist, back in 1925, discovered that elimination of whole groups or families of food – like cereals or citrus fruits – could lead to relief of conditions, such as headaches, stomach aches and asthma. But it was some years later that another American, Herbert Rinkel, discovered the important difference between a chronic and an acute allergy. An acute reaction leads to immediate discomfort of a short-term nature every time a particular food is eaten. A chronic allergy could have more dire, deceptive, and long term effects.

Rinkel said that if someone became allergic to a food he ate every day, such as bread or potatoes, he would at some point cease to suffer a bad reaction (which he may never have associated with those foods anyway) and a pick-me-up feeling, every time he ate them, would occur instead. After a period of time, maybe years, the regular eating of the food would cease to provide a 'pick up' and lead to exhaustion and feelings of illness. Rinkel came to these conclusions after isolating the effects of particular foods on individuals in tests.

This work has been taken further by a few psychiatrists who are convinced that severe long-term allergy to certain common foods is the cause of up to a third of all apparent mental illness. They have claimed successes with patients suffering from severe depressions and uncontrollable violence, all of whom ceased to need drugs or any other treatment once their diets had been corrected.

Forensic Psychiatry

Forensic psychiatrists specialize in treating and giving medical opinions on mentally ill people who commit crimes. They are very often called upon to give expert evidence in court, concerning a defendant's state of mind in relation to the crime. (See **insanity**.)

Free Association
see **Freud**

Free-Floating Anxiety
see **Anxiety**

Freud

Sigmund Freud is the father of **psychoanalysis**. The cohesive personality theory which he developed is still the basis for all psychoanalysis, although many of his disciples have broken away from strict Freudian lines of thought. It is to Freud that we credit the concept of the unconscious mind, not because he was the first to 'discover' it but because he was the one to formulate all existing knowledge as well as his own ideas and beliefs into a psychoanalytic theory.

Freud was born in Freiberg in 1856 and was the apple of his mother's eye. She was convinced he would be a great man and, with her encouragement (he was given the only oil lamp in the house when he wanted to study), he learnt Spanish, Latin, Greek, French, Hebrew, Italian and English. Freud admitted later that the expectation of success, kindled in him by his mother, led him to achieve it in reality.

At seventeen, he went to study medicine at the University of Vienna and worked with Ernst Brucke, a leading physiologist of the time. It was here that he learned that energy cannot be destroyed, only transformed, and this had a great bearing on his later ideas about the personality. Later he worked at the Vienna General Hospital where he practised various aspects of medicine and first gave serious study to mental disorders. In 1885 with a grant from the hospital he went to study under the renowned Jean Charcot, director of a neurology clinic at an insane asylum in Paris. Here he discovered that **hysterical** disorders which manifested themselves in paralysis of a limb or sudden blindness could be cured by **hypnosis**.

Viennese physician Josef Breuer, another teacher and friend, also had a tremendous impact on Freud. He too was experimenting with hypnosis and Freud was working with him when he learned that a patient under hypnosis was able to reach below his or her ordinary consciousness and recall painful old memories that had a strong relevance to current mental troubles. This realization convinced Freud that hysteria was caused by repressed memories. This revolutionary idea came to affect the whole course of psychology. When one of his own patients, by relaxing and letting her mind run free, found she too could get back in touch with painful memories that till then had been locked away from consciousness, *without* hypnosis, Freud was on the way to developing the system which has become psychoanalysis today.

Using his knowledge about the nature of energy, he decided that the mind is made up of three levels, distinct but interrelated: the *conscious* mind, the *pre-conscious* mind (which houses thoughts and feelings just below consciousness and easily brought into it) and the *unconscious* mind. It is a dynamic theory, meaning that Freud presumed a constant movement between the levels, with some feelings and experiences slipping away from conscious awareness and others intruding from the unconscious, in the form of dreams. He also believed in *multiple determination*, that there are numerous causes for any one event. Accordingly, nothing, to Freud, could be an accident; slips of the tongue (see **Freudian slip**) were all determined and were the result of something in the unconscious mind trying to find its way back into an individual's awareness.

Freud explained human behaviour by the assumption that every personality has three vital strands, the *id*, the *ego* and the *superego* (the first being totally unconscious, the latter two being a mixture of unconscious and conscious). The id is the 'boiling cauldron' of the personality, the animal energy which is concerned with immediate gratification of basic desires for sex, food, etc. It is such a strong force that its energy sometimes finds expression in fantasies. It houses the instincts, love and death wishes, and blindly follows the pursuit of pleasure with no sense of 'right' or 'wrong'. Love, aggression and greed all emanate from the id.

To prevent the id from having its own irresponsible way, we have the ego, the guiding force of which is not pleasure but reality. The ego controls the id, allowing it only to fulfil those desires which it isn't detrimental to fulfil. It is ego control which teaches us to delay gratification, to 'wait' for things, when it is expedient to do so. The ego is a personal value system whereas the top layer of the personality is the superego, an amalgam of belief systems based on external standards set by society. Its main role is to suppress the unseemly desires of the id by forcing the ego to ignore all the id's baser urges. The reward for so doing is societal approval.

The three centres of our personality are therefore always warring for superiority, looking for consensus through conflict. So we can love and hate simultaneously. As there is a set amount of energy in a closed system (and Freud saw man as a closed system), one of the three has to come off 'best' at the expense of the others. If the id has most of the energy, an individual is impulsive or even amoral; if the ego, he is realistic; if the superego, he is an ultra-upright moral citizen, entrenched with others' belief systems.

Because, said Freud, the sex instinct is our strongest motivating force (see also **libido**), our psychosexual development has tremendous, all-important bearing on our adult personalities. Freud believed that all neurosis derived from sexual repression. (See **psychosexual stages**). It is with all this material that Freud set to work in psychoanalysis, trying to uncover unconscious motivations arising from the repression of unsatisfied needs. After dropping hypnosis, he used *free association*, whereby a client would say whatever came into his mind. The theory is that the unconscious will take over, forcing itself into awareness through the expression of, maybe, apparent trivia – which really has deep significance (see **psychoanalysis**).

Freud also believed that clues to repressed painful experiences could be found in dreams – where unconscious feelings would express themselves in disguised forms. (The disguise was necessary to satisfy the refusal of the subconscious to face disturbing thoughts.) So Freud worked out a complex system of *dream symbolism* (the symbol might be the compression of several feelings or events) in order to interpret dreams. Although he believed that dream symbols were very individual, some he decided were universal: the dream of being naked in public and ashamed represents natural sexual desires, the fulfilment of which society inhibits; dreams in which a person, usually a parent, is dead represents the dreamer's unresolved conflict with his same-sex parent, who had rivalled him for the love of the opposite sex parent (see **psychosexual stages**).

For other elements of Freudian thought, see **defence mechanisms, dissociation, fixation, libido, resistance, sublimation** and **transference**.

Freud, Anna
see **Ego Psychologists**

Freudian Slip

Freud believed that we are all a mass of conflicts, because we all have conscious and unconscious minds (see **Freud**). Painful experiences and memories are locked away in the unconscious, along with baser desires which our conscious minds, steeped in the mores of society, are reluctant to admit. But the unconscious is always trying to fight its way through to the conscious and, according to Freud, this is the origin of what we call mistakes or accidents, such as slips of the tongue, but which are really intentional acts – the intent being that of the unconscious.

So when someone writes 'bridal' instead of 'bridle', it has a significance (perhaps something to do with sex and surrender) – presuming, that is, that they do know how to spell. Freud mentions someone who said she would be back in a 'movement' instead of a 'moment', and it turned out she was bothered about constipation. In each case, the unconscious is trying to tell us something we have repressed (and psychoanalysis is a method devised for uncovering exactly what it is that has been repressed, using Freudian slips as clues).

Freudian slips don't have to be verbal. So, if we lose some papers that are vital for a business meeting, we may think it is an accident but, in Freudian thinking, really we are expressing hostility to the individual who has forced us to take such responsibility in our jobs and hope, unconsciously, that ineptitude will lead to our being relieved from it.

Frigidity
see Sex Disorders

Fringe Therapies

Since the mushrooming of the personal **growth movement**, so many 'ways to self-knowing' have come on to the market that it is difficult to find a term that can adequately describe them. Therefore I am using fringe therapies to cover all the modern techniques which purport to help individuals get more in touch with themselves but which fall outside orthodox approaches to the task, such as psychiatry and psychoanalysis.

So this includes humanistic therapies, such as **Gestalt** and **Rogerian**; learning therapies such as **rational-emotive therapy** and **reality therapy**; and **body therapies**, such as **bioenergetics, primal therapy, rebirthing**, etc. But it also includes those techniques which concentrate not just on getting in touch with one's real emotions but on finding one's spiritual core. Individual offerings of this nature are too numerous – and often too transient – to mention, but main ones include Arica, a forty-day intensive that supposedly leads to a total self discovery, **est** and now Insight Training

Seminars, a new techinque which has received the blessing of writer Arianna Stassinopoulos and which claims to combine all the 'best' of approaches to higher consciousness along with a little bit more of its own. As one of its guides (their word for trainers which is est's word for leaders) claims, 'it gives you a deep experience of being alive; it's a consciousness of what I call loving'. The aim is not to teach but to help individuals find their own truths 'for wisdom is inside us all. There are eternal truths we just keep forgetting'.

Other groups which are hot on enlightenment but less concerned with therapeutic techniques I have listed under **cults**.

Future Shock

In 1970 Alvin Toffler published a book called *Future Shock*. Its theme is that new learning and new discoveries of all kinds, converging on us from all directions and all at one time, are taking their toll on us psychologically. We are struggling to cope with the implications of space travel, computer technology, and new theories about behaviour. We are suffering from over-stimulation and the loss of old anchors in our lives as everything succumbs to change and, says Toffler, we just cannot cope with it. This is future shock.

He makes the plea for people to make conscious efforts to find new ways to anchor themselves in society, now that the old values of family, community and religion are no longer meaningful to many. People must learn to understand the significance that all the wider changes have on their own lives. They must become aware of and face the individual stress factors they cause and make sure they have 'stability zones', such as secure emotional ties, as buffers against the flux.

G

Genes

Genes determine vital characteristics such as general body shape and the way bodies function. Blood types, fingerprints, eye colour, hair colour and skin texture are all associated with particular genes. Genes may also, to a certain extent, determine our behaviour.

There are billions and billions of cells in our bodies and each contains genetic material called chromosomes. In every cell, bar the reproductive cells, there are twenty-three pairs of chromosomes. Every single chromosome contains more than 1000 genes. Each member of a pair of chromosomes is called an *allele* (an alternate) and these pairs influence specific characteristics, such as hair colour. When a cell divides in two during growth, it duplicates its genetic material exactly and sends a copy into each new cell. Long string-like substances of molecules called DNA and message-carrying chemicals called RNA are responsible for the actual transmission of traits.

The reproductive cells (*gametes*) have twenty-three single chromosomes instead of twenty-three pairs because these chromosomes will pair up with those of the opposite sex partner after an egg is fertilized. The result is a single cell called a *zygote* which then divides and grows. It is this union that determines hereditary variations among individuals. For instance, in a newly formed pair of chromosomes, one allele may be for blue eyes and the other for brown. Someone who has one allele of each will have brown eyes because brown is the dominant gene. The allele for blue eyes is said to be recessive, or not dominant, and may only find expression, in blue-eyed children, if both parents have a recessive blue gene. Other dominant characteristics are dark hair, curly hair, large ears and freckles.

Of the twenty-three chromosomes in each sperm or egg, one pair establishes a child's sex. The female carries an identical pair of chromosomes, called XX because their shape resembles those letters. The male carries a pair called XY, so named for the same reason. The reproductive cell has a single chromosome. The cell of the mother will always carry an X, whereas the father's may carry an X or a Y. Dependent on which, the child will be a girl (X) or a boy (Y).

It is purely a matter of chance which gamete merges with which, but that chance dictates many of the physical characteristics of a child. Many genes often work together to determine one particular trait (polygenic traits).

But we are not totally the product of genetic inheritance – even though we'd still each be unique if we were. For each reproductive cell of twenty-three chromosomes contain over 30,000 genes. The possible combinations of 30,000 characteristics from the mother merging at random with 30,000 characteristics from the father are way beyond imagination. However, environmental factors influence the way we look and behave as well. The kind of food we eat, the climates we live in, can produce differences in physical characteristics. Size and weight, for instance, are influenced by a combination of hereditary and environmental factors.

The higher the species on the evolutionary scale, the more difficult it becomes to isolate the two. How do we know that characteristics are inherited at all? Purely because careful examination of family trees has revealed clear inheritance of such factors as blood types, body types and hair colour. To study the degree to which more complex features of our make-up are inherited, twins have been a godsend to geneticists. Identical twins, developed from one egg, are presumed to have identical genes, whereas unidentical twins, formed from two eggs, do not. The two can be compared to see how far environment and how far heredity influence certain intangible qualities, such as intelligence.

There is much controversy about the basis of intelligence but research has shown that there is some genetic influence, indicated by some very similar intelligence scores amongst identical twins. The pattern of the menstrual cycle also has a clear genetic basis, although environmental factors get very entangled here. The age at which menstruation starts has dropped over the past few decades because of improvement in nutrition. But research involving identical twins has shown that they still tend to start to menstruate for the first time within three months of each other. In unidentical twins, the time lag is as much as a year.

Certain diseases are known to be genetically inherited. Cystic fibrosis, for instance, is caused by a single pair of faulty recessive genes. Huntington's Chorea, a progressively degenerative disease of the nervous system, and haemophilia, where blood fails to clot properly, are also genetically inherited. Haemophilia is carried by women but only inherited by men. (No woman could survive haemophilia because she would bleed to death at menstruation.)

One area where war wages between the environmental and genetic schools is over the inheritance of schizophrenia. One school of thought, originally led by Dr R. D. Laing, maintains that it is purely the product of environment and certainly research in England has linked incidence of schizophrenia with poverty-stricken areas. On the other side, twins have revealed yet again that, where one of two identical twins develops schizophrenia, there is a sixty per cent chance of the other developing it too. But that is hardly conclusive evidence of heredity.

Genetic influence remains a very difficult area. While the advances we have made in understanding how our genes work are quite astounding, suggestions that some races, for instance, may be intrinsically less intelligent than others because of genetic factors have only caused outrage. And understandably so, for genes do not determine any individual level of intelligence, only ultimate potential, which few of us ever realize anyway. Genes cannot flourish without the right environmental nourishment and stimulus. It is up to each of us to flesh out the structure and to make the best of what we've got.

Genetic Engineering

The words 'genetic engineering' tend to conjure up images of rows of pre-conditioned babies, some programmed to be the world's great thinkers and leaders (see **eugenics**), others to be the menials who deal with the dreg-ends of society's needs without ever asking for a pay rise. Unlikely, we hope, but not so far-fetched, for this area of science is the study and practice of creating life outside the womb and altering the genetic material that imprints an individual. While such knowledge can be put to the good, by enabling us in the future to correct the defective genes that cause diseases such as mongolism or haemophilia, it could also be subject to obvious abuse. (Little did Pavlov know that his discoveries about **conditioning** would find expression in brainwashing techniques.)

In the early 1950s a sperm and an egg were for the first time fused outside of the female body, in a test tube. The egg lived for six days. Now, twenty years later, we are seeing the world's first test tube babies, developed from eggs that are fertilized outside the womb and then returned to it to develop and grow. It is a discovery that has brought hope to childless couples where one partner is sterile.

But the possibilities of genetic engineering far exceed that. In 1978 Dr Arne Gyldenholm in Denmark suggested that women could conceive without men being involved at all. The method, tested on frogs, is to remove a nucleus from the ovary and replace it with a nucleus from elsewhere in the body. The new nucleus then guides the life cycle of the egg and embryo which will ultimately grow into an exact likeness of the mother. This is a similar idea to cloning, in which a cell is taken from a male or a female and is activated so as to divide and grow (every cell in the body has the potential to grow into an entire human being). Cloning produces an organism exactly like that which donated the original cell and has been successfully achieved with frogs. It is envisaged that within fifty years we could have the first clonal human.

Geneticists see a future possibility of our buying frozen embryos, free of defect and labelled according to essential characteristics, such as sex, hair and eye colour, intelligence level, etc., ready for later implanting. Others imagine further genetic discoveries enabling us to put an end to cell deterioration and senility and prolonging life – or even re-constituting someone who had died a century before.

The possibilities are frightening and exciting. Whilst many of the advances are still embryonic themselves, they will soon be real enough to warrant extensive debate on the ethical issues that will come to affect us all.

Genital Stage
see **Psychosexual Stages**

Gestalt Therapy

Gestalt is one of the many humanistic therapies, which have as their goal self-understanding and the uncovering of creative potential through free self-expression.

Gestalt therapy was developed by psychiatrist Fritz Perls in the late fifties and its techniques are very often applied in **encounter** groups. The essence of Gestalt is in its name – a German word, the nearest equivalent of which is 'wholeness', 'completeness' or 'form': we are all a 'wholeness' that is greater than the sum of our parts and Gestalt aims to put us in touch with it. In keeping with this idea, it sees the mind and body as inextricably linked and a sense of wholeness can only be achieved by paying attention to both.

Gestalt therapy can be individual or take place in groups. But when the latter, it involves one person at a time being in the 'hot seat', the centre of the therapist's and the group's attention. The therapist will try to make the person aware of the defences and barriers he puts up to the world – in his words and his thinking, as well as in his body, by rigid posture or inability to allow himself to be touched. Awareness must precede change. By drawing the person out, the therapist will be encouraging him to 'be himself' and accept himself, instead of conforming to what he thinks others require of him. Perhaps this is best expressed by Perls' 'Gestalt Prayer':

> I am not in this world to live up to your expectations
> And you are not in this world to live up to mine.
> I am I and you are you
> And if, by chance, we meet each other, that's fine.
> If not, it can't be helped.

Gestalt therapy concentrates on the 'here and now', rather than on the idea that we are what we are because of some dreadful experience in our childhood. Perls has even said that infantile trauma is an excuse, hung on to in order to justify unwillingness to change. But the 'here and now' approach doesn't dismiss the past. Gestalt thinking has it that we carry much of the past with us. We have never resolved it and so it is still a part of our present. Just another, more modern-sounding expression of the old psychoanalytic ideas? No, for the Gestaltist is not interested in trying to track back and find out what really did happen when his client was three. (The word client is used in preference to the more passive 'patient'.) It is the effects on an individual's current life of some past, unresolved (and therefore still present) anxiety that will be uncovered in therapy. The 'why' is irrelevant, it is the 'how' that counts.

Gestaltists refer to unresolved past experiences as 'unfinished business'. By tackling the defence system first, the wounds emerge in the here-and-now of therapy.

One of the Gestalt techniques for assaulting defences is to encourage an awareness of the different roles we play and the effects they have on our behaviour. So the client may be asked to perform a kind of duologue in which he plays both parts, e.g. the aggressive part of himself arguing with the timid self. Emotions which surface, such as anger, are given release in a safe way – an individual is invited to pound a pillow and express hate feelings that he says he feels, say, about his mother.

Dreams are also an important part of Gestalt therapy. But they are again treated in the 'here and now', not analysed as by the Freudians and interpreted according to set principles. A Gestalt therapist encourages a patient to interpret his dreams in his own way and even to speak with the voice of one of the main features of the dream – a hill he was trying to climb, or a person from whom he was seeking attention. The idea is to open the client to a new perspective that may give him insight into himself.

Another Gestalt concept is that of the top dog and the under-dog. We all have elements of each but one has the upper hand. The top dog is authoritarian or bullying; the under-dog is whining and full of excuses for himself. Gestalt therapy aims to unite the two in such a way that they merge and change, producing a personality that is realistic and understanding, instead of dominant or submissive. 'Wholeness', as already said, means more than just a sum of parts.

Graphology

Over ninety per cent of anyone's personality, from emotional make-up through to sexual responses, can be assessed from handwriting – if you apply the rules. At least, that is what graphologists claim and graphology, the science of reading handwriting, is no longer dismissed as a quirk of cranks. It is taught in several universities in Europe, and even in more conservative countries, such as Britain, it has an increasing role to play in personnel selection, vocational and personal guidance.

Working from the thesis that every physical writing movement reveals the tensions and drives of the personality, the graphologist concentrates on the way letters are formed, and the speed and the pressure used to form them. Critics protest that we don't invent writing style, we are taught it and that, of course, handwriting changes. The graphologist will reply that retention or variation of taught style is a significant personal choice and that of course, handwriting changes. It changes, even imperceptibly to the layman, with every changing circumstance of our lives.

Intuition is not the guiding spirit of graphologists. On the contrary, there are specific rules for the analysis of handwriting the learning of which, along with experience, could make a graphologist of anyone.

The pointers that a graphologist looks for in handwriting are too complex to ennumerate in detail, but some of the indicators can be briefly described here, to give an idea of the process. However, as graphologists are careful to stress, analyses are made by an overview of *all* the personality indicators; nothing can be judged from just a single stroke. Also, as we are all a mass of contradictions, every aspect of our writing can be given a positive or a negative interpretation. Nothing in our handwriting is inherently good or bad.

Graphologists look at the slope of writing (backwards shows inhibition, forwards extraversion); the regularity of the baseline (the more irregular, the more emotional the writer, whereas a straight baseline shows level-headedness). Other indicators are size of letters, width, connections between letters, fullness or leanness of letters, pressure and speed. As mentioned, there are positive and negative interpretations for all of these, and the correct interpretation can only be judged by the overview of the writing as a whole. Speed, for instance, can express spontaneity, generosity and self-confidence; or it could equally well indicate aimlessness, flightiness and rashness.

Illegibility does not affect a graphologist's ability to judge a handwriting – in fact, it may be all the easier to interpret because the writing is usually produced fast and is therefore uncontrived. For that reason, shorthand is very revealing.

Graphologists are not even fooled by people who 'try hard' to produce impressive script. It seems that duplicity is impossible to keep up. Ends of letters and sentences start trailing away into normal hand and that's what the expert looks for.

A graphologist can only tell a writer's *psychological* age and sex, so when approached for a personality analysis, he asks to be given the writer's actual age and sex as a guide, and a fairly long sample of writing.

Group Pressure

We probably all like to think of ourselves as fairly independent individuals with views of our own. However, group pressure often has a stronger hold on us than we imagine and non-conformism is very hard to maintain if there is *no* social support for it at all.

Solomon Asch carried out a revealing experiment in 1965. He showed students a card with an eight-inch line drawn on it. Then he asked them to say which of three other cards had a line the same length as the first. Only one had an identical line, the others were quite clearly shorter or longer. However, in each group of students, all bar one were 'set up' to give the same wrong answer. The genuine subject didn't know this. And, although the stooges were obviously giving wrong answers, the pressures of being a social isolate were too much.

The size of the group played a part in the results. With only one stooge, the real subject usually gave the correct answer; with two he sometimes conformed and, with three, he was unlikely not to conform. However, if in a larger group one other stooge was 'set up' to give the correct answer, so would the genuine subject. So a little social support is enough to encourage an individual to make a stand.

However, overall, the findings are alarming. If people can be swayed on such trivial and self-evident matters, how easily can we be swayed in matters of political, social or moral import? (See also **social psychology**.)

Group Therapy

Group therapy is any therapy where groups of people are involved. Whilst the therapy itself may come in many forms, the distinguishing factor is that the grouping encourages people to share emotions, ideas and experiences with others who may have had similar experiences or who may be supportive and caring. The **growth movement** therapies, such as **encounter, bioenergetics** and **gestalt**, tend to take place in groups, with or without leaders, and group **psychotherapy** in hospitals is also common.

But groups do not always generate caring and sharing. One person in a group may become the focus of the others' negative emotions, suffering criticism, hostility and even rejection. It takes a skillful leader to ensure that no individual leaves with their self-image shattered!

A group's success also very much depends on the motivation from within it. If people are too nervous or unwilling to open up, a session may pass with no one saying anything at all – especially if the therapist believes in non-directive techniques. But whereas the therapist may think that there's insight to be gleaned even from silence, a whole hour spent uncomfortably shuffling one's feet does little to promote the patient's confidence in the method!

The Growth Movement

The growth movement, so called because its accent is on personal growth, developed from the ideas of **humanistic psychologists**, notably Abraham Maslow. Humanistic psychologists believe that everyone has free will (instead of being governed by purely

114

unconscious forces or the conditioning of the environment) and this will should be freely expressed. But, till Maslow, no one really thought that ordinary, seemingly healthy people needed a special environment in which they could explore their deeper needs or 'wills' and come to fuller understanding of themselves. That sort of thing was reserved for ill people.

The result was the mushrooming, first in America and then in other countries, of growth centres to which ordinary people could go for a day or a weekend to 'explore' themselves, to come to terms with deep-seated hostilities, prejudices or fears which didn't prevent them from carrying out their daily lives, but which did prevent them from developing their full potential.

Growth centres borrowed techniques from a variety of therapies to facilitate the purpose: e.g., bioenergetic exercises, gestalt techniques, Reichian massage. These have been supplemented by an ever-increasing number of alternatives. A look at a programme run by a growth centre (which may have a special name and not be called a growth centre as such) may reveal intriguing courses in creative dreaming, howling, Chinese dancing, primal scream-ing, meditative techniques, sexuality workshops, peer counselling and a whole host more. The uniting factor is that each and every technique is supposedly a method via which ordinary individuals can get more in touch with themselves, strip off old defences and lead a new, freer life, where everyone is allowed to 'do their own thing'. In its zeal to abandon psychoanalytic jargon, with its condescending 'professional' overtones, the growth movement has developed an extensive vocabulary of its own (see **psycho-babble** and **encounter groups**).

Guilt

Guilt feelings are very closely tied to childhood learning and the development of our own moral codes. Once a code is learned it is very difficult to shake, which is why feelings of guilt can sometimes be so inexplicable in later life: the feminist, for instance, who despite fully believing in female independence and autonomy, still feels guilty if she is late getting her husband's dinner. Her guilt does not indicate that women are not intended in the higher scheme of things to be independent and autonomous; more that early, entrenched convictions cannot always be shaken by later, intellectual understanding.

The most formative years are those between nought and five.

This is when a child learns 'the rules'. He knows something is wrong if he gets told off for it; he is quick to process such information and formulate it into a working code. The code will vary from child to child, of course, which begs questions about whether we have a fundamental sense of Right and Wrong. For, the child who picks up from his parents that it's natural to try and cheat the system – out of tax or television licence payments – but wrong to cheat your friends will develop a very different code from the child whose parents instil it with the idea that to cheat anyone or anything is wrong. The first may learn that loyalty to intimates comes before everything; the second that external standards of right behaviour govern even one's faithfulness to one's friends.

It is from our own moral codes that we develop conscience. Our conscience nags us if we break our rules and then we feel guilty. Freud recognized this conflict between what we want to do and what we feel we ought to do and said that, if unresolved, it could find two secondary forms of expression. We either defuse our guilt by projecting it outward, on to someone else, as justifiable anger (the feminist feeling guilty about serving dinner late may deal with her guilt by abusing her husband for expecting to be waited on hand and foot) or we may turn it inwards, resulting in self-reproach and loss of self-esteem.

Guilt is a very powerful drive. It can be a positive force, enabling us to live peaceably with each other because conscience dictates that we take account of each other as well as ourselves. Or it can be destructive, if we fail to come to terms with it. But it is vital, however unpleasant it may feel. A person who experiences no guilt is amoral – and the totally amoral personality is that of the **psychopath**.

H

Halo/Horn Effect

This intriguing-sounding concept refers to the human tendency to allow one overriding impression about a person to colour their general judgement. This then makes any change in attitude difficult.

Someone may be interviewing applicants for a job when he notes, on one form, that a candidate is interested in model railways. Being a railway enthusiast himself, the interviewer may then become more disposed to notice the candidate's good qualities.

That's halo. The converse is the horn effect, where a person's bad qualities or a bad initial impression sets the tone for future interraction. If a job candidate's first action on entering the interview room is to trip over the doorstop, the interviewer might become unswervable from the belief that the applicant is clumsy and inept in every way. In other words, we see what we expect to see and expectations are very quickly set up.

Hawthorne Effect

This completely un-self-explanatory and technical sounding term describes a discovery that is basic to psychological experimentation. It is named after the Western Electric Company's plant in Hawthorne, near Chicago, which was the setting for a research experiment into productivity in 1927.

Using six women workers as the subjects of the experiment, the researchers installed them in a special workroom, away from the rest of the workforce, and then systematically altered their working conditions in various ways to see the effects on productivity. They tried implementing five-minute rest periods twice a day, then ten minutes, then ending the work day at various times between 4 p.m. and 5 p.m., amongst other things. After each variation was tried, the women had to report their views and the effect on their productivity was monitored.

After a year, productivity had definitely soared but the psychologists could not figure out exactly what it was that had done the trick. They realized that the women were actually responding to all the attention they were getting from the researchers and that the rest periods et al had little to do with the rise in efficiency at all! At least that discovery enabled them to suggest that attention and expressions of interest from the supervisors would have the same effect. But, more importantly for psychology as a whole, they had realized that the mere act of being observed changes the way an individual behaves, often for the better as far as performance is concerned.

It sounds obvious now but it had them fooled for a while at Western Electric.

Heredity
see **Genes**

Hermaphrodite

A hermaphrodite is an individual with mixed sex characteristics. The condition is rare and draws its name from the Greek youth Hermaphrodites who became fused with a nymph he fell in love with.

There are three forms of hermaphroditism. Firstly, there is the *female pseudohermaphrodite*, so called because the individual is quite clearly female genetically, with all the internal female sex organs (ovaries, fallopian tubes, vagina and uterus) but she has an extremely enlarged clitoris which may look like a penis. The cause is usually an over-production of particular male sex hormones (androgens) and can be corrected by the administration of counteracting hormones.

Secondly, there is the *male pseudohermaphrodite*: here all the sex hormones are male and the individual is genetically male but sometimes external male organs are lacking. The condition may not then be discovered until a doctor is consulted about lack of onset of menstruation, for, to all intents and purposes, the individual will have been living as a female. Surgery can extend the 'vagina' but the person will of course be sterile. In most cases of male pseudohermaphrodism, however, the external organs are mixed or may be indistinguishable from the female pseudohermaphrodite's.

Genuine hermaphrodites (the third category and very rare) have fully functioning testicles and ovaries. But the external organs will again be mixed instead of fully male and female. Generally the hermaphrodite is 'sexed' according to the appearance of the external sex organs, even if sex glands and chromosome balance do not correspond with it.

Heterophobia

Heterophobia is a general term for fear of the opposite sex. It can encompass a range of problems, often more to do with lack of social skills than attraction towards one's own sex.

A man may be heterophobic if he becomes anxious at the idea of performing sexually with a woman, even if he is quite comfortable relating to her on a purely social, conversational level. Or the sexual anxiety may prevent him from relating comfortably to women at all, even in unthreatening situations, such as at work. If the problem is limited to fear of sexual communication, not social, sex therapy or a sympathetic girlfriend may help. In the second case, the man may need a course in social skills, so that he can learn how to relate to women as people, make conversation and feel at ease in their company.

Homosexuals may not be heterophobic at all. Although their sexual preference is for their own sex, they may be perfectly at ease relating to women as colleagues and friends.

Heterosexuality

A heterosexual is sexually attracted to people of the opposite sex. Clinically, heterosexuality has always been seen as 'the norm' (after all, it leads to procreation) and little research or analysis has been made of the state, whereas homosexuality has been the subject of tomes. However, in the modern permissive sexual age, heterosexuals are no longer the good guys and the others the deviants. More and more, heterosexuality is seen as one option, amongst many, for sexual expression. And many people who call themselves heterosexuals, in that their main source of sexual interest is the opposite sex, have in fact experienced homosexual sex in adolescence or adulthood.

But while modern sex therapists and sex researchers stress that there are no rights and wrongs in sexuality, the psychoanalysts disagree. Freud and even modern analysts, such as Arthur Janov (of **primal therapy**) and Alexander Lowen (of **bioenergetics**) see heterosexuality as the desired norm and homosexuality as a deviation caused by an inability as a child to identify with the same sex parent.

Lowen goes further and says that even heterosexuality – or the seeming sexual interest in someone of the opposite sex – can in fact be disguised homosexuality. He claims that men who are too concerned with providing satisfaction for their female partners and whose own excitement depends on the female's arousal are acting out a homosexual attitude. Mature heterosexuality, for Lowen, depends on mutual respect for each other and an ability to work towards mutual pleasure, instead of concentrating on 'servicing' or helping each other to reach orgasm, at risk of one's own.

Homoeopathy

Homoeopathy found its beginnings in the late 1700s, when a German doctor, Samuel Hahnemann, tried a drug which was recommended for certain forms of fever and discovered that he developed symptoms of fever himself. He supposed, therefore, that the drug's usefulness in curing fever was due to the fact that it could also *produce* it. From here, Hahnemann and colleagues went on to test a whole series of drugs and, from their adverse effects on healthy individuals, ascertained what illnesses they might help cure.

Opposition to such a theory of medicine was, of course, strong. But, although homoeopathy is still on the fringe of medical practice today, certain similar practices are common in orthodox medicine: for instance, inoculation against a disease by injecting a mild dose of the disease into a person's system is known to stimulate the body's natural defences against infection.

The homoeopath is aware that the same general illness can take many forms. Sinus infections, for instance, may affect the nasal passages or the throat or the ears. Colds may affect the eyes, the nose, induce headaches or produce cold sores. It is the symptoms that he treats rather than the illness, so treatments for the same basic illness may vary.

Hahemann discovered very early on that too much of a similar-acting drug aggravated the illness he was trying to cure. He found that reduction of the dosage still produced therapeutic effects but prevented any bad ones and this dilution approach is still important in homoeopathy today. When an improvement is noted in the patient, the dosage is reduced or even stopped altogether.

Homoeopaths claim the treatments are preventative as well as curative and will benefit the general health of a patient. They stress the particular benefits of homoeopathic remedies for nervous disorders, for, while it is difficult to establish the causes, the *symptoms* are all too apparent.

Homoeopathic medicines are all of animal, vegetable or mineral origins.

Homophobia

Homophobia is a fear of the same sex, often manifested as a fear of homosexuals. It also encompasses fear of homosexual thoughts and behaviour and homosexuality in oneself. A 1969 Harris Poll in America revealed that ninety-three per cent of those questioned considered homosexuality a disease and sixty-three per cent thought it was harmful. An over-intense reaction against homosexuality, particularly in males, is thought by analysts to be the result of unconscious homosexual desires.

Homosexuality

A homosexual is attracted sexually to members of his or her own sex. The word comes from the Greek *homo*, meaning 'same', not the Latin word meaning 'man' and is applied to both sexes. However, in colloquial usage, the word homosexual tends to refer to a man and the word lesbian is used for a woman who is sexually attracted to women.

For a long time homosexuality was thought to be a disease and much psychiatric time was given to trying to cure it. Freud believed that if a child didn't learn to identify with his same-sex parent, he might well become a homosexual. Psychoanalysts today still believe that homosexuality is an abnormal sexual development, caused by some early childhood block. Modern analysts, such as Arthur Janov, who developed **primal therapy**, and Alexander Lowen, father of **bioenergetics**, claim that homosexual patients who have experienced their therapies have ceased to have homosexual orientations.

Another school of thought is that homosexuality is the product of hormonal imbalance. There is some evidence that male homosexuals have lower levels of the male sex **hormone** testosterone than male heterosexuals. And recently some medical researchers found the level of testosterone to be higher in lesbians than in heterosexual women. But here it was also found that older heterosexual women had less testosterone than youngers ones while the reverse occurred with ageing lesbians. The researchers could not elicit whether the level of the hormone was a cause or a response to homosexuality. And certainly testosterone levels do seem to be affected by circumstances. British researcher Glenn Wilson reported that they dropped in long-term prisoners, perhaps as a self-defence against frustration.

Popular modern thinking has it that homosexuality is perfectly normal. It is found in all species and amongst primitive peoples as well as in civilized societies. Sex researcher Alfred Kinsey collected statistical information on the sexual behaviour of thousands of men and women, which was published in 1948 and 1953. He

121

found that only a half of American adults were totally heterosexual; at least thirty-seven per cent of males and thirteen per cent of females had experienced homosexual relationships at some time.

The 1960s saw the first campaigns for gay equality, vocal and highly successful attempts to counter ostracism because of sexual orientation and to break down the stereotypical image of the male homosexual as effeminate, promiscuous and incapable of forming long-term relationships. It is not in the least uncommon for homosexuals to have long-term loving monogamous relationships, although promiscuity is higher amongst homosexuals generally – probably because of the difficulties of meeting the like-minded and maintaining relationships in the face of disapprobation and, till recently, prison sentences for unlawful sexual activity.

With the rise of the women's movement, radical lesbian feminists have also made their voices heard. They have had to fight not only societal stigma but accusations of being unfit for motherhood. Many women who enter lesbian relationships may be divorced mothers with children. However, one recent piece of research may help in the battle of homosexual mothers to retain custody of their children and to break down the idea that children are affected by the sexual preferences of their elders (a belief that makes life difficult for gay teachers). American researcher Richard Green, well respected for his work on childhood gender identity, studied thirty-seven children raised by female homosexuals or transexuals. Thirty-six had heterosexual preferences (the orientation of the thirty-seventh was unclear). None had homosexual or transexual fantasies although all knew of their parents' orientation. Green suggests that parents' sexual preferences do not affect infant sexuality because children are equally influenced by their peers.

While the fight for minority rights all too often leads to an extremism and an exclusivity that can be destructive (gay social workers, gay socialists, gay psychologists against the world), there is still a good way to go before jobs and status, for example, are not affected by sexual orientation.

Hormones

One of the great debates within the psychiatric profession is whether particular kinds of mental illnesses have an environmental or biochemical basis. Advocates of the former blame emotional disturbances on social surroundings, the latter claim that they result from hormonal abnormalities of some sort.

Hormones are essential to the functioning of our bodies. They are chemicals secreted by the *endocrine glands* which are responsible for keeping the body functioning efficiently whatever changes may occur in the outside environment. Because the hormones are secreted directly into the bloodstream, the endocrine glands are sometimes called ductless glands.

The endocrine glands are situated in various parts of the body and each has a different function, although all also interact. The *pituitary* gland is the pinnacle of the system because it releases at least six different hormones and has an influence on all the rest of the endocrine glands. It is found at the base of the brain and its hormones are mainly concerned with stimulating growth, controlling metabolism and regulating body fluid, as well as, in females, directing the uterus to contract at birth and stimulating the secretion of milk.

The *thyroid* gland and the *pancreas*, situated, respectively, close to the larynx and between the stomach and small intestines, are both mainly concerned with metabolism. The *adrenal* glands, found on top of the kidneys, are concerned with helping us respond efficiently to stress by the release of **adrenalin** and noradrenalin.

The sex glands are called the *gonads* – the *testes* in males and the *ovaries* in females. The main sex hormone produced by males are the *androgens*, and *testosterone*, a hormone particularly connected with sex drive, is one of these. In females, the main sex hormones are the *oestrogens*, which also influence sex drive and play a part in pregnancy and childbirth. But males also have oestrogens and females have androgens. The sex glands are responsible for stimulating the growth of external sexual characteristics, including body hair, voice levels and distribution of fat. Research now indicates that hormonal influences within the brain also cause psychological sex differences (see **sex differences**).

Although much is now known about the functioning of all these glands, more mysterious is the *pineal* gland, found within the brain itself and seemingly responsible for our individual **body clocks**. It secretes the hormones *melatonin* and *serotonin* which respond to light and dark and therefore influence our waking and sleeping patterns and stimulate all cyclical body activities, such as enzyme production and menstrual rhythms. Links have recently been

123

found between high levels of serotonin and anxiety and depression (see **air ions**).

In its entirety, the endocrine system is extremely complex and delicate. Hormonal functioning affects our psychological state but external factors, such as depression, can also affect hormones, slowing down their activities.

Adjustment of hormone levels has been claimed by many in the medical profession to be an effective way of reversing some of nature's ills, such as severe pre-menstrual tension (see **menstruation**) and an uncomfortable menopause (see **hormone replacement therapy**). Others, biochemically inclined, have asserted that **schizophrenia**, **manic depression** and **psychopathy** are caused by some irregularity of hormone production. It is a contentious area for, though it would be extremely comforting to attribute all such illnesses to a chemical cause that is easy to correct, critics protest that mental illnesses are too complex to be so simple in origin. They are, they say, caused by a variety of factors and to isolate hormonal imbalance as the explanation is erroneous.

The use of hormones to correct behaviour is particularly contentious in the case of sex offenders. As testosterone affects sex drive (the higher the level of the hormone, the higher the drive), some prisons condone the practice of neutralizing these hormones with primary female ones. This causes the development of secondary sex characteristics associated with women, such as breasts, which in many cases has required surgery to correct. But the psychological effects of such development cannot be so easily annihilated.

Our knowledge of the effects of long-term hormonal treatments is still limited, although it is now thought that the Pill and hormone replacement therapy to correct debilitating effects of reduction of oestrogen production in menopause may be linked with cancer.

Hormone Replacement Therapy

Oestrogen therapy, to reduce the unpleasant physical and psychological side-effects of the menopause, has enjoyed a great vogue over recent years, particularly in America. It has even been proclaimed as a 'youth' pill, opening the way to a whole new energetic life. Now it is under attack as yet another cancer risk.

Two of the more unpleasant symptoms of the menopause, hot flushes and vaginal dryness, can be caused by the dramatic fall in oestrogen production which occurs when menstruation ceases. As the hormone oestrogen has an important function in pregnancy and childbirth, in later life it no longer needs to be produced in such high amounts by the body. Loss of oestrogen can also make bones brittle and induce curvature of the spine.

Oestrogen replacement therapy, given in the form of pills, injections and implants, can reduce these effects and, as accompanying insomnia, irritability, nervousness and depression often decrease too, the responsibility for that relief has also been attributed to the therapy. However, recent research shows that there is no scientific proof for oestrogen effects on psychological symptoms. Often enough, the irritability, depression, etc. may be caused by lack of sleep caused in its turn by the discomfort of alien physical sensations. Of course these will reduce if the physical effects are treated but it will not be the oestrogen that is actively responsible.

Fears of detrimental side-effects from the therapy have always been voiced but, in recent years, it was thought that risks of heart disease, hypertension and cancer were only linked to synthetic-based oestrogens; 'natural' oestrogens, taken from mares' urine, were believed to be clear.

Now, two studies on women who have taken any oestrogens, natural or not, for more than five years, running independently at Boston University and the University of Pennsylvania, show quite clearly that incidence of uterine cancer is far higher in these women. The Pennsylvania study places the odds at women being fifteen times more prone to get cancer if they have used the therapy for five years, reducing to six times more likely if they have used it for less. It is believed by the doctors at both universities that oestrogens should only be used, if at all, to cover women for a short period, whilst suffering their most uncomfortable hot flushes.

Women are not necessarily to be reconsigned to an uncomfortable menopause, however. There are some claims for homoeopathic remedies, Vitamin E, herbal remedies and yoga as methods to deal with the hot flushes. Whether they really work or not, at least they don't have side-effects.

Horney, Karen
see **Neo-Freudians**

Humanistic Psychology
see **Growth Movement**

Humour

Psychologists have been accused of wasting a lot of time trying to measure and quantify the unquantifiable – such as why and how we fall in love – but until recently the study of what makes us laugh wasn't one of them. Then a well-attended international conference on humour and laughter held in Wales in 1976 revealed that a great many psychologists have indeed turned their attentions to this intriguing question after all.

And at the moment there are, in fact, more questions than answers. One study revealed that the average person laughs fifteen times a day. But why and when? Investigation many years ago revealed that most people laugh in the presence of other people and the laughter-inducing events are witty remarks, stupidity or amusing antics. Funny books and magazines account for far less laughter time. Howard Leventhal and colleagues at Wisconsin University found that women judged the humour value of jokes by how long they laughed at them; men, however, were just as likely to laugh long and loud at a joke they knew well or didn't find particularly amusing.

The American magazine *Psychology Today* ran a readership survey in 1978 to find out what makes people laugh. About 14,500 readers rated thirty widely-differing jokes and from their responses the magazine drew several tentative conclusions: the men were more amused than the women; sexual humour was the most popular with men but fanned the fumes of feminists; ethnic jokes came second in popularity; older readers were more likely to have found the jokes funny than younger ones; and people who described themselves as funny, socially aggressive, pleasure-seeking and with above average sex drives were most likely of all to have got a kick out of the cracks. Social class, religion and race were found to have no bearing on how funny the readers found the jokes.

Laughter, of course, can be a defence mechanism or a reaction to anxiety. We may accompany some rather hard-hitting statement or pointed remark with a little laugh, in an attempt to take the sting out of the sentence. We laugh to cover embarrassment. And children, particularly, laugh in relief when an anxious

126

moment has passed or in triumph at having achieved a particular end, such as placing building bricks one on top of each other.

British psychologists Tony Chapman and Hugh Foot, organizers of the Wales conference, have made studies of children's laughter. They found interesting sex differences. Boys, it appears, use laughter as a means of breaking their attention away from companions while girls use it to maintain or restore attention. They concluded that boys were less able to tolerate close relationships and when things became too intense they tended to try and break the tension by laughter. Girls seemed to thrive on the attention that comes from close encounters and used laughter to strengthen the closeness. They looked at each other directly when laughing whereas the boys threw back their heads and looked away. The researchers also found that individual children varied greatly in the extent to which they laughed and smiled and that this seemed to be linked to birth order. Later-born children seem to laugh and respond more than first-borns.

Whatever the researchers have so far found, the value of humour cannot be under-estimated. A joke is funny because it offers the unexpected, the seeming contradiction in the punchline. We have to suspend disbelief to laugh at a joke and, in so doing, we can break out of rigid patterns of thinking. Fables and teaching stories use this aspect of humour to open the mind to a different view of reality.

As Plato said, 'Serious things cannot be understood without humorous things, nor opposites without opposites.'

Hypnosis

Hypnosis is a state of deep relaxation, sometimes trancelike, which can be induced by oneself (auto-suggestion) or by another person. Although the state resembles sleep – and was called hypnosis after the Greek word for sleep by an Englishman, James Braid, in the nineteenth century – the hypnotized person is really awake and alert, but so relaxed that the deeper parts of his mind become accessible to him.

Although he never used the word, hypnosis as a technique is usually traced back to a man called Franz Anton **Mesmer** who originally thought his success was due to the use of a steel magnet and then later discovered he could achieve the same affects by his own 'animal magnetism'. (We now credit the process to auto-suggestion.)

There are many ways to induce a hypnotic state: the hypnotist can get the subject to concentrate on the swing of a dangling watch or on a fixed point on the ceiling or else he can stare into the subject's eyes and tell him he is getting heavy and sleepy. And the effects are various too. Subjects can experience time distortion, hallucinations, forgetfulness, cessation of pain or **regression** to childhood.

It is commonly believed that not everyone can be hypnotized as individuals vary tremendously in their suggestibility and their willingness to allow themselves to relax. People who, once told a fact such as 'it is getting warm in here', then start to feel warmer, are highly suggestible and strong candidates for successful hypnosis. Others are completely resistant. Research by Ernest Hilgard at Stanford University indicates that up to ten per cent of the population is highly suggestible and the same number are resistant, with the remaining eighty per cent falling in between. He also found that people with vivid imaginations and the ability to act out roles were particularly susceptible to hypnosis, as were individuals who had had a strict upbringing, where punishment led to obedience.

But the idea that some people are resistant to hypnosis altogether is now being questioned. Professor Joe Barber of the University of California in Los Angeles Medical School claims that everyone is susceptible – it's just that the approach needs to vary according to the personality of the individual. Some people, he says, are hostile to the low, lugubrious tone that most hypnotists use to induce trance and react defensively to direct commands such as 'You will feel drowsy', 'You will relax'. Whereas, if the hypnotist keeps the tone conversational and just suggests ideas such as, 'I wonder if you are surprised at the ease with which your eyes are getting heavy', the subject usually responds. Professor Barber tried this 'naturalistic' approach with 27 people and then subjected them all to extremely painful electrical stimulation of the nerve fibres in the teeth. Not one of them felt a thing. Yet the usual success rate for inducing hypnosis is held to be one in four.

Hypnosis has its uses in medicine and as a means of dulling pain and fear in the dentist's chair. It is also a route to the unconscious. The method works by allowing the subject to become so relaxed that he lowers his defences and gets in touch with feelings and memories that he has repressed. This is called hypnotherapy.

Hypnotherapists are usually also trained psychotherapists and do not interpret or advise their patients. They use their skill in hypnotism purely as an aid in eliciting the causes of a person's problems. They ask questions and listen and even help a person to put himself into hypnosis, so that he can recall facts from his past more easily. The aim is to provide the wherewithall so that the patient can get in touch with and resolve the causes of his own difficulties.

Hypnotism is known as a method for curing addictions, such as drinking, smoking and over-eating. But medical hypnotists reject the 'amateur' approach of suggesting to a hypnotized person, 'You will never want to smoke again'. Instead, they treat the addiction as symptomatic of an underlying problem and use hypnosis purely to help the patient open up and discover the real root of his habit.

Hypnotherapy
see Hypnosis

Hypochondria

Hypochondria is a preoccupation with physical health, and fear of disease. It may lead people to rush off to the doctor at the first sign of any strange symptom and little comfort will be derived once they are told it is all in the mind. It may also be unfair to suggest that the symptoms *are* all in their imagination. Patients who appear to be hypochondriacs may often, in fact, be experiencing anxiety symptoms, which, because they have no obvious cause, the patients don't recognize as concomitants of anxiety. Anxiety symptoms can be very real and physical indeed, ranging from the pounding heart to dryness of the mouth, heavy perspiration, tight bands around the chest and dizziness. Sometimes they can be part of a depressive illness. It is not surprising if someone who experiences such feelings regularly mistakes them for a sign of serious physical illness. Rather than being dismissed as a hypochondriac and an annoying drain on the medical profession's time and resources, he needs to be given help for his anxiety, either drugs or an explanation, at least, of what it is that's happening to him.

Hysteria

Someone with a so-called hysterical personality tends to dramatize things and over-react. Simple setbacks are shattering, any form of pain is torture, a moving film is overwhelming and stunning. The hysteric tends to be flamboyant in his or her constant attention-seeking and is somewhat self-absorbed. The word itself comes from the Greek for womb and was coined by Hippocrates because he ascribed the condition to a wandering womb, alleviation of which could be brought about by marriage! (Hysterical symptoms were considered to be a female thing.)

A feature of hysteria is the conversion of some emotional problem into the loss of a physiological function – usually suitably dramatic, such as paralysis of a limb, blindness or deafness.

On investigation, no physical causes for the condition can be found; in fact, the condition itself may only be a waking phenomenon. The hysteric with a paralysed arm can usually move it during sleep, for instance. The paralysis, blindness or whatever can be cured temporarily by hypnosis or more permanently by encouraging the patient to get in touch with and discharge the emotional trauma that is the real cause. (See **abreaction**.)

Another form of hysterical reaction is to dissociate oneself completely. Dissociative reactions such as amnesia and sleep-walking are hysterical in base.

Hysterical reactions are relatively rare. Unfortunately, the label of 'hysteria' is too often used for patients when doctors can't find an obvious physical cause for their problems. But research has indicated that the vast majority of 'hysterics' turn out to be suffering some definite physical brain damage.

I

I Ching

The I Ching or Book of Changes is an ancient Chinese book of oracles. It consists of readings for 64 hexagrams, figures made up of a combination of six broken or unbroken lines and which, taken together, are supposed to symbolize all that happens in the universe. Broken lines (–/–) symbolize the female principle **yin**, and unbroken lines (—) symbolize the male principle **yang**, which are the two complementary forces of the universe present in all things. (See also **Tao**.)

The 64 hexagrams evolved from an earlier system called

the *Pa Kua* or eight trigrams, which were eight figures made up of different combinations of three lines and which stood for fundamental elements of the universe, such as earth, water, wind and fire and the different attributes associated with them. The idea of the eight trigrams was supposedly inspired by the markings on the shell of a tortoise.

The I Ching is very popular in the West. People throw coins or toss yarrow sticks in order to 'ask' it information. The more usual method is to use coins, three of which are thrown six times. Heads are counted as three and tails as two. If the sum of each throw makes an even number, that represents a broken line; if it is odd, it represents an unbroken one. When the thrower has his combination of six broken or unbroken lines, he looks up that hexagram in the I Ching. First, however, he will have written down the question he wishes to ask, which can be on any matter at all. For instance, 'Should I make some drastic changes to my life?' or 'Is my relationship with Jill/John right for me at this time?'.

The hexagram that is formed from the throw of the coins represents the interaction of the forces yin and yang at the very moment that the coins fall. The explanations of the hexagrams in the I Ching are couched in poetic, mysterious and ambivalent terms. So the questioner must try to interpret the words, using his own intuition, to get the answer to his question. The process therefore requires an individual to suspend his logical mind and 'feel' his way towards meaning.

The workings of the I Ching are based on the idea of simultaneity: many things converge to create a single event and nothing is static. So a person who throws his coins and reads an answer to his question, then throws more coins and asks the same question may well get a different answer the second time. This is supposedly because of the ever changing nature of the yin/yang relationship; and because the individual's reasons for asking that question again will no longer be quite the same.

Id
see **Freud**

Identity

Identity is one of those concepts which are impossible to define closely and yet everyone has an understanding of their meaning.

We all talk about so-and-so having a strong sense of identity or someone else undergoing an identity crisis.

Loosely, identity refers to one's sense of self. If a person is confident about his abilities, can take criticism for what it is worth, feels emotionally secure, communicates well with others and doesn't depend on approval of others for his belief in himself, he is thought to have a strong sense of identity. He knows who he is. If, however, someone is nervous, unconfident, constantly in need of praise and affirmation, unsure what he is good at or what direction he is heading in, he is lacking a sense of identity or – if the situation is extreme – undergoing an identity crisis.

How do we develop our identities? It all goes back to our early childhoods and our first learning experiences. If a mother is warm, affectionate and ever-available, the baby will start to experience a sense of trust and security and feelings of self-worth. If she is dismissive of his needs or treats his care as a duty rather than an act of love, this will communicate itself to the child and make him untrusting of his environment and people in it and unsure about his own role and value.

Similarly, a mother who is uncomfortable with her own sexuality and who happily tickles the palms and tummy of her baby but studiously avoids the penis or clitoris, will instil in the child a sense that certain parts of the body are 'not nice' and any feelings arising from them must be repressed if mother-love is not to be forfeited. So arises sexual confusion.

Each stage in a child's development affirms or denies identity. (See **developmental psychology**.) If the child is encouraged to feel independent as it first starts to walk and to explore, it will develop feelings of confidence; if it is over-protected or gets scolded for creating what to the child is a feat of inventiveness and what to the mother is just a mess on the kitchen floor, it will learn to doubt and distrust its abilities.

At each stage of learning, children are dependent on parental approval and encouragement for their sense of right and wrong. If given, they can be sure of themselves and develop a sense of identity that no longer requires them to seek approval. If withheld, they may grow up increasingly unsure that what they are doing is 'right' and perpetually looking for reinforcement or validation from others.

Impotence
see **Sex Disorders**

Industrial Psychology

Industrial psychologists are specifically interested in people at work, whatever their work setting. They focus on work efficiency, decision-making procedures, management-worker relationships, job satisfaction and effects of morale on productivity. Sometimes they are employed in personnel departments, drawing up criteria for personnel selection.

Their work may involve them in assessing worker motivation and suggesting a system of productivity bonuses to increase it; or they might investigate morale and find that workers would derive more job satisfaction if their physical surroundings were made more pleasant or if they had a system where complaints could be made direct to management. They might also be concerned with devising training schemes and assessing how best to retrain workers whose jobs have become obsolete.

One of the biggest modern challenges for psychologists interested in this area is the phenomenon now known as 'assembly line hysteria', the most recent 'industrial disease'. Although documented incidents are few, it is not that rare for an outbreak of sudden inexplicable illness to spread rapidly through a factory. In Ohio, for instance, a woman suddenly became dizzy, light-headed and nauseous. Within minutes, about forty other people were led off to the sickroom with the same symptoms. But investigation revealed no physical cause – no leaks, no fumes, nothing. Investigators can only surmise that underlying boredom, home stresses or general tension, kept within bounds until some catalyst appeared as an 'explanation', all erupted to the surface together. The catalyst could be a strange smell or a woman suddenly collapsing for no apparent reason. At the moment there are no answers, either as to how it all happens or what can be done to prevent it.

Inferiority Complex
see **Complex**

Inhibitions

In the social sense, an inhibited person is someone who holds in his feelings and won't let go, for any of a number of reasons. He may be inhibited about speaking in public, for instance, because, on some previous occasion, he made a complete fool of himself. Or he may be inhibited about appearing on the beach in bathing trunks because he thinks he has an unsightly scar on his leg. Sexual inhibitions may be due to fear of failure or deeply entrenched moral convictions.

In psychology and physiology, however, the word inhibition has very specific meanings. In the nervous system, when a weak impulse (e.g., pain caused by a knock on the knee) is drowned out by a stronger impulse (e.g., simultaneous message of pain caused by a gashed wrist) the weak impulse is said to have been inhibited.

In memory, there are two specific forms of inhibition. *Proactive inhibition* refers to the phenomenon whereby old learning interferes with new learning (e.g., it's more difficult to learn a second language because of fluency in the first). *Retroactive inhibition* is the reverse: old material is forgotten once we learn new stuff. Of course if something is important enough for us to want to remember it (i.e., the motivation is strong enough) we'll remember it regardless of whether old or new information could confuse us.

Inkblot Test
see **Rorschach Test**

Insanity

Apart from its usage as a legal term, the word 'insanity' has no technical meaning in psychiatry and it fails to appear among the myriad of names that designate all the possible thought disorders and emotional disturbances. It is an antiquated term, once used fairly lightly to pigeon-hole all sorts of seemingly wild or inexplicable behaviour, and conjures up unpleasant memories of the old insane asylums where people were kept in the most horrific conditions, chained to walls or howling in cells.

In law, however, it does have a place and an important one. In criminal law, an act is not automatically a crime if the doing of it has resulted in the breaking of the law. To qualify as a crime that is punishable by prison sentence or any of the other avenues open to a court, the law must have been broken *knowingly*. This raises problems in the case of some severely mentally ill people, and was first come to grips with as the result of a British case in 1843. Daniel M'Naughten was brought to trial for shooting and killing another man. However, his disturbed state of mind led the jury to find him not guilty by reason of insanity and he was sent to a mental hospital where he remained till his death twenty-two years later.

A precedent was set by this ruling, thereafter called the M'Naughten rule: that a person cannot be held responsible for criminal acts if he does not understand the nature or effects of what he is doing or if he cannot see that what he is doing is wrong.

A successful plea of 'not guilty by reason of insanity' now leads people to be designated as mentally abnormal offenders and sent to maximum security mental hospitals instead of prison. They do not receive a sentence and they are kept in hospital, under secure conditions, until treatment is deemed to have made them capable of returning to live outside. In some people's minds, this seems as though it is synonymous with getting off lightly. It is far from that: a person who has admitted to an offence but whose mind was disturbed at the time is likely to spend far longer in a mental hospital than he would have stayed in prison had he been sentenced. A British study showed that for non-serious offences, the average prison sentence given by the courts was six to twelve months. For the same offences the average period of detention in a maximum security mental hospital under a restriction order (meaning only the Home Secretary, not the doctors, can authorize release) was six to eight years. (More serious offences, such as arson, manslaughter, wounding or any act endangering life, still only brought prison sentences that, with remission, amounted to between one and a half and two years.)

As mentioned, the mentally abnormal offender receives no sentence. His discharge date is linked to that intangible entity, his recovery. He may, therefore, end up serving life in the real sense of the word. Sometimes it is because of a political decision, not a medical one: if the front page of the newspapers have recently been ablaze with the gory details of tragic murders committed by a psychopath, the Home Secretary is unlikely to authorize the release of other once-violent psychopaths, which might fan public outrage and demands for our streets to be kept free of dangerous killers.

There is a strong case for getting the 'therapy' to fit the crime. Gross abuses of justice have been committed on both sides of the Atlantic. In America someone once spent twenty years in a mental hospital because she claimed to be clairvoyant and someone in England was sent to a secure mental hospital because he had stolen a cabbage worth four pence (but was disturbed at the time). We may have deleted 'insanity' from our medical vocabulary but we still work by other rules that are just as archaic.

Insomnia

One interesting seventeenth-century suggestion as a cure for insomnia was the application to the forehead of the juice of a lettuce, mixed or boiled with oil of roses. Innocent though it sounds, it was not advised for those who suffered from short-windedness or who spat blood! The modern remedy is the sleeping pill and all too many people reach to take them without stopping to think whether they really do have a sleeping problem at all.

For many people believe they need more sleep than they really do and think that they are waking too early because of a sleep problem. Old people, who are known to need less sleep, often go to bed earlier than most, through boredom or a need to conserve heat and lighting, and then worry because they are awake in the early hours.

Much so-called insomnia is in fact pseudo-insomnia, caused by false expectations about the need to sleep long. Often people who get an interrupted night's sleep, due to traffic, partners' snoring or vociferous neighbours, worry that they are not getting their full quota. But interrupted sleep should not be a source of worry because it is quite possible to be awakened regularly during the night, fall back to sleep and wake again, and still get sufficient rest. Often we think we have had less sleep than we did, just because the periods of wakefulness seemed much longer than they really were.

Real insomnia is habitual and goes on night after night, for weeks. It starts with perhaps just a little difficulty in dropping off, then becomes a major difficulty and soon less and less time is spent in sleep, with the result that the insomniac next day is full of tension, irritability and inability to concentrate. This is chronic insomnia and is usually caused in the first place by worry and anxiety. Gradually the lack of sleep itself becomes a worry and the person is caught in a self-perpetuating cycle: worry causes sleeplessness which causes tension and worry which causes sleeplessness. To deal with the insomnia, it is important to deal with the worrying factors that have caused it in the first place. If the worry has long been resolved and the only worry remaining is the sleep cycle, the syndrome needs to be broken, perhaps by learning to relax, checking that the bed is warm and comfortable enough, that there is enough air in the room and so forth. Sedatives may help but they need to be treated with caution as they may lead to dependency and inability to sleep without them.

Acute insomnia is not at all uncommon. It simply refers to the inability to get to sleep because of some particular pre-occupation, such as exam nerves or excitement about going on holiday. But it can become chronic if it persists for a few nights and the non-sleeper forgets that something particular – and passing – is keeping him awake and starts to think he has a problem. Sometimes insomnia can be an accompanying factor of some other disorder, such as depression. But here it is the depression that needs treatment, not the insomnia. In very rare cases sleep loss is due to an actual neurological disturbance. This does need treatment.

Instinct

Instinct is generally defined as a complex automatic response (as opposed to a simple, automatic response, such as the reflex action of blinking when a strong gust of air hits our eyes, or a learned form of behaviour, such as reading).

Instinctive behaviour is easy to isolate in animals and birds – hibernation and migration, for instance, that is common to certain species, or certain signals that are vital for survival (wolves bare their necks when they are demonstrating submission to another of their own kind). But it wasn't until Charles Darwin showed that humans are a different higher form of animal that it became popular to consider that we also exhibit certain set responses common to our own species.

In fact, so popular did the instinct theory become in the early nineteen hundreds that psychologists started producing mammoth lists of all kinds of behaviour they were now convinced were instinctive. Amongst the several thousand instincts they ended up with were secretiveness, resentment and fear of noise (from American psychologist William James) and self-abasement and pugnacity (from his fellow countryman William McDougall)!

Freud also believed that man's actions were the product of innumerable instincts but he later settled for the less messy idea that they all derived from the two basic instincts of love and death.

But naming instincts did little to actually explain them and, in 1914, behaviourist John Watson reacted against it all. He maintained that all so-called instincts were in fact the product of learning or conditioning. For, in humans, there are no responses that are performed absolutely identically by each of us. We may all be motivated by hunger to seek food but we may choose different things to eat or ignore the signal altogether.

This theory wasn't utterly convincing either but it is now more commonly accepted that human instincts, if we have them, are very difficult to detect because we have so much opportunity for learning and becoming conditioned in our responses to external stimuli.

In short, instinct is by no means a clearly agreed or simply observable feature in humans.

Intelligence

Intelligence as a word has no clear, universally accepted meaning. Yet, on the basis of this one word, the lives of thousands are shaped for the future. Children are streamed according to intelligence at a very early age.

Dictionaries offer vague synonyms such as 'intellect' or 'understanding'. Modern-minded psychologists suggest intelligence is the capacity to learn, to apply that learning, to benefit from new experiences and to be generally alert and aware. This broad approach to intelligence is a far cry from that taken in intelligence testing (IQ) which concentrates on verbal and performance skills. IQ tests are now agreed to be a very limited way of testing intelligence, emphasizing to the exclusion of all else the logical abilities of the mind. Yet they are still used. An average IQ is 90–110. A score of less than 70 leads to the designation of a child as educationally subnormal (with those with an IQ of less than 40 being designated mentally handicapped).

While it is relatively easy to assess brilliance and severe retardation by IQ tests, it is less easy to make accurate assumptions about people who fall within the middle range. Skills in logic do not necessarily mean effective reasoning power. Edward de Bono has shown that lateral thinking can lead children with relatively low IQs to solve certain problems faster than university lecturers (see **lateral thinking**).

The discovery in recent years that the two hemispheres of the brain have specialized functions – the left being concerned with logical, analytical skills, the right with spatial, visual skills – has further complicated the understanding of what constitutes intelligence. (See **split brain**.) In the west we have over-emphasized

138

the work of the left brain and tend to devalue the skills associated with the right. Yet a sense of intuition, creativity and space also has a part to play in our capacity to be aware and alert and receptive to new information. Differences between the skills of males and females seem to be partly related to differences in brain organization (see **sex differences**).

But there is more to 'intelligence' differences between males and females than that. Social learning plays a strong part for, traditionally, girls have been taught that men are threatened by a clever woman, that attractiveness is more important than a quick mind, etc., and are therefore under societal pressure to play down at least their intellectual capacities. Accordingly, it is difficult to come up with meaningful distinctions between the inherent intelligence of the sexes, although many have tried.

Similarly, it has been suggested that there are definite differences between intelligence levels of different races. This view is based on the idea that intelligence is genetically inherited. (IQ tests on identical twins give some support for inheritance as their scores are similar, whereas non-identical twins, formed from separate eggs in the uterus, show distinct IQ differences. See **genes**.) American Arthur Jenson drew forth a flurry of protest when he found that, on average, the IQ of black people is up to twenty points lower than that of white people. (He did point out that this referred to racial groups in general, not to individuals within them.) Critics said that Jenson could not possibly have accounted for the effects of environmental learning and the lack of motivation resulting from years of discrimination against blacks.

Interpersonal Attraction
see **Attraction**

Introverts
see **Extravert**

J

Janov, Arthur
see **Primal Therapy**

Jealousy

Jealousy is a powerful emotion. In its weakest form, it is unpleasant to experience; in its strongest, it can be lethal. Sometimes we put a nicer name on it – it's a crime of passion when a woman guns down her unfaithful lover – but it all comes back to the same thing. When we feel threatened in some way, we experience jealousy.

Anthropologists have shown that, in the same way as animals protect their territory, we protect our property and have strong ideas of ownership; we believe we have rights to a person's affections or to a particular function at work and we feel threatened and jealous if they are taken away from us. Much jealousy is due to thwarted attention needs, and is learned early on in childhood.

Freud believed there were three types of jealousy; the first was normal, competitive jealousy and, according to Freud, anyone who seemed to be free of it had really repressed it. It was normal, he claimed, for someone to feel resentment against a lost lover, to hate the rival and to reproach himself. The second and third forms of jealousy were not so normal, and resulted because the people concerned couldn't handle natural manifestations of jealousy. They would either deny they were jealous at all, or become completely obsessed with jealousy (e.g. the man who keeps watch on his wife's office block and believes that every man who enters it is his wife's lover).

Rather than deny jealousy or disguise it under a host of more flattering-sounding motivations, we have to learn to accept it and cope with the consequences.

Jung

Carl Jung was born in Switzerland in 1875 and his work is often referred to as *analytical psychology*. He was practising medicine when, in his twenties, he read **Freud**'s work on dreams and wrote to him. As a result Jung went to meet Freud, was hailed as his most brilliant pupil and the two kept in correspondence for thirteen years. But then an irreparable rift came between them because of Jung's refusal to lay all neurosis at the door of repressed sexuality and his over-enthusiasm for the occult. (Freud much later became interested in paranormal phenomena himself but he feared that any mention of mystical thought would harm the respect that psychoanalysis was accruing.) The rift with Freud probably contributed to Jung's subsequent denunciation of Jews in Nazi occult literature.

Jung's main deviation from Freudian thinking was in his belief in the *collective unconscious*. He maintained that the whole personality, the *psyche*, had three levels: the *ego*, which is the conscious mind; the *personal unconscious*, in which is stored all our repressed fantasies, dreams and desires; and the collective unconscious, which belongs to the primordial past and which each of us inherits. So our memories are stored with age-old ideas and this reveals itself in feelings which may be irrational but which take their genesis from time long past – e.g., fear of the dark. The collective unconscious has a strong influence over the other strands of our personality.

It is from the collective unconscious that we derive our image of *archetypes*, Jung's name for the symbols of common, important experiences. The archetype of the mother, for instance, is warm and life-giving and protective; the father is the symbol of power and authority. These images have crept into all ancient mythologies. Other symbols represent life events such as birth and death.

Amongst the important archetypes are the *anima* and the *animus*. The anima is the feminine part of the personality, soft and accepting but also seductive, irrational and betraying; the animus is rational, strong but also tyrannical and stubborn. All men and women are imbued with both. Co-existing, in the collective unconscious, is the *shadow*, primitive, base, animal but also creative. It is the shadow in us that personified by the devil and evil. But, because it is creative too, Jung believed that it must be acknowledged and accepted as a legitimate part of our personalities.

Jung also talked of the *persona*, the mask we each wear or role we play in particular social situation, such as work or domestic life. But it is just a mask, necessary for survival within society and not to be mistaken for one's real self.

141

Real *self* is at the core of the personality, drawing towards it all the opposing forces of good and evil from the collective and personal unconscious. When it has absorbed and resolved its own opposites, accommodating both maleness and femaleness, conscious and unconscious, the self is at one with the universe. This is in keeping with Eastern philosophies about the nature of man, sharing a life energy with the universe. Jung called the process of integrating all aspects of self by the name *individuation*.

Some Jungian terms have found their way into common usage. The concept of **extravert** and introvert was his and also the concept of **complexes**.

K

Kirlian Photography

This is a process which claims to capture life energy on film. It was discovered in 1939 by Russian researchers, Semyon and Valentina Kirlian, who refined a photographic process that required no camera, lens or source of light. Instead, the method involves a high-frequency electric discharge between the object to be photographed and an electrode. They discovered, to their amazement, that brilliant patterns of colour emanated from the leaves they photographed this way and that these colours varied in intensity in different pictures: when a leaf freshly cut from its stem was photographed, the colours around it were bright. But in subsequent photos, as it withered, the lights faded away.

The couple took photos of their own fingers and found that the colours emanating from them differed according to their states of mind. When they were nervous or hurried, the colours were indistinct, when they were calm, the colours were bright and clear.

Their discovery led intrigued Western researchers to beat a track to their door and, amid the excitement, it was proclaimed that the Kirlians had found a way to capture energy on film. Experiments with healers showed that while healing, there was a definite, visible, transmission of radiance moving towards the patient.

Further experimentation revealed that the radiance around the finger of a healthy person was blue and different states of mind caused an infiltration of red blotches into the blueness. People under hypnosis or meditating radiated more brilliant colours which extended further than normal from their bodies.

Recent American tests have shown that tighter control on experimental conditions eliminated the changes that had been attributed to altered states of consciousness, though interested researchers still believe that more sensitive equipment will iron out the inconsistencies and reveal Kirlian photography to be a reliable aid as a diagnostic tool in medicine.

Klein, Melanie
see Ego Psychologists

L

Labelling

Labelling, as a general practice, can be extremely useful. In libraries, museums, even home-freezing, grouping materials according to general or specific categories can do much to facilitate their retrieval. But, in the field of human behaviour, labelling is a subject of controversy.

It is a fact that labels stick. So children who are classified as slow learners or dyslexic absorb that image of themselves and teachers or psychologists who encounter them also expect poor academic performance.

In psychiatry, a label can follow one all one's life. It is not uncommon to be told that a diagnosis of severe (albeit temporary) depression written on to a medical card still prevents someone getting a job even twenty years later. Labels such as **psychopathy**, which are so all-embracing that they can mean different things to different doctors, have even more damaging effects on an individual's attempts to rehabilitate himself after hospital treatment. For psychopathy means uncontrollable violence in the public mind.

One school of thought has it that labels are self-perpetuating, as people are made to fit them, rather than vice-versa. A famous experiment by David Rosenhan of Stanford University had eight people report to a mental hospital claiming to hear voices. All eight were diagnosed as schizophrenic. Once admitted, all the patients proceeded to act absolutely normally and gave correct life histories to the staff. But they were still held there for between seven and fifty-two days, given a total of more than 2,000 pills and none were ever found *not* to be suffering from schizophrenia! Rosenhan concluded that once someone had been designated mentally ill, all behaviour was viewed in that light. So an angry retort, for example, which would be dismissed in the outside world as a moment of pique, in hospital becomes the immature acting out of hostility.

This is not the only kind of blinker that operates where labelling is concerned. It is a common complaint from women who have had some history of emotional disturbance that their family doctors are very likely to dismiss any complaint of a physical ailment as being just a neurotic reaction.

Supporters of the classification process, however, go to ever further extremes to refine the art. The American Psychiatric Association's definitive guidebook to the diagnosis of mental disorders ends up grappling in each edition with the validity of new labels such as 'post-Vietnam combat disorder', 'caffeinism' or 'tobacco-use disorder'. Needless to say, such proposed entries provoke uproar in various quarters. One American psychiatrist was prompted to comment sourly 'I trust that missing a three foot putt on the eighteenth hole will also be classified as a psychiatric disorder'.

Laing, Ronald
see **Anti-Psychiatry**

Language

Language is one of the most exciting and puzzling of human attributes. It isn't just synonymous with speech, although it is remarkable enough that a child of two has a vocabulary of nearly 1000 words and, by the age of four, is perfectly at ease with sentences. Language is concerned with meaning and the meaning of what is said is often not communicated by the words spoken alone. So if someone says, 'That's a terrific piece of work,' but they are wearing a sneer or the inflection in their voice is down rather than up, they are quite clearly saying that the work is particularly poor. Often we communicate without words at all, letting our expressions and body gestures do the talking for us (see **body language**).

Meaning is also dependent on context. The words 'We're out of juice' have a different meaning if the speaker's car has just ground to a halt from that implied if he were standing by the fridge in the kitchen. Once we have a firm grasp of language, we instantly adapt our understanding of words to the situation in which they are spoken and can cope quite easily with shorthand speech. *Diner in restaurant*: 'Roast pork and potatoes, please.' *Waiter*: 'Sorry, it's off.' A literal approach rather than a meaning-approach to language is what causes all those gaffs in foreign language phrase books.

We presume that language ability evolved thousands of years ago, with the physical development of the vocal cords to enable us to form words. Whether language itself actually began with humans imitating the sounds of other animals or whether it is an innate ability in all of us is still a matter of controversy.

The **behaviourists**, led by B. F. Skinner, believe that language is a learned response. Children start to make sounds which, to adults, sound like parts of words ('da' for 'daddy'). So the adults finish the words off, the children imitate them and, delighted by the approval they receive for doing so, learn to say them again.

Others maintain that language is far too complex an ability to be just a simple response to a stimulus. Leading critic of this approach is Noam Chomsky, linguistics professor at Massachussetts Institute of Technology. He believes that language is too universal a skill to be linked to a reward system based on parental approval. All children, regardless of the complexity of the country's language they speak, process verbal information in the same way.

Chomsky says that language has two components; the sounds which make up individual words, and a deep grammatical structure that determines semantic content. Chomsky maintains, therefore, that the latter, the deep structure (*grammar*) of language is innate and only the 'surface structure', the particular sounds and words of the language that is spoken in one's own country, is learned.

These ideas are borne out by the fact that many sentences have double meanings, which are decided by the grammar. One of Chomsky's examples is the sentence 'Flying planes can be dangerous'. The word flying could be an adjective or it could be a gerund, a form of noun. The sentence has to be understood before the traditional grammatical labels can be put on each word. A child will not know formal grammar but it will know what

145

it is possible to say and what is not. Chomsky illustrates the understanding of deep structure of language by inserting a clause. So we can have 'Flying planes, which are a nuisance, is dangerous' which is acceptable. But 'Flying planes, which is a nuisance, are dangerous' is not. We know which is right and which is wrong automatically.

This idea of surface and deep structure might well be illustrated by the differences in language use that exist between well-educated and poorly educated people. The latter may say, 'I ain't coming' which isn't good English, but his understanding of spoken language, with all its complex clauses, phrases, etc., is perfectly adequate. The better educated person has a wider choice of vocabulary, a more elegant style of sentence formation; the poorly educated counterpart has purely a workable knowledge of structure without the frills.

But acquisition of language is different from use of language. Researcher Basil Bernstein talks of a restricted code (the shorthand we use in speech) and an elaborated code (formal, grammatically constructed sentences). Educational success depends on the ability to use an elaborated code for the organization of ideas and experiences and the tasks of problem solving. This depends on childhood learning. People who do not have an extensive vocabulary, which includes abstract ideas, are unable to develop the intellectual skills necessary for studying. Other research has shown that meanings given to particular words differ from one economic and cultural group to another, with resultant differences in thinking and reasoning processes.

Anthropologist Benjamin Lee Whorf believes that our perception is determined by language; that we only see what we have developed words to describe. Eskimos, for instance, have a number of words for different types of snow, whereas we just see 'snow'. But this theory isn't popular. It is more likely that because snow is particularly important in Eskimos lives, they have invented several words for it. But it is certainly true that our ability to put things into words affects our ability to think about them. Thought involves abstract concepts, only denotable by words, as well as visual images.

Latency
see **Psychosexual Stages**

Lateral Thinking

This is a creative thinking skill, a technique devised by Edward de Bono, doctor, researcher and inventor extraordinaire. De Bono shocked teachers with his idea that thinking should be taught in schools. Originally dismissed as ridiculous, 'thinking' is now on the curriculum in 4000 schools in various countries.

De Bono has pointed out the basic fallacy that thinking skill is totally tied up with knowledge and logic and demands a high IQ. While knowledge is important for thinking, the accumulation of knowledge is not enough. What counts is how we apply it. Those of us who are not lateral thinkers can fall into definite traps when thinking. We make instant judgements and then use logic to back them up instead of exploring alternatives; we focus on one narrow aspect of a problem and refuse to 'confuse' our thinking with 'extraneous' material (this is known as tunnel vision); we imagine that if we can prove another person wrong, we must be right; we are so convinced that the logical approach to problems is the right one that, if we reach a deadlock, we just flounder instead of going back and questioning whether the first few logical steps were really the only ones possible.

Lateral thinking is not concerned with logical, progressive motorway thought. It is about shooting off down all the side roads, some of which may lead nowhere. The idea is to consider a problem from every possible angle and eventually come up with a right solution. Lateral thinking teaches perceptual skills and a self-organizing information system that allows incoming information to form itself into patterns. Like humour, it is about alternative ways of arranging available information.

Jokes depend for their funniness on the unexpected development, the non-linear approach to a situation. 'Lady Astor to Sir Winston Churchill at a dinner party: "Mr Churchill, if I was married to you I should put poison in your coffee." Mr Churchill: "Madam, if I was married to you, I should drink the coffee."' Creativity and insight work the same way – an idea shoots into the mind unexpectedly. But, as de Bono says, humour, creativity and insight can't be taught. Lateral thinking can.

Learning lateral thinking involves the practice of numerous exercises. Experience has shown that children with low IQs can become highly successful problem-solvers through lateral thinking. Academics at Harvard took eleven minutes to solve a block-arrangement puzzle that lateral thinking schoolboys solved in thirty seconds.

One of the techniques is Plus, Minus and Interesting (PMI). Children are given a statement such as 'Children should be paid for coming to school' and are asked to look at the pros and cons. Whereas initially all children support the statement, after trying to find 'minuses', they realize there could be a lot of unpleasant ramifications to getting a wage (parents may reduce pocket money, schools would start charging for things, etc.). To counter the protest that we all look at pros and cons anyway, de Bono says we only do that if we are in doubt about the virtue of a particular idea.

Another technique is to take a problem, such as 'How can I make better use of my time?' And then to think of any word at random, e.g., orange. Now the thinker has to find as many relationships, however bizarre, between oranges and time-organization as he can: e.g. 'Oranges have no sense of time and they still grow. Maybe I'm too time-obsessed.' Sometimes a useful idea may flash into the mind which throws new light on the problem.

Edward de Bono is founder-director of the Institute for Cognitive Studies in Cambridge and he is a consultant to several industrial, financial and scientific bodies. Lateral thinking has helped him to come up with a variety of practical solutions to everyday problems. To reduce the red tape over illegal parking, for instance, he suggests free parking be allowed at a meter as long as a car's lights are left on, indicating (and ensuring) that the car will only be there a few minutes. Would you have thought of that?

Learned Helplessness

What do dogs who quietly accept the administering of electric shocks without trying to get out of the experimentation box have in common with certain seriously depressed people? A great deal, according to American psychologist, Martin Seligman. Both are the victims of 'learned helplessness'.

Some years ago, Seligman and colleagues discovered the phenomenon of learned helplessness when they were testing a particular learning theory on dogs. The test involved the administration of electric shocks to dogs which were strapped down and therefore couldn't escape it. (The shocks, we are told, were painful but not physically damaging.) Later the dogs were placed in compartmentalized boxes from which they could escape, when given shocks, and the researchers expected them to learn to jump over the barriers. At first, the animals ran around the box trying to get out. But extremely quickly they gave up and resorted to quiet whining while suffering the shocks.

The researchers were amazed. Then they realized that the dogs were reacting to their previous experience of being totally unable to control what was happening to them. They couldn't escape the shocks when they were strapped down. So now, they very quickly assumed that they wouldn't be able to escape shocks in any environment. The dogs had learnt that their actions had no effect and that they were helpless.

Seligman sees this same syndrome in people suffering from a reactive **depression**. Reactive depressions are those that have some obvious external cause, such as loss of a loved one, failure to get promoted at work or pass exams at school. People who experience setbacks over which they have no control may well learn to think that they can never have control, never have events turn out the way they would like them, and therefore give up trying. They see themselves as failures and suffer loss of motivation, lack of interest, self-denigration and misery – all symptoms of depression.

Experiments run by Seligman on humans have confirmed this learned helplessness link. Students who were subjected to the experience of being unable to turn off a loud, unpleasant noise, no matter what knobs they twiddled, on a different occasion didn't even bother to try to control it, even when they could have. Similarly, learned helplessness breeds the expectation of failure which leads depressives to avoid learning to cope with their environment.

Therapy for learned helplessness, says Seligman, needs to concentrate on showing the depressive that he can operate on his environment and be effectual. Some therapists work by encouraging a display of anger in the patient – as anger is a powerful visible force for controlling others. Others concentrate on getting depressives to succeed in simple tasks, then harder tasks, to build up their confidence and break their conviction that nothing they do works.

But learned helplessness can be very entrenched, and for adults very difficult to overcome. Seligman suggests that knowledge of the learned helplessness syndrome should help us to take a preventive approach. Candidates for this sort of depression could be identified in childhood and, while still at school, given aid to help them develop the coping mechanisms that are necessary for dealing with demands of everyday life.

Learning

Every single activity or behaviour we engage in as a result of practice or experience is a learned behaviour. Because of learning we change our ideas, our reactions, our expectations as well as developing new skills. Learning, therefore, involves not just memory and processes of reason but our emotions, our sense of humour and our fears.

Learning theory varies, of course, according to the theorist. One theory is conditioning. An early Russian physiologist, Ivan Pavlov, discovered that **conditioning** by particular stimuli from the environment causes us to react in a certain way, and that we can learn to make associations. By ringing a bell whenever he brought his dogs food, he conditioned them to associate bells with food and found that they would therefore salivate at the sound of the bell, even if no food were provided.

The famous behaviourist psychologists John Watson and B. F. Skinner developed this discovery to explain all behaviour (see **behaviourism**). Skinner posited the idea of reinforcement: if we do something and get a 'reward' for it (approval from a parent for putting toys away), we will repeat it. If the consequences of an action are not pleasant (a child wanders off from the house, gets lost and frightened) we will not repeat it. All behaviour is therefore, initially, a case of trial and error. We do something or something happens to us and, according to the result, we learn to repeat or avoid the circumstance.

Skinner thought that reward was a far more successful way of teaching children acceptable behaviour than punishment. If something nice happens to them when they learn their letters or tidy their playpens, they are more likely to internalize that behaviour than if they are punished for not attending or tidying up. A hard thwack on the leg or an enforced early night may effectively stop the child doing something bad but he is quite likely to suppress his activity, rather than drop it altogether (he waits till his parents are out before raiding the fridge), or develop strong feelings of hostility and anger.

Skinner denied that intangibles such as free will and goodness

150

existed independently: everything was governed by reinforcement from the environment and if 'goodness' brought pleasant societal approval, then goodness would be learned.

Few psychologists would nowadays claim that all behaviour is a result of simple stimulus-response learning, although they accept it is an important part. Social psychologist Albert Bandura, for instance, believes that we are not passive respondents to environmental stimuli; we make choices, based on our own experience and insight. We have the opportunity to watch other people, to decide what behaviour of theirs we wish to imitate and to see the consequences. We model our ideas on those of others and exercise judgement about which are acceptable to us. Bandura believes that cognitive factors – internal processes of thinking, memory and reasoning – are involved in this particular kind of learning.

Cognitive psychologists are interested in how people actually think and solve problems. On the premise that we have built-in processes for thinking, etc. in our brains, they investigate how we actually apply them. We all receive a perpetual bombardment on our senses from the sights, sounds, smells, etc. of the outside world. Yet we perceive our environment as essentially stable. We draw consistency out of confusion. Much processing, selection and categorizing of information received from our senses must therefore go on in our heads and the mechanisms involved are the interest of the psychologists. Computers have been particularly useful in this line of research, as they can simulate, to a certain extent, the processes involved in cognition. (See **artificial intelligence, memory, language, perception, brain.**)

German psychologist Wolfgang Kohler thought that, besides conditioning and reasoning processes, learning involves insight – the sudden flash of knowledge or understanding that seems to come from nowhere. He came to this conclusion after observing chimpanzees trying to solve particular problems – e.g., how to reach a banana outside the cage when all the hollow sticks they had inside were too short. One sat down and looked at the sticks, and suddenly fitted one just inside the other, making a long stick, and thus pulled in the banana. Although Kohler saw this as sudden insight, others have maintained that the chimp was really making use of experience: he was familiar with sticks. But perhaps Kohler, who was working in the early 1900s, was ahead of his time. There is a strong school of thought today that believes the right hemisphere of the brain is concerned with intuition and insight, and has a special role to play in the learning process (see **split brain**).

It has been suggested that there is a limit to the amount of information a human being can process; that we must all unconsciously filter out a great deal that reaches our sense organs. Studies in this area have shown there are limits to concentration span, for instance, and to the ability to listen to two people talking about different things at once. But these conclusions are now being questioned.

Researchers Ulrich Neisser, William Hirst and Elizabeth Spelke have recently demonstrated that it is possible for people to learn to read and write simultaneously without losing concentration. They believe that mental processes can change so fundamentally if given practice, that there can be no fixed assumptions about the limits of brain capacity. Their subjects had to read short stories and, at the same time, take down dictation about something else. Whereas they found the task impossible at first, after six weeks, their reading speeds were normal and their dictation correct. They were tested for understanding of both what they read and wrote, to check that one had not become an automatic activity, allowing concentration to be devoted to the other. The subjects showed that they had absorbed all material.

The researchers think their findings are significant, not because they expect simultaneous writing and reading to catch on and enable us to achieve two hours' work in one, but because their experiment undermines fallacies about brain capacity and implies that there are no doubt other mental barriers of our own making which could be broken down.

This idea fits in with the current interest in consciousness. Are there different ways of receiving and interpreting information which could widen our experience of the world or the universe? New discoveries about brain function (see **split brain**, **biofeedback**) imply that we could open ourselves to hitherto untapped knowledge if we only 'learn' how. (See also **consciousness** and **mysticism**.)

Leboyer, Frederic
see **Natural Childbirth**

Left Hemisphere
see **Split Brain**

Lesbianism
see **Homosexuality**

Leucotomy
see **Psychosurgery**

Libido

Psychoanalyst Sigmund Freud coined the name libido for what he saw as the energy force behind the life instinct. He claimed the libido, most commonly expressed in the forms of sex and love, to be the strongest motivating factor in all human behaviour. It is the libido which directs us to seek sexual and (ideally) emotional satisfaction, as well as of course being responsible for the propagation of the species.

Fellow analyst **Wilhelm Reich** also used the term libido to express what he saw as the drive at the core of all human action. But for him libido meant specifically sexual energy, which he believed was suppressed first by parents and then by society in general, with resultant debilitation and deadening of all feeling.

Libido, as we use it today, means sex drive. It is now thought that it can vary between individuals, not necessarily because of neurosis, but according to sex hormone levels.

Lie Detector

The lie detector, or polygraph, was invented by Leonard Keller in the 1920s. It monitors changes in the nervous system brought about by stress. The theory is that, when lying, an individual will experience a speeding of the heart rate or other revealing physiological changes. Changes in heart rate, blood pressure, respiration and skin temperature are monitored on graph paper by pens attached to the polygraph. The operator takes account of the fact that just the taking of the lie detector test itself can cause stress and therefore looks only for very pronounced physical deviations from a norm.

The lie detector has now been banned from many courts in America (it is not used in England), for it is feared to be too easy to deceive. Senator Sam Erwin, during the Watergate hearings, dismissed it for that reason, claiming that a guilty person could pass one with ease and a truthful person might fail one.

153

His words have been borne out by the findings of researchers in Texas who discovered that people trained in biofeedback and autohypnosis techniques for relaxation could all beat the polygraph. Their training enabled them to control their own levels of physiological arousal whilst lying through their teeth. The researchers have used their findings to challenge American business firms which still use the lie detector as a basis for hiring and firing employees.

Limerance

Limerance is a word coined by American psychologist Dorothy Tennov to describe what we usually term romantic love. Those fluttery sensations and tuggings within the breast are not just the prerogative of the writers of romantic fiction. They are, says Tennov, a genuinely observable state. What is more, some people are limerant and others are not.

Limerance, it appears, is characterized by the involuntariness of the feeling, intrusive fantasies (normally non-sexual) and obsessiveness about the loved one. Limerants have two types of fantasy: the first is a flash image of the moment when a limerant object reciprocates the emotion with a meaningful look or a clasp of the hand; the second is a detailed fantasy of the events leading up to that instant. The consummatory moment – when the handclasp or look takes place – is as significant and as overwhelming as any anticipation of sexual contact.

Non-limerants are incapable of understanding such a state and tend to dismiss romance as rubbish.

Lobotomy
see Psychosurgery

Love

In 1978 American senator William Proxmire bestowed one of his Golden Fleece awards for ridiculous waste of tax payers' money on the National Science Foundation, which had provided a grant of 84,000 dollars for research into why people fall in love. True, the researchers, Elaine and William Walster, didn't come up with any shattering insights, but their work did enable them to knock a few myths on the head. For example, people who are aloof and

154

tantalizingly unattainable are not generally seen as more desirable partners than individuals who respond affectionately to advances. Goodbye *la belle dame sans merci*.

Love may be difficult to subject to psychological testing – and ill-advised may be the attempt – but animal behaviour has taught us much about the different forms of loving we all need to experience if we are to be mature, well-adjusted adults. Harry Harlow's work with monkeys in the 1960s led him to define a hierarchy of loving: maternal love, infant love, peer love, heterosexual love and paternal love.

Maternal love is the caring and nourishing bestowed on a child by its mother. The child responds with infant love which seems to be deeper than just a need for the source of food and milk. Monkeys who had the choice of contact with a cloth mother substitute that didn't produce milk and a wire version that did all chose to spend more time with the cloth mother despite this meaning a brief period without food. The comfort that comes from warmth must therefore be as important as the gratification of hunger and thirst.

When a child becomes more independent, it is ready to experience peer love, which shows itself in play and affectionate rough and tumble. In animals, this period is also associated with sexual posturing and Harlow maintains that peer love is a necessary precursor to adult heterosexual love. Monkeys which were deprived of the opportunity to play with peers became aggressive when, as adults, they were presented with a monkey of the opposite sex. This is mirrored in humans in the 'social misfits' who never made satisfactory friendships as children. Eminent American developmental psychologist William Hartup once said that 'poor peer relations in childhood are amongst the most powerful predictors of later social and emotional maladies'.

The final form of love is paternal, associated with protection and called paternal because that is the father's primary role, whereas the mother's is nurturing. But the qualities of paternal love can and are equally well provided by the mother.

But what is love? It is a question that numerous philosophers, analysts and psychologists have given thought to, amongst them Abraham Maslow and Erich Fromm. Maslow talks about B-Love, which is genuine love of the Being of another person, unselfish and undemanding love, and D-Love which is Deficiency-Love, and conditional upon the lover meeting one's needs. B-Love is the profound love.

Erich Fromm says that without love an individual is alienated and not fully alive. He also questions a common belief that loving is a sacrifice, a giving up of personal freedom, a transaction that is only desirable if something definite is received back. Fromm says the giving in itself is the joy of love – the sharing of everything that makes one what one is.

Philosopher A. R. Orage calls such love conscious love, and says it is rarely found. Conscious love is totally selfless and needs knowledge and power to guide it. Love alone is not enough. ('I love you,' said the man. 'Strange that I feel none the better for it,' said the woman.) To love consciously means 'to take hold tightly, let go lightly'. Every tragedy of love arises, he says, because the lovers seldom know the moment or the way to take hold of each other and even more rarely do they know the moment or the way to let go. (See also **attraction**.)

Lowen, Alexander
see **Bioenergetics**

LSD
see **Psychedelic Drugs**

M

Manic Depression

Manic depressives experience excessive mood swings, going from the depths of despair one day to wild heights of elation the next. In a moderate form it is probably a phenomenon we are all familiar with but in a severe form it can be absolutely crippling.

While in a state of manic high, which may last months, the person usually suffers from delusions of grandeur, is over-elated, hyper-active, full of babble and bright-eyed. Everything is urgent, everything must be done now and the consequences can be quite dire. It seems to be a feature of the manic phase that the sufferer become quite blasé about money, distributing bounty that he doesn't even possess.

He may buy a whole wardrobe of expensive clothes, lavish large bunches of red roses on all and sundry, decide to hire a chauffeur-driven car for a week.

If his plans are thwarted, he can get angry and violent. But, because it is so hard for him to keep his attention on any one thing for an appreciable length of time, it is quite easy to distract him from his fury by throwing in a neutral remark about the weather or a friend. The manic person is so busy with his strange schemes, he has little time to sleep and consequently gets physically exhausted.

Then the mood may swing to the depths of depression, where he is consumed with guilt, self-hatred and inability to motivate himself to do anything. If the mood swings between highs and lows occur frequently, the condition can be very hard to bear, for the person feels he is never in real control of himself or his actions. It is also a difficult condition to treat because the patient needs to co-operate in monitoring his own symptoms so that appropriate drugs can be given. However, there are now certain drugs which lift depression and reduce mania simultaneously and electroconvulsive therapy (ECT) can also help.

Manipulative Therapies

Osteopathy and chiropractic are the two major manipulative therapies, both concerned with malfunctioning of the skeletal structure. Although they are used because of physical problems, such as lower back pain, the root cause is often psychological. It is now known that stress can express itself in many physical ways (see **psychosomatic medicine**).

Osteopathy and chiropractic achieve the same end but approach it from different ways. The chiropractor talks in terms of restoring normal alignment of the spine by adjusting vertebrae. He does this by short, sharp blows. The osteopath talks of restoring normal motility (movement) to a joint. He makes gentle, repetitive movements to loosen the soft tissue around the fixed vertebra and only later specifically manipulates the joint concerned. However, in the process, the chiropractor also restores normal motility and the osteopath restores normal alignment.

If the stiff neck, locked shoulder blades or bad backache is caused by tension that has an emotional base, the patient may well experience a release of unexpected emotion once the physical problems are ironed out. So the osteopath or chiropractor has to be sensitive and sympathetic to such reactions or, where necessary, refer to patient to psychotherapy. (See **rolfing, reichian therapy**.)

Marathon Group
see **Encounter**

Marijuana

Marijuana is the mildest form of the consciousness-expanding drugs. It is derived from the Indian hemp plant *cannabis sativa* and although it has a long history as an innocent folk medicine in many parts of the world it shot to notoriety in the West as the social drug of the sixties, hailed by the hippies and frowned on by the state.

It became one of the symbols of the peace-and-love era because of its physical and psychological effects – a deep sense of relaxation, a heightening of feeling, a distortion of time-sense, all of which often combined to create an experience akin to the mystical. It is in many ways an extremely unsocial drug, as it tends to lead the user to withdraw into himself. It affects thought processes and in large amounts makes normal mental functioning almost impossible. But reactions to marijuana vary from user to user and, according to researcher Charles Tart, personality, motivation and expectation all play their part in whether a person gets pleasantly high or remains fairly unaffected. Many people nowadays smoke marijuana in the same way as others enjoy a drink, just as a pleasant way to relax.

Marijuana is in most places illegal. Legalize-it campaigns stress that it is not physically addictive, is less harmful than alcohol and tobacco and quote research that shows it has a place in medicine for the relief of pain, insomnia, anxiety, asthma, epilepsy, glaucoma and the side-effects of cancer treatments. But the difficulty of retaining the potency of THC, the chemical responsible for marijuana's effects and the by no means conclusive evidence of research results so far imply that marijuana is not yet destined for the chemist's shelf.

Other researchers claim that marijuana usage definitely does impair memory and, with it, the ability to carry out responsible jobs. Because reactions to the drug are subjective, no doubt research will only convince whichever side the latest findings support.

Martial Arts

Man has always fought; against the elements, against animals and against fellow man. But nowhere has fighting been developed as an art in the way that it has in Asia. Complete systems involving the use of bows, ropes, swords, sticks and many other weapons, as well as empty hands, have been in use for centuries in countries such as China, Japan, Burma, Thailand and Indonesia. In some, the martial arts developed purely as a system of defence; in others physical prowess became linked with a spiritual system, inspired by **Zen** and **Tao**, and the skill involved was a medium for achieving harmony with the universe.

The martial arts most familiar to us in the West are those of the Japanese, particularly the 'ways of the empty hands', i.e., karate, judo and aikido. Although taught here purely as sports, they are all spiritual in base.

Often also called 'the ways of the breath', the important element in these martial arts is *ki*, the life energy that is believed to make up everything in the universe. But it obeys a mind that can direct it, causing it to flow and concentrate on any one desired area. This is how karate experts develop the strength to break bricks with just a blow of the hand.

The three ways of the breath have their own systems for developing mastery over ki but central to all is *hara*. Hara is the centre of gravity in each of us, a spot just below the navel. When relaxed, strength naturally sinks to this point. Complete physical and mental co-ordination can only result if one is in touch with one's hara. Those with total mastery of hara can, for instance, draw a perfect circle freehand. And a person who is able to let his strength centre at the point of hara can be impossible to lift, even if he is tiny and his opponent is large and strong.

Traditional masters of these martial arts were concerned with the relationships between the different natural rhythms of the universe, the ebbing and flowing of tides, the turning of dark to light. Movement and action is a way of attuning to these rhythms, to work in conjunction with them instead of against them. So mastery of the martial arts, it is claimed, brings harmony with the universe. The student must learn to see without concentrating; to co-ordinate all energy in one totally effective movement. The man who can direct ki, the force of the universe, can take on one opponent or ten.

Aikido, karate and judo find their direct root in the Chinese system *T'ai Chi*. Based on the principle that energy, of which breath is one form, penetrates everything in the universe, T'ai Chi is a method of controlling breathing and actions, involving sequences of dance-like movements that are elegant to watch. As the movements flow, the breath becomes a source of energy. In aikido, karate and judo, the actions of the body are also an extension of the breath. Mastery of breathing leads to mastery over all the body. The student must first learn to relax and free his energy, to open himself up. Once freed from inner tension, the individual becomes both the centre of and outlet for a universal energy. Throwing an opponent is simply one way of expressing that mastery.

Maslow, Abraham
see Self Actualization

Masochism

Freud considered that there were two forms of masochism: perverse masochism in which clear sexual pleasure is derived from the experience of pain and humiliation; and moral masochism in which a person unwittingly manoeuvres himself into uncomfortable situations. The word itself is derived from the name of a nineteenth-century novelist, Leopold von Sacher-Masoch, who wrote about the sexual domination of men by women.

The perverse masochist is one who finds sexual release only when he is being abused, physically or verbally. He derives intense sexual pleasure from experiences such as a whip on his bare flesh and salt being rubbed into the wound, or from being given an electric shock or having hot candlegrease dropped on to his testicles.

The moral masochist is more familiar to most of us. He's the one who always gets involved in relationships that others can see are doomed to failure right from the start; or he seems perpetually accident prone; or he indulges in self-destructive acts such as smoking and excessive drinking. Moral masochism, in its own way, can be as extreme as the sexual kind – the person who develops inexplicable illnesses, for instance, and contrives to get himself repeatedly operated on.

According to the psychoanalysts, both kinds of masochism derive from the same basic root: usually the experience in childhood of being dominated by one's parents and not being allowed to break away and form one's own identity. For, although the masochist may appear to be a hapless victim, what he is really seeking is control over his own life.

The perverse masochist, if a man, is saying that, even under the most severe of pain and humiliation, his manhood and potency can still triumph (i.e., he can have an orgasm); the female (more rare in perverse masochism) is also effectively declaring that nothing can break her.

Meanwhile the moral masochist is seeking control by unconsciously steering his way into situations which have a sure outcome. He knows deep down that his relationships won't work or that he'll break his leg, but the fact that he is making it happen puts him firmly in charge of his fate. Or so he imagines.

Another parallel theory about the root of masochism is that the individual wants to get his own back and play the part that his dominating parents played – i.e., inflict hurt on others. But, because he feels guilt, he uses himself as victim and inflicts the hurt on himself.

People who resort to perverse masochism are notorious for being unable to fantasize. Despite their seemingly 'creative' approach to sex, they in fact stick to very limited rituals. This poverty of imagination, according to analysts, comes from a disturbed early child–mother relationship where the child fails to draw from his mother, through play, fantasy and safe physical contact, the experiences necessary to create a rich inner life.

Liberal thinking has it that any form of sexual contact between consenting adults is all right. But that doesn't mean that any sexual practice, such as extreme perverse masochism, is a natural form of sexuality. It is, in the final analysis, a defence against some deeply hidden hurt. (See also **sadism**.)

Masters and Johnson
see **Sex Therapy**

Masturbation

A great many people still think masturbation is harmful – not surprising, perhaps, when one thinks of the wealth of child-rearing literature put out over the last centuries, complete with dire warnings about the horrible consequences of the practice (blindness and baldness, to mention only a couple). One Dr Shreber

(1842–1911) recommended that children should do windmilling exercises with their arms one hundred times daily, just so that their minds shouldn't stray towards unchaste occupations.

Fortunately, we now know that there is nothing harmful about masturbation. At a very early age, babies become aware of pleasant feelings in the genital area, when being rubbed dry after a bath perhaps, and they go on to explore those feelings for themselves. At this early age, they enjoy a general feeling of eroticism throughout their bodies. But this declines and interest in genital pleasure, specifically, only revives around puberty. Most boys and, it is now realized, most girls, masturbate in some form during adolescence and a great many masturbate to orgasm.

Masturbation is a way of exploring oneself and becoming more attuned to one's own sexuality while, giving every individual the freedom to experience sexual release, whether he or she has a partner in love or not.

It is only in recent years that masturbation has been hailed by women as the way in which they have discovered their own sexuality and ability to reach orgasm. A survey of the sexual experiences of over 3000 American women in 1976 led psychologist Shere Hite to conclude that masturbation is more satisfying than vaginal penetration for most women. Sex researchers Masters and Johnson had earlier found that, while intercourse was usually preferred because of the human contact involved, for intensity of orgasm masturbation could not be excelled.

Analyst Wilhelm Reich maintained that, while masturbation in itself is not important, the *inability* to masturbate with satisfaction is. For this indicates a deep and basic sexual guilt which all the most uninhibited sexual intercourse in the world cannot hide.

Meditation

Meditation is a way of stilling the mind. By turning the attention inwards and using the resources of concentration to block out the normal barrage of sights and sounds from the environment, the meditator achieves a state of alert relaxation. Experienced meditators speak of transcending the boundaries of self and feeling at one with the universe – enlightenment. Although an integral part of Eastern philosophies, such as Zen, Yoga and Sufism, with enlightenment as the goal, meditation is also now acclaimed in the West as a means of relaxation and reducing stress.

Meditation techniques vary. They include the use of breathing exercises, the focusing of attention on an object or a word, the repetition of a word or a movement or a combination of physical and mental exercises. Systems vary according to the philosophy they belong to and can only be of real benefit if practised as an integral part of that life philosophy. Different people have different needs, as regards meditation, at different stages in their development. But a system of meditation that was specifically devised for general usage in the West is **transcendental meditation**.

Research indicates that meditation is physically beneficial, as well as mentally, because it induces relaxation which dissipates the anxiety that is generated by stress, and calms the nervous system. It has been found that meditators can not only reverse the effects of stress, they can also deal with it better at the time. Once a challenge or a threat has passed, they can instantly relax, whereas non-meditators remain aroused for far longer. Other claims for the benefits of mediation are fewer **psychosomatic** problems such as headaches, and an increase in creativity and drive.

According to American psychologist Robert Ornstein, the workings of the central nervous system play a strong part in the seeming sensory black-out induced by meditation. The nervous system needs constant and changing stimulation if alertness is to be maintained. We cease to hear the ticking of a clock, but we 'hear' the silence if it stops. So when a meditator is concentrating on staring at a vase, for instance, the prolonged sameness of the visual experience eventually results in the viewer ceasing to 'see' the object. This blocking-out frees the meditator to experience an inner calm and to be receptive to signals that are normally overshadowed by external stimuli. ESP experiences are much more common in the meditative state.

Megavitamins
see **Schizophrenia**

Memory

People often moan, 'I have such a bad memory', but they're wrong. We all have the most terrific memory powers. Think, for instance, of all the words you know, all the objects you recognize, all the events from your life or scraps from your schooldays you can still call to mind. Our memory potential is in fact astonishing. How on earth do we do it?

We have three types of memory, *sensory*, *short-term* and *long-term*. The first stage, sensory, occurs at the point when we take in an impression from our ears or eyes. We see an image, for instance, for a fraction of a second after it has actually passed out of sight. During this fraction of a second, the image is being held in the memory's sensory store, whilst higher brain processes are deciding whether it's worth coding or not.

If it is coded, it passes into short-term memory, which consists of information that we need to retain for a short time. A telephone number that someone calls out across the room for us to dial is held in short-term memory. We are likely to hold it in our heads just time enough to dial it but forget it shortly afterwards. If, however, we repeat it to ourselves several times, we may be able to retain it as long as the information is useful. It has been estimated that we can keep a list of up to nine related items in our short-term memories but one way to increase on that is by *chunking*. For instance, if we are told the names of twelve politicians, we are unlikely to be able to repeat them all back. But if we group them in chunks, e.g., four from three different parties, we may improve recall by remembering the sections.

Long-term memory is thought to be limitless. Most of it remains out of awareness but ready to be summoned to the surface if needed. Here are all our memories of facts, books, experiences, formulae etc. that we have collected over a lifetime. It is not clear how these pockets of information are actually created but it is believed that we code according to meaning, sounds and patterns and that some permanent chemical change takes place in the nerve cells involved. Because each nerve cell connects with countless others (see **nervous system**), one memory may spark off a host of others. If we recall certain significant words spoken to us on one occasion, we may also recall the occasion itself, the room where the words were spoken, the expression of the speaker and so on.

The concept of separate short and long term memory systems is appealing but is it just a hypothetical division rather than a real one? Apparently not. A man called Henry M had a part of his brain removed, including the *hippocampus* (see **brain**), because of severe epilepsy. He could, as a result, remember everything that had happened long before, showing long-term memory, and he could hear a number and repeat it a few seconds later (short-term memory). But he could not remember information after about five minutes. It seemed he had lost the ability to transfer items from short- to long-term memory and that the hippocampus is therefore involved in this.

Our ability to memorise depends on several factors, some unconscious, some we can deliberately apply. For instance, it helps if we are interested in the material to be learned, or it stands out in some way, or we pay full attention when learning it. Particularly helpful strategies are rehearsal and mnemonics. If you are studying something, after an hour, try repeating it or looking through it again. Do the same a day later and then a week later and then a month later. The material will stay in your memory much longer. Also, as it is known that we remember beginnings and endings of things but forget middles, it is worth cutting down the chunks you learn at one time, so that there is less of a middle to sag.

Mnemonics are a way of coding material according to meaningful associations. The sentence 'Richard of York gave battle in vain' is easy to remember: and the first letter of each word jogs our memory for the colours of the spectrum – *red*, *orange*, *yellow*, *green*, *blue*, *indigo*, *violet*. Other mnemonics depend on visual links. If you need to recall a long list of unconnected words, you link each to the next in some bizarre and memorable fashion. So, if tree, television and dog are on your list, you might imagine a television up a tree and then a dog jumping out of a television. Mnemonic systems are innumerable.

There is an important distinction in memory between recognition and recall. It is easier to recognize something as having been heard or seen before than it is to summon it to mind unprompted. And, even though it is easier to recognize, we often forget where we saw something or the exact words that were written down. We may think we've read something before because the meaning is the same as something else we've read. This may not matter but mistakes in visual recognition can have vast repercussions in courts of law. Nebraska Professor Kenneth Deffenbacher has shown the tricks memory play. People who see photos of complete strangers may believe, when they see them in the flesh, that they have met them before. For this reason, he believes police, when showing witnesses mug shots of possible villains, may be prejudicing their ability to recall whether the person they see in court is one they really saw or just one viewed in a photo.

We also tend to reconstruct memories. As time goes by, we

recall events more as we would like them to have been: we recall unbalanced shapes as symmetrical, people as more attractive, events as more propitious. This is an active process of our own for the memory itself is not distorted and doesn't decay. A Canadian neurosurgeon called Dr Penfield showed that, when a particular area of the brain is stimulated electrically, a whole vista of events from the past is relived as if for real. All the detail is there, just as it happened, so retention itself is perfect. It is retrieval and recall that is not.

What makes us forget things? The popular theory is interference. Things we have learned before or learn later may interfere with our ability to recall a particular fact or event (see **inhibition**). But there is also the idea of deliberate forgetting, the suppression of anything connected with events and feelings that are too painful to face. The process is unconscious, of course; the person who 'forgets' his dental appointment may really have been motivated by fear.

How and where in our brains are items coded as memories? Information travels to our brains from our sense organs via the electrical activity of nerve cells (see **nervous system**). But quite what happens then is still unresolved. Some researchers point to genetic links. Because RNA, which forms the message-carrying chemicals that are part of our genes, is higher in animals that have been taught new skills, it is thought that it is connected with memory. As RNA helps to synthesize protein and protein is important for many bodily activities, perhaps protein is also responsible for the storage of information.

Neuro-chemist Georges Ungar believes information becomes coded in molecular chemicals in the brain and can be transferred. He taught mice to fear the dark (normally they seek out dark places) and isolated particular chemicals in their brains which he then duplicated and fed to untrained mice. They too became afraid of the dark.

Does this mean we'll eventually be able to have memory transplants and 'eat' intelligence, so to speak? Unfortunately there are still too many chemical questions that remain unanswered. (See also **amnesia, primary effect.**)

Menopause

The menopause is the cessation of periods and ability to bear children which occurs usually in the late forties/early fifties. For many young women looking ahead, it is a private dread, a time when sexual identity and life purpose both grow uncertain. Little research has been undertaken into women's actual reactions to the menopause and perhaps that is why a number of myths are perpetuated. For, from what little is documented and what more has been gleaned from female experience, the menopause does not deal such a crushing blow to womankind as had previously been thought.

Physically, the experience may be uncomfortable. Periods may cease suddenly or become further and further apart and then stop, as the ovaries lose their ability to produce eggs and less of the female sex hormones (oestrogen and progesterone) is produced in the body. Women commonly report 'hot flushes' – thought to be caused by a combination of lowered hormonal levels and resultant emotional tension – and sweats, as well as emotional disturbances, such as anxiety, depression and irritability. But the emotional factors may well be the result of the physical ones (e.g., sleep interrupted by hot flushes and discomfort may lead to tiredness and irritability next day.)

Sociologist Bernice Neugarten studied menopausal women in the 1960s and discovered that they were more concerned about getting older than about losing their ability to bear children. For most women, sexual relations became more important or were unaffected after menopause. (Many positively enjoyed the freedom from fear of pregnancy.)

As times change and women come to see that they have an identity beyond that of childbearer, the onset of the menopause has less crippling psychological effects. ('Traditional' views about roles can have an equally strong effect on ageing men: if they have seen their own value as family breadwinner, they too may experience a loss of identity a little later on, when they retire.)

A recent survey in Boston revealed that younger women were often fearful about the idea of menopause, the colloquially-termed 'change' emotively signifying a profound alteration of their identities, while older and post-menopausal women were far more mater-of-fact about the experience.

Women who experience painful menstrual symptoms or pre-menstrual tension as well as difficulty with pregnancy and child-birth tend also to experience a more difficult menopause. One of the currently hailed 'treatments' for this is **hormone replacement therapy**. But scepticism has overshadowed the initial euphoria with which this corrective was greeted in some quarters, as there is now evidence of its association with an increased cancer risk.

Menstruation

From time almost immemorial, menstruation has been linked with mystery, ritual and taboo. Alien to men, it is for them an essential but inexplicable element of the female mystique while for women its attendant miseries long ago earned it the name of 'the curse'. For, although casually dismissed as 'women's problems' by the other half of the human race, pre-menstrual tension is a very major stress. It is estimated that at least fifty per cent of the world's women suffer this affliction in some form for a quarter of their thirty or forty potentially child-bearing years.

There are two forms of menstrual pain: spasmodic, which is usually characterized by colicky pains in the abdomen, and congestive, which covers a variety of symptoms experienced before and sometimes during menstruation. The symptoms include physical sensations of dullness, heaviness, nausea, backache, headaches, breast pain and emotional disturbances such as irritability, listlessness, depression and anxiety – commonly known as pre-menstrual tension. The link between menstruation and emotional upset is the hypothalamus, a part of the brain which governs the emotions but which also plays a part in the menstrual cycle. The change in a woman's personality, if she suffers severe pre-menstrual tension, can be so complete that she doubts her own competence as a human being and certainly performs less well at school or work or acts unpredictably in relationships.

London doctor Katharina Dalton maintains that all severe menstrual pain is caused by faulty hormone production and can be corrected by taking extra oestrogen or progesterone (according to the nature of the pain). Hormone treatments have been found effective for many women but it is still too early to assess long term risks, if any.

Meanwhile, recent years have seen the rise of a new menstrual psychology that stresses the *positive* aspects of this part of woman's lot. An English couple, Penelope Shuttle and Peter Redgrove, after diligent research into the subject, have concluded that menstruation can be a source of increased sensitivity, sensuality and energy. For many women, it is a time when they are functioning at peak, though they may have been totally

168

unaware of it. Shuttle and Redgrove maintain that understanding of the menstrual cycle leads to important self-knowledge, the acquisition of which can lead to empathy with others. Shuttle and Redgrove recommend that the menstrual cycle should be studied, not shunned, and all women should tune in to their own moods and body changes during each month. For these moods affect all the family.

But, while they are urging women to tune in to these cycles, another lobby maintains that, far from being natural, menstruation is almost abnormal. British gynaecologist Dr Caroline Deys has pointed out that, before the advent of contraception, women spent most of their reproductive years being pregnant or breast-feeding – during which time they were unlikely to menstruate. The only time they had periods was between puberty, which was later than it is now, and marriage, which generally occurred much earlier.

Research now indicates that Western women are far more prone to breast cancer than women elsewhere and that the later a woman has her first child, the more likely a candidate she is. Dr Deys believes that the modern menstrual cycle, with its monthly hormonal upheavals, may be the cause: the breasts, ovaries and uterus were not designed to cope with it. Dr Deys and other gynaecologists who support her believe that the menstrual cycle should be suppressed artificially. To counter the outcry against such a seeming act against nature, they maintain that it is no more unnatural than contraception and may redress the body balance.

Research into the possibilities is at early stages but, should it produce results, there will still be another hurdle to cross: for, despite complaints about the curse, it would seem that women are somewhat attached to their periods. The World Health Organization undertook a study in twelve countries which revealed that young women welcome menstruation as a sign of womanhood and women over thirty treasure it as a reassurance of continued fertility.

Mental Handicap

A mental handicap is a malfunctioning of the brain with which a person can be born and for which there is no cure. It is completely different from mental illness, which is mental or emotional breakdown that *can* be cured.

Many conditions can create a mild or severe mental handicap. Sometimes there is a malformation of chromosomes which cause a child to have limited mental capacities. Physical abilities and co-ordination may also be affected, as messages from the body are not received and processed correctly by the brain. **Mongoloid** children have a chromosome abnormality.

Certain diseases such as German measles suffered by a mother during pregnancy can communicate themselves to a child and result in a mental handicap at birth. Also, the likelihood of a mother giving birth to such a handicapped child increases as she ages – for ageing affects the ovum. The use of forceps during a difficult delivery may also damage the brain.

The demands made upon parents by a severely mentally handicapped child are great and the children may need to be cared for in a special environment. All too often this has meant big, rambling mental hospitals where, for lack of staff or resources, the children receive limited individual attention and so are not helped to develop what potential they possess. Now the trend is to try to care for less severely mentally handicapped people in smaller groups and to teach them, as is possible in a great number of cases, to meet their own needs and even to work at jobs in which their reduced mental abilities are not a real drawback.

Many people mistakenly believe that a mentally handicapped person will be violent. Very rarely is this the case, though some may appear 'out of control' because of their poor body co-ordination.

Mental Health

Mental health is an even more woolly concept than **mental illness**. Whereas mental health should be the criterion against which mental illness can be measured, more often it is itself defined, rather unhelpfully, as the state of not being mentally ill.

Some brave souls have tried to come to grips with it. Mental health, it is suggested, is the state in which we feel independent, emotionally secure, confident of our abilities, filled with a sense of direction, free to develop and express our creative potential. Few of us feel we actually possess these qualities in such abundance, yet neither would we class ourselves as mentally ill.

Strangely enough, mental health as a word mainly enters the vocabulary as a nice way of talking about mental illness. Institutes and associations for mental health spend most of their time researching into, publicising and meeting the needs of the mentally ill and handicapped. In recent years, many such groups have entered the area of so-called preventive mental health which doesn't refer to the desire to prevent mental health but to bring to public attention the nature of the stresses that can lead to mental illness. So confusing is it all that, when I worked with such an association, I used to receive letters from people complaining that they suffered from mental health. Would that we all did.

Mental Illness

Mental illness is by no means a simple concept. We usually know when the body is malfunctioning because we experience pain or discomfort but that criterion doesn't work where the mind is concerned.

To define mental illness – and the legal profession has tried – one ends up grappling for something to measure normalcy against. Are we mentally sick if we cease to be able to function as a responsible member of society? No, shout the **anti-psychiatrists**, who claim that it is society itself that is sick and those that break down under the system are in fact those with a sense of sanity.

Are we mentally sick if we cease to be able to look after ourselves, to take responsibility for our own lives and function as independent entities? That is closer to the model on which modern psychiatry works – at least in the West – even though anti-psychiatrists might again claim that any such breakdown is due to the pressures of a suffocating society.

Letting definitions be what they may, there are certain symptoms which come in many combinations and which indicate that all is not well with an individual. The person experiencing them may or may not be aware that something is amiss. All significantly disruptive mental aberrations that are *not* of a physical nature (see **mental handicap**) come under the umbrella term mental illness. These include severe clinical **depression**, **schizophrenia**, and **psychopathy**.

We all experience ups and downs in our lives, emotional highs and lows, uncomfortable phases of insecurity, feelings of worthlessness, desires to opt out of responsibility. While these feelings may bring us down or, on the bright side, be the catalyst for

171

our making changes in our lives, they do not comprise mental illness unless they really start to consume us, prevent us taking any interest in or responsibility for our affairs and make us withdraw further and further from our normal sense of reality. Then some kind of help becomes necessary: perhaps the prescription of psychiatric drugs or a course of ECT to alleviate the pressure first; or a period of asylum somewhere (using asylum in its true sense of a place of refuge); or a course of therapy that involves talking out and coming to grips with underlying problems.

For all the advances of recent years, mental illness is still little understood. Theories as to its causes abound and treatment will vary according to the views of the practitioners. Some claim it is caused by intolerable living conditions, some attribute it to family conflicts, others are convinced it results from some chemical imbalance. The word 'mental illness' still has for many people unpleasant and frightening associations with madness, although most mental illnesses are now either curable or containable. But that old fear is perhaps not surprising. If the so-called experts argue amongst themselves as to the correct approach to cure or even the correct naming of the disorder, mental illness still remains a dark spectre on an uncomfortably close horizon.

Mental illness, because of its amorphousness, only has any real significance as a word because of the need for a legal definition. There has to come a point where, for the protection of an individual himself or for others a person can be held temporarily in a hospital against his will. Many is the suicide that has been prevented because of such powers, with the suicidal person himself grateful that he was prevented from taking that final step while in a temporary deep bout of depression. But human liberty is at issue here and it is the requirement of a just society that such compulsory powers should be impossible to abuse. Unfortunately, even now, vagaries in the law enable albeit well-meaning mental health professionals to use the powers as a time-saving short cut or as an administrative convenience.

We may condemn psychiatric practices in the Soviet Union but a blinkered approach to care-and-cure can also perpetuate a subtle abuse of human rights in the West.

Mental Set

How often have you sat reading a book and just as you are finishing a particular sentence, someone else in the room or a

172

voice on the radio says one of the very words you have just read? Our usual reaction is 'what a coincidence' but really the phenomenon has more to do with mental set.

When the mind is set on one particular activity, idea or even object, it tends to pick up on it, wherever it may occur. So someone who has just had her long hair cut short may notice that other people she knows have also had their hair cut. If it isn't because the style has suddenly become all the rage, it is because her mind has focused in on hair and is therefore noticing it when normally she might have been oblivious to it.

If we expect to see something, we recognize it much more quickly. So, at a fancy dress party we will know that Santa Claus is Uncle Fred whereas, if we didn't know he was doing the job, we might fail to recognize him playing Santa for the children in a big store at Christmas.

Our minds can remain 'set' for something even if we imagine we have long put that particular matter out of our heads. We may spend half an hour trying to remember the name of a particular actor and fail. Then, days later his name will crop up in some completely different context and we'll remember that that was the person we were trying to think of. Our minds have remained 'set' for that name.

Political opponents are set to see only their own point of view, no matter how convincing a contradictory argument. A person who is convinced he has a large nose will be set to notice the noses of other people and perhaps even see a nose as someone else's distinctive features when other people would notice they had one green eye and one brown one or flaming red hair.

Mental set can help in medicine. If people are set to believe that a certain drug will cure them of their illness, they may well recover – even though, unknown to them, they were given a placebo (a substance that looks the same as the drug it is meant to be but which really has no curative properties).

But the advantages to be accrued from mental set don't have to be unconscious. We can 'programme' ourselves to alter our approach to a great many aspects of life if we only learn how to use it. (See **positive thinking**.)

Mentally Abnormal Offender
see **Insanity**

Mescaline

see **Psychedelic Drugs**

Mesmerism

Anton Mesmer, a Viennese doctor in the 1760s, came up with the idea of 'animal magnetism', a vital fluid or force which he imagined to exist in the universe, in the human body and in magnets. Sickness was caused by an imbalance of this all-important fluid but health could be restored, he claimed, by the use of magnets. So he used to sit his patients around tubs filled with iron filings from the midst of which protruded metal rods. The patients, by holding these rods, had the necessary magnetism restored to their bodies.

The treatment process was somewhat dramatic. Soft music was played and then, suddenly, in swept Mesmer dressed in a long lilac silk coat. In the dimly lit room there was silence whilst Mesmer touched or stroked his patients with his wand. The effects varied. Some people experienced nothing at all, others fell into wild convulsions, after which they claimed they were cured.

Although he obviously did his utmost to create a mysterious, magical atmosphere, Mesmer declared that his methods were based on natural scientific principles. Later he discovered he could achieve the same effects without the paraphernalia of the rods and filings. The heightened emotional atmosphere of the occasion made it quite easy to induce trance and collapse. In short he mesmerized people.

So, while Mesmer was wrong about the magnets, he did provide the background for the discovery of hypnosis and the power of suggestion. It was a follower, Englishman James Braid, who, while experimenting with 'animal magnetism' on his own, decided that the phenomenon was nothing to do with that at all and it was all psychological. He coined the word **hypnosis**.

Metal Bending

Uri Geller sprang to international fame when he went on television to demonstrate his ability to bend metal just by stroking it. Millions watched agape as he made keys and cutlery curve; even the sceptics paid attention, when Geller was willing to re-enact his fantastic feats in the supposedly fraud-proof atmosphere of a laboratory investigation.

Then scientists who had initially suspended their disbelief started to revive their criticisms. Professional magicians could do what Geller had done and, worse, it came out that Geller himself had once been one of their number.

But, for some other scientists, investigation of the phenomenon has continued to be treated seriously and they are by no means convinced that metal bending is fraud. One such is John Hasted, professor of physics at Birkbeck College. London. He initially ran experiments using Geller as subject and then found others in whom similar powers had been awakened once the phenomenon was publicly identified. (Many people watching Geller on television discovered they too could bend cutlery.)

Hasted's best subjects have been children, and often they don't need to touch the metal but just concentrate on it. Paper clips imprisoned in glass domes have duly bent into a tangle of metal, along with keys suspended in the air and connected to monitoring electrodes. Hasted, who has taken care to eliminate all possible means of fraud, clearly believes metal bending is genuine. But he doesn't know how it happens or why the ability is most pronounced in children. Something would appear to be happening at molecular or atomic level in accordance with laws that are not yet understood.

Similar research into metal bending is also being carried out in Australia, Japan and France and those engaged in it are respected academics in orthodox disciplines.

Migraine

Migraine is the name given to a particularly intense sort of headache and is suffered by at least one person in ten. Its causes are not really known and probably what one person designates as migraine another person might well call a headache. Migraine is not the prerogative of the sensitive, the highly strung or the artistically inclined: it can strike anyone.

Although the causes are unclear, medical science has isolated a number of symptoms which, broadly speaking, can be categorized to form two varieties of the complaint. Classical migraine is the crippling variety, and fortunately the less common. The sufferer experiences intense throbbing pain around one eye, accompanied by distorted sense of vision and hearing, giddiness, nausea and even hallucinations.

Common migraine, the more usual sort, as its name implies,

also results in pain on one side of the head but doesn't have any of the other symptoms. Still, the head pain with this variety can be stronger and last longer than chronic migraine.

The head pain is caused by a constriction of blood vessels in the brain. One cause of this can be an over production of the hormone adrenalin, which is itself caused by stress. So it is not surprising that relaxation methods – particularly **biofeedback** techniques – have had some success in alleviating migraine.

But stress is just one of the known triggers of migraine. Changes in body chemistry can also be caused by blood sugar deficiency, for example. Certain foods, as varied as chocolate, alcohol, dairy products, citrus fruit and fried foods, can set the migraine off for some people. Fatigue and hormonal changes, particularly in women, can trigger it off and noise, stuffy atmospheres or intense light often play a part.

All that the medical profession can suggest at the moment is that sufferers attempt to identify their own triggers and then try their hardest to avoid them.

Milieu Therapy

Milieu therapy consists of providing psychiatric patients with a stimulating environment in which they can participate, with the staff, in taking responsibility for themselves. This might take the form of setting up patients' committees, devising and fulfilling work rotas, taking turns at helping make decisions about the running of the ward or the community (see **therapeutic community**).

Milieu therapy came into being as a way of preventing the destructive effects of institutionalization. Patients used to be left to sit around wards with nothing to do, were given no stimulation of any kind and were relieved of the responsibilities of looking after themselves, because meals were provided and cleaning was done by domestic staff. Milieu therapy provided the opportunity for patients to learn to take back some responsibility for themselves again but within a supportive and understanding environment.

The term milieu therapy is sometimes used in a slightly different context. Maximum security hospitals, for patients with a violent disposition, often claim to provide milieu therapy when they actually mean the following: a person suffering from mental illness will be helped merely by being in the particular surroundings he is in. Maximum security hospitals are not noted for being the most pleasant of places, yet this is the milieu in which some patients are expected to show signs of spontaneous movement towards recovery.

For some, being taken into such a sheltered environment where one is freed from responsibility from one's own maybe inexplicable and frightening actions may indeed be the first step on the road to insight and change. Others, suffering the indignities of crowded facilities, resultant loss of privacy and a 'sentence' without the security of a definite date for discharge, may feel milieu therapy is a little bit laughable.

Mind

What, if anything, is the mind? Where does brain stop and the mind start? Or is the mind part of the brain?

It is an unanswered series of questions that has given rise to different philosophical and psychological schools of thought down the ages. Scientific discoveries about the seemingly limitless potential of the brain and its role in the experience of emotions, perceptions and thought have encouraged many workers in the field to believe that mind is just the complex amalgamation of a whole variety of physiological processes. Others believe that an understanding of the processes of the brain can never explain the individuality of man expressed in his intuition, reasoning powers and creativity: that there is mind, a mysterious entity that is inextricably linked with the body but cannot be reduced to a series of reflexes or neuronal connections. How else can we appreciate beautiful music, experience deep love, have a sense of self-consciousness? Where does abstract thought come from? Is there a cosmic **consciousness** of which our minds are a part? Individual convictions abound but there are no universally accepted solutions.

Mnemonic
see **Memory**

Mongolism
see **Down's Syndrome**

Monoamine Oxidase Inhibitor
see Psychotropic Drugs

Mood-Changing Drugs
see Psychotropic Drugs

Motivation

Motivation is the driving force that prompts us to do something, and we are motivated by a need. We eat and sleep, for instance, to satisfy biological needs that are vital for survival. The acts of eating and sleeping therefore have *primary motives*. Included with primary needs are sensory needs, such as stimulation and contact. A child needs to be touched, if its development is to be normal.

But other needs have their basis in social learning. We develop the need to be held in esteem by our peers, for instance, motivating us to be high achievers at work or to be loving, understanding people. These are *secondary motives* and though survival does not depend upon their being met, emotional stability does. Secondary needs, being rooted in social learning, obviously vary from culture to culture. More importantly, they vary from individual to individual, as the effects of social learning and experience are highly personal. An individual may be motivated, on occasions, to eat not to satisfy hunger but as a comfort against loneliness or as a means of avoiding dealing with anxiety.

Multiple Personality

The emergence of multiple personalities in one person is a rare form of **dissociative reaction**; while successfully burying the cause of anxiety from his or her conscious mind, he ends up expressing them through a different personality.

One of the most famous cases of multiple personality is that of the American woman Chris Sizemore, whose story became the subject of the film *The Three Faces of Eve*. The three faces were Eve White, an excessively demure and lifeless housewife, Eve Black, a fun-loving, outgoing, good time girl and Jane, a calm, attractive and capable young woman. However Chris Sizemore's autobiography, published in 1977, showed that she had known

178

no less than 22 different personalities, (though none as long lasting as those characterized in the film).

Her childhood was fraught with traumatic experiences of pain and death which probably helped trigger her particular anxiety-coping mechanism. Before even her teens her life was populated by young strangers all of whom were really her and whom she 'saw' as from a distance, living out her own life. It was they who strayed out of bounds or who hurt her kid sister and she was always surprised to be scolded for their misdeeds. Later, in adulthood, the personalities took over her whole life and she would involuntarily switch from one to another. Most of the personalities knew of the existence of the others and each had distinct characteristics: one couldn't drive (although Chris could); one was left-handed; another couldn't even talk.

Munchausen Syndrome

This term refers to people who go from hospital to hospital complaining of illness when there is nothing physically wrong with them – and they know it. Those that are really good at it sometimes even manage to get operated on before they are found out.

The name Munchausen comes from a famous eighteenth-century teller of tall tales who himself became the subject of some very exaggerated stories, but modern-day Munchausens are real enough. The syndrome has been noted both in England and in America – in the latter, one master Munchausen has been admitted to 32 hospitals, at a cost to them of nearly £18,000.

Alan Maltbie, an assistant professor of psychiatry at a university medical centre in America, has made something of a study of the syndrome. He says that the patients arrive with plausible medical history and plausible symptoms. But when the doctors, after thorough investigation, suggest psychiatric rather than physical treatment, the patients leave.

Sometimes the Munchausens make their case even more plausible by swallowing razor blades, coins or other objects. But doctors have little chance to discover what is behind all the feigning, because of patients' quick exit once found to be fabricating.

Still, Maltbie is convinced that faking illness *is* an illness and though the patients may go to great and unbelievable lengths to corroborate their stories, it is only themselves they are deceiving. Doctors who have actually been fooled into performing endless

179

tests or even operations do not feel quite so charitable about it all.

Mysticism

The Oxford dictionary, after its entry for mysticism, has 'often derogatory' in brackets. This is symptomatic of Western man's opinion of those esoteric arts which aim to concentrate the attention on inner awareness and, in so doing, encourage the experience of sense of oneness with the universe.

Mysticism is the term often applied to describe the practices of Eastern systems, such as **Zen**, Buddhism and **Sufism**. Practitioners are concerned with opening themselves to 'objective' or 'cosmic' consciousness, the sensations of other than ordinary, environmental stimuli. Whereas we unconsciously ignore all impulses bar those of ordinary consciousness, mystics consciously block out ordinary sensory stimuli and concentrate on inner, holistic awareness.

Their **meditation**, dancing and chanting are not meaningless rituals; they are specialized ways of focusing inwards and deactivating the normal sensory organs. This change of awareness is not totally unknown to us in the West. Fasting for a few days, or extremely energetic activity or the use of mood-changing drugs can all affect our perceptions. That 'twilight zone' between waking and sleeping and even dreams themselves provide a sensory awareness that is floaty rather than functional.

In the West we think in terms of time and sequential patterns. We are logical rather than **lateral thinkers**. In the East, there is more emphasis on time being ever present, on intuition and a sense of wholeness, oneness. Discoveries about the specialized functions of the left and right hemispheres of our brain have shown that the left side controls verbal, logical, thinking whilst the under-used right side is the intuitive and creative centre. (See **split brain**). It would seem that what we term mysticism is a sensory focus that is available to all of us, if we can waive our ordinary patterned thinking and allow the other side of us to surface. (See **Zen, Tao, Sufism, consciousness.**)

N

Narcissism

Narcissism traditionally means love of self to the exclusion of others, deriving its name from the Greek boy, Narcissus, who caught sight of his reflection in a pool and was so entranced by its beauty that he couldn't tear himself away – with the result that he starved to death.

Freud used the term narcissism to describe a stage that all children go through, around the age of three, when they are totally absorbed by themselves; he claimed that this was a natural and necessary precursor to learning to love others.

In recent years psychiatrists have revived their interest in the narcissist but as an adult personality type. American psychoanalyst Otto Kemberg is one of the chief formulators of a theory about pathological narcissism. Whereas a certain degree of desire for attention and approval is normal, pathological narcissism results in over-intense self-absorption.

The narcissist's opinion of him or herself is totally dependent on the attention and admiration he is given by others and so he courts interest and praise by being, often, extremely affable and attractive. But in reality he has little real feeling for other people himself and fails to appreciate others' feelings. Often the narcissist will appear to be particularly productive and creative, holding high positions in management or performing as an entertainer. But his abilities in reality lack depth, for he uses them merely as a ploy to attract and maintain attention.

Narcissists, according to Kemberg and others, lack emotional depth too. Their emotions are quick to arouse and quick to fade and they rarely experience anything lasting. Even loss of a friend is felt not as sadness but as resentment. Few have really been in love.

However rather than self-love, it is self-hatred that the narcissist is trying so hard to counter by courting the attentions of others. Kemberg says the narcissist also experiences intense, unconscious envy that makes him want to spoil and belittle what others have and particularly what others have to give, in terms of love. This means that the narcissist can never be truly satisfied by what he receives and so remains empty inside.

Kemberg has found that the pathological narcissist has had a very particular kind of childhood. Consistently there has been a mother-figure who had an indifferent or aggressive attitude towards the child. It may be the parent's coldness that leads the child to seek admiration elsewhere. Or the mother may herself have used the child as a source of attention-getting from friends. Very often the narcissist, as a child, showed brilliance and promise and was exploited for it.

Narcissists are only interested in what they themselves can get out of a situation. They expect favours without feeling the need or desire to reciprocate and are always surprised and resentful if someone won't do just what they want. So, instead of feeling long-term love for one person, the narcissist moves between many relationships and settles for sexual excitement. But, as he feels the need for conquest always, the need to make someone succumb to him, he loses interest once the challenge has been met.

While all this may seem fun to the narcissist when he's still young, even he gets disillusioned by the transience of it all in middle age. Then, says Kemberg, the narcissist often loses almost all interest in sex and can start to see for the first time how empty and shallow his life has been. It is in middle age that the narcissist may benefit from therapy and finally come to terms with himself.

Natural Childbirth

Natural childbirth stems from the idea that pregnancy and birth should be allowed – and helped – to proceed with the minimum of outside interference. More and more evidence is coming to light to show that hospital routines, with their inevitable emphasis on expediency, can do much to harm the relationship between mother and child. Where labours are induced, for administrative conveniences, the mother is unconcious during the process and too hazy to appreciate the first glimpse of her child. Hospital practice of whipping the baby away to be washed prevents mother and child experiencing the immediate skin-to-skin contact that is now known to be so important in fostering a healthy rapport and promoting mother–child co-operation in breastfeeding.

The natural childbirth lobby emphasizes the mother-to-be's need to learn to relax her muscles, through simple relaxation techniques or by yoga, so that she can reduce her fear of labour pains and experience the birth without drugs. And new ideas about the birth itself are now gaining acceptance, as a result of the work of French obstetrician Frederick Leboyer, who drew attention to the unfortuitous atmosphere into which a child is normally born.

With an interest sparked by re-experiencing his own birth trauma in psychotherapy, Leboyer denounced the standard delivery room practice of bringing the new born out into glaring lights, noise and bustle, brusquely cutting the umbilical cord and inflicting a resounding slap on the bottom to encourage respiration. He believes this sort of thing does nothing to alleviate birth trauma. Instead, he recommends subtle lighting, and the elimination of as much noise as possible. At birth, the child should be placed on the mother's stomach and gently massaged, leaving the umbilical cord unsevered for at least five minutes. Next the baby should be bathed in warm water, to aid the transition from the cushioning of the amniotic fluids in the womb to life in the great outside. Then the baby goes back to the mother to suckle and rest.

This practice, says Leboyer, helps produce a happy, secure child. The idea is pooh-poohed by many of the medical profession but mothers who have experienced this 'gentle birth' claim their children are more settled and have fewer eating or sleep problems.

Natural Selection

Sir Charles Darwin, father of the theory of evolution (the single most important discovery from which our knowledge about biology and psychology stems) posited that all species produce more young than nature can provide for and so, through a process which he called natural selection, only those that can adapt themselves to an ever-changing environment will survive. The adaptations necessary for survival are numerous – not only have humans, for instance, needed to adjust to changing climates (with appropriate skin colour and hair growth), develop the 'tools' to defeat predators (e.g., evolution of the thumb which enabled us to fashion and use weapons) and adapt to illness, so that health can be restored, but also to cope with psychological stresses caused by personal factors.

Whole species that have failed to adapt have died out – nature's way of keeping the numbers down. In the animal kingdom, anything that is malformed or diseased at birth is likely to die extremely quickly, unable to cope with the demands of survival.

For humans, of course, the advances of medicine and surgery have meant that deformity or congenital disease is no longer a death warrant. This has produced a moral controversy of its own. Should children born with gross physical or mental defects be kept alive in order to live out their lives with paralysed limbs, permanent incontinence, severely retarded mental faculties and perpetual need of support? Whilst it is a question that may never be able to have a legal answer – where could one ever draw the line between a life that's 'worth' saving and one that is not? – many doctors have in recent years admitted to taking the decision into their own hands, removing life support systems from the severely handicapped and sometimes even actively administering drugs aimed to speed death. Outrage at such 'infanticide' has to be tempered by recognition of the fact that few families are able to cope with the extreme demands of seriously handicapped children and few resources exist for their effective care. Saving life may, in many circumstances, simply mean consigning such individuals to a living death.

Naturopathy

Naturopathy is a means of preventing disease by correct eating, with the resultant elimination from the system of toxic substances that cause illness. It is a form of self-healing based on the belief that all living cells, if unadulterated by the infiltration of artificial chemicals, work towards the maintenance of a healthy body and the rejection of harmful waste products.

Naturopathy claims to put man back in touch with his natural energy processes so that he can live a healthy life, in harmony with nature. It is concerned with wholeness and so sees the body as interdependent parts, all of which are affected by each other. Disease is not a particular condition but the result of some general blockage in energy flow. It may manifest itself in one particular organ but it is the whole body that needs treating, not the site of the symptom.

So naturopathy concentrates on purification of the whole system by correction of diet, although there is also an accent on adjusting any skeletal problems, such as those caused by poor posture. The removal of toxic waste products that are responsible for disease is achieved by fasting, intake of Vitamin C, application of hot and cold water to the skin to help elimination of waste, and massage. After the period of fasting, under the guidance of a naturopath, vitality is restored to the body by adjusting the diet. All refined foods are out; emphasis is on fresh green vegetables, fruits, beans and grains, etc., with specific recommendations made for an individual by the therapist. Often supplementary vitamins and minerals are required to be taken for a while to build up body defences.

Once people are set back on the right track, naturopaths say they can sense their own health requirements, knowing automatically what substances are harmful for the human organism. But they warn against over-eating even the right foods. For it doesn't follow that the more right food we eat, the more energy we'll derive. On the contrary, too much food of any kind reduces vitality and slows down the system.

Neo-Freudians

The followers of **Freud** all based their ideas on his personality theory but refined or altered it according to their own findings and beliefs. These people are sometimes called the Neo-Freudians. Amongst them are disciples **Jung** and **Reich**, but both altered Freud's ideas so extensively that they are usually considered as having developed a branch of analysis all to themselves.

Other disciples included Alfred Adler, who was a student of Freud but who chose to play down the significance of the unconscious mind and concentrate on social development and each individual's need to control social relationships. Individual weaknesses, he believed, led to the attempt to compensate for them in other areas. So a very short height-conscious man may become the leading light of the amateur dramatic society, full of verve and wit. (See **inferiority complex**.)

Karen Horney did not study under Freud but was heavily influenced by him. She laid her accent on a child's need for security (her own home life was very troubled) and the behaviour patterns that can result from lack of it. She also challenged Freud's views on penis envy (see **psychosexual stages**) and claimed that if women felt inferior it wasn't for lack of a penis but because of society's attitude towards them.

Erich Fromm is a renowned analyst also influenced by Freud but who has applied a political perspective to his theories. (See **aggression**). For others who broke away from strict Freudian thought, see **ego psychologists**.

Nervous System

All physical and mental activities are dependent on the nervous system, a complex mass of nerve cells transmitting information throughout the body. We are able to think, feel and make sense of what we see due to the activity of the nervous system.

The human nervous system is divided in to two parts, *central* and *peripheral*. The central nervous system is made up of the **brain** and the spinal cord, the structures that house most of the body's nerve cells. (There are ten billion nerve cells in the brain alone.) The spinal cord co-ordinates information passed to·and from the brain and the rest of the body but its own special concern is with reflex actions. If a light blow is received on the knee, the spinal cord receives information about the sensation and activates nerve cells specifically concerned with movement, so that they can carry the message to the leg muscles to extend.

The peripheral nervous system consists of nerve cells that carry messages from the central nervous system to the rest of the body. It is sub-divided into two parts. Firstly the *somatic* system, containing nerves that carry messages to the surface of the body and to muscles that we are consciously aware of. Secondly there is the *autonomic* nervous system which contains nerve cells that connect with internal organs and is involved with unconscious activity such as breathing and digestion. The autonomic system operates independently of our conscious awareness. However it is now known that, though its functions do not require conscious control, we are capable of influencing the autonomic system and altering our heart rate, blood flow, etc. (see **biofeedback**).

The autonomic system is also divided into two parts: *sympathetic* and *parasympathetic*. The sympathetic system is concerned with gearing the body to meet and withstand stress. It instigates the secretion of the hormone **adrenalin**, speeds the heart rate and slows digestion (see **fight or flight reaction**). The parasympathetic system is concerned with restoring the body functions to normal rate after the stress situation has passed. So the two systems work together to keep the body in balance.

All of the work of the nervous system is effected by the intricate network of nerve cells that serve each part of it. The nerve cell, or *neuron*, is the core of the whole system. Neurons, which consist of a cell body and a long connecting fibre, called an axon, vary in length according to function: one type, stretching from

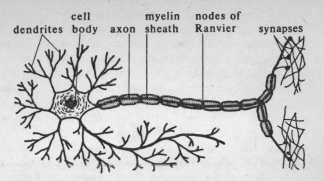

cell   myelin   nodes of
dendrites body   axon   sheath   Ranvier   synapses

Fig 4. Simplified diagram of typical neuron. Electrical charges are received from other cells by the dendrites. Their overall effect on the cell body governs the rate at which impulses are sent out via the axon and transmitted to the dendrites of other cells at the synapses.

the spine to the foot, is over three feet in length whilst some neurons in the brain are considerably shorter than an inch.

There are three types of neuron: *sensory* neurons which carry information from the sense organs to the spinal cord and brain (sights, tastes, smells, etc.), *motor* neurons, which carry information between muscles and glands and the brain and spinal cord, and are responsible for physical movement; and *association* neurons which connect one neuron to each other and aid in the transmission process.

Information is conveyed through the body in the form of an electrical charge. Extending from the nerve cell body are branching fibres called *dendrites*. These receive an impulse from a sense organ, muscle or adjacent neuron. This impulse is then carried into the cell body and on down the length of the axon until it reaches the *end branches*, which look similar to the dendrites. Between the end branches of one neuron and the dendrites of the next there is a space called a *synapse* filled with fluid. The neuron signals its impulse to the next neuron by releasing a chemical called a *neurotransmitter*. This chemical will then ignite the next neuron or deaden its activity, according to need. (For instance, if one set of neurons are signalling for the arm muscles to flex, the impulses will fail to ignite those neurons concerned with telling the arm muscles to contract. If all neurons were igniting together, movement would be deadlocked.)

Not all stimulation of the nervous system provokes activity. The stimulus has to be strong enough to ignite the receiving neuron and prompt it to send out an impulse. The synapse too has a threshold which governs how readily the impulse is accepted by the adjacent neuron. For reflex activities, the threshold is low, allowing impulses to cross easily. Synapses are vital to the efficient and swift transmission of information because they provide the link with a number of adjacent neurons. A single impulse from a single neuron sets off a whole wave of communication in progress, with hundreds of neurons receiving and transmitting.

The stronger the chemical transmitter, the easier the message is passed. Adrenalin, released in times of stress, serves to lower the synaptic threshold and enables us to act and think faster. One school of psychiatric thought has it that certain mental disorders are caused by faulty and weak transmitters. Extra doses of the relevant chemical transmitter can speed up reactions or slow them down, according to need. Similarly, artificial substances such as caffeine in coffee serve to lower synaptic threshold and enable us to function more efficiently, whilst nicotine has the reverse effect. It raises the synaptic threshold, making impulses more difficult to transmit, and so its calming effect comes from the resultant deadening of reactions. Mind altering drugs, such as LSD, can also interfere with synaptic transmissions, giving rise to distorted perceptions.

Neurology

A neurologist specializes in abnormalities of the nervous system or diseases that affect its functioning. His concern is with diseases that are known to be of organic origin, such as epilepsy or Parkinson's disease, not with emotional disturbances that affect brain function. A neurosurgeon, who performs any necessary operations on the brain, usually works closely with him.

Neurosis

One very short definition of the difference between neurosis and **psychosis** is: neurotics build castles in the air, psychotics live in them. Simplistic it may be but it makes the essential point that while neurotic people may distort reality, they are not completely out of touch with it.

Neurosis is a broad term to describe emotional disorders that

188

are all basically characterized by **anxiety**. The anxiety may be acknowledged and openly expressed or else it may be so deeply hidden that it manifests itself in other forms, such as sleepwalking.

People suffering some form of neurosis do not hallucinate nor are they incapable of carrying out their domestic responsibilities or jobs (unless their neurosis takes the form of, say, obsessional handwashing which may well get in the way of a lot of ordinary activities). But they are unhappy, unfulfilled, often threatened people. They are usually perfectly aware that their reactions to particular situations are inappropriate (fear or distrust of a colleague's actions, perhaps) and if their behaviour is bizarre they know and are uncomfortable about it.

Neurotic behaviour can take many forms, mild or severe. Free-floating anxiety is one, where an individual feels panic and fear for no known reason. Others are **phobic** reactions (excessive fear of spiders, heights, lifts, etc.); **obsessive-compulsive** behaviour (carrying out rituals like checking and re-checking and re-re-checking door locks); and **hysterical** reactions. In some cases the anxiety expresses itself through **dissociative reactions** (ways of closing off the threatening thoughts or feelings from consciousness).

Freud and the psychoanalysts thought neurotic behaviour derived from unconscious conflicts and suppressed guilt and **psychoanalysis** was necessary to uncover its source. The behaviourists take the anxiety as manifested as their starting point and try to change an individual's responses to the kind of circumstances that arouse it (see **behaviour therapy**). Drugs may be useful as a way to suppress the discomfort of anxiety but **psychotherapy** is more effective (less time consuming than psychoanalysis), as a way of getting to the root of the anxiety and dispelling it.

Nicotine
see **Addiction**

Non-Verbal Communication
see **Body Language**

Normality

We are very preoccupied these days with what's normal and what's not. 'But is it normal to feel like this?' whines the woman in the doctor's surgery. 'It's not normal in a boy his age,' says the father of his bookworm, girlfriendless son.

As British psychiatrist Tony Whitehead has pointed out, there are two kinds of normal: the statistical normal and ideal normal. The statistical normal is based on a finding that a particular attribute or action is common to a large number of people. It is a statistical norm for men in Britain or America to grow to a height of between five and six feet. It might also perhaps be a statistical norm for people to leave home late for work and rush to the station, thus incurring stress symptoms which lead to heart attacks. The fact that it might be a statistical norm doesn't mean that it's normal in the sense of desirable.

The ideal norm, however, involves a societal consensus, or majority view, about the attributes and behaviour that should be considered healthy. It is seen as normal, for instance, to cry at the death of a loved one and distinctly abnormal to go off and play darts instead of attending the funeral.

As far as behaviour goes, the concept of normality can only ever operate as a flexible yardstick. The ideal norm, as regards mental health, may be a person who is happy, independent, responsible and creative. But it is also normal to be unhappy at times. Unfortunately, many people have come to associate the experience of misery with being unwell, not normal, and seek treatment to alleviate the 'condition'.

Nymphomania

Traditionally, a word for a woman who is always looking for sexual gratification. In colloquial usage, it refers to any woman with an incredibly high sex drive who goes to almost any lengths to get her own sexual needs fulfilled. In medical usage, it actually means a woman who is incapable of deriving sexual satisfaction and it is her *inability* to achieve orgasm that drives her to try to find fulfilment in one sexual relationship after another.

O

Obsessive-Compulsive Behaviour

Obsessive-compulsive behaviour is the involuntary repetition of some thought or action, or both, usually in an unconscious attempt to ward off feelings of anxiety. We have all probably experienced the mild obsessive thought – maybe a line of a song that we can't get out of our heads – or the need to carry out some little ritual, such as checking that the door's locked, several times over. Obviously this sort of behaviour isn't a sign of mental illness. It is only when the obsession takes over and interferes with a person's ordinary life that it warrants some form of treatment.

The anxiety that underlies obsessive behaviour may be quite obviously connected with it, as in the case of someone who ritualistically checks window locks and alarm systems because of a fear of burglars; but in other cases the individual doesn't realize why he's anxious. Whichever way, if the individual is prevented from carrying out his ritual, extreme feelings of anxiety and impending doom ensue.

The most common or well-known instance of compulsive behaviour is repetitive handwashing. Here a person is obsessed by the thought that he and everything around him are covered with germs and so resorts to frenetic and compulsive handwashing, innumerable times a day. Someone who suffers from this obsession to this extreme is obviously being incapacitated by it; he can hardly carry out his work or domestic duties if he keeps having to wash away contagious microbes.

But there are many other bizarre kinds of obsessive behaviour: the person who has to pick up all the pieces of broken glass she sees on the road – something of a nuisance if she happens to be on a bus at the time; the individual who has to go through certain complex mathematical calculations every time a particular make of car passes him on the road. One psychiatrist tells the tale of how, when he walked into his ward one morning, he found that all the patients had gone back to bed because one of them, who had an obsession about getting out of bed according to some particular sequence with the other patients had done it wrong. He needed everyone to start again so that he could do it right!

Having an obsessive personality does not automatically lead to the need to comply obsessively with strange personal rituals. A great many people are obsessive in a mild way, needing to live by the letter of the law, be scrupulously tidy and religious about routine. They are perfectly happy that way and, though they may never become the world's most creative thinkers, they are in no way ill. Whereas those whose behaviour is so bizarre that it affects their normal functioning are miserable (because they know that they are making a laughing stock of themselves) and need help. The obsessional behaviour may be superficially effective as a way to avoid the original anxiety but it creates a whole lot more of its own.

Drugs can be useful to allay the anxiety. But the most effective way known to treat obsessions is by **behaviour therapy**. If it is a thought the person is plagued by, the therapist tries to condition him to replace that thought with another – a difficult process. Less difficult to deal with is obsessive behaviour; the therapist prevents the patient carrying out his ritual and then helps him to handle the ensuing floods of anxiety by reassurance and support.

Occult

Traditionally the occult has referred to black, evil forces beyond our understanding; witches engaged in animal sacrifices, devotees at candlelit rituals summoning up the devil and the casting of evil spells.

Now, however, the occult has a much wider, less demonic meaning. It is used to cover all aspects of the paranormal, such as ESP, astrology, faith healing, numerology, psychic surgery, etc. and is the subject of much scientific research by parapsychologists trying to understand the forces involved.

The occult really means anything that isn't easily explainable in terms of our usual five senses. And even witchcraft and wizardry, so long associated with the occult, are now thought to have had much more innocent origins than the activities of certain demented modern-day cults would suggest. Witches first came to be thought of as evil in the Middle Ages when the Church hit upon the idea of possession by the devil as an explanation for any abnormal behaviour. In keeping with this idea, it seemed that someone had to be responsible for letting the devil in in the first place and the blame was placed on 'witches', any unfortunates who had any superior talents or behaved in a slightly bizarre way.

Many of these were people who had highly developed senses;

192

some were able to heal people or others to foretell the future. Witchcraft as such was a folk cult that stressed home crafts, such as weaving, cooking and growing herbs, and the worship of the forces of nature. Most modern day witch cults concentrate on the development of these interests rather than blatant sex rituals and gory sacrifices to darker forces that are usually associated with magic rites.

Occupational Therapy

Occupational therapy is an important ingredient in a psychiatric hospital's programme to rehabilitate a patient and prepare him or her for normal living outside in the community again.

Modern occupational therapy encompasses a broad spectrum of activities, from silk-screen printing to leather work, not just the basket-weaving and knitting associated with its earlier days. In fact, it used to be used just as a time-killer in some hospitals, offering only boring, repetitive work. Used properly, however, it can supply stimulation and meaningful occupation, aid manual dexterity, promote self-confidence and generally be enjoyable. Art therapy, dance therapy and drama therapy all fall under the general umbrella term of occupational therapy and industrial therapy is a variation of it too.

In industrial therapy, hospital patients are taught, or helped to maintain, skills that will enable them to get jobs in the community, should they need them, when they leave. The work may, however, be simple and monotonous, such as packaging or putting tops on bottles, and it is often on a sub-contract basis from a local factory. Sheltered workshops of this kind (i.e., work done outside of a competitive open market) offer useful occupation particularly to chronically mentally ill or mentally handicapped patients, as part of a normalization programme. But to be of use to those whose breakdown has been of only a temporary nature, industrial therapy needs to provide challenges and the chance to master increasingly difficult tasks as well as graduated exposure to the kinds of pressure which have to be coped with in open employment.

Oedipal Complex
see **Psychosexual Stages**

Oestrogen
see **Hormones**

Operant Conditioning
see **Conditioning**

Optimism

Only humans have hope. We hope that a baby will give us a smile or that our children will be successful in school; we have hope, according to our beliefs, that society can be changed, a cure will be found for cancer, that there is life after death.

Degrees of optimism vary. Some people are almost insufferable in their easy-going belief that everything will turn out all right in the end. But, say American researchers, Margaret Matlin and David Stang, we are all more optimistic than we think. From their studies it seems as if our brains edit out much unpleasant information and concentrate on the brighter side of life.

They found, through extensive tests, that people take longer to recognize unpleasant or threatening stimuli; they communicate good news more frequently than bad; they use words that denote pleasantness more often than words with unpleasant associations; people report more pleasant than unpleasant things, even if they have in fact been equal in number; likewise, they recall pleasant events occurring more often than nasty ones, even if they were equal; when people make lists of colours, individuals they know, TV programmes, etc, they put the ones they like first; people remember the details of nice things better than unpleasant things; past events grow more pleasant with the passage of time; they tend to rate other people positively more often than negatively.

Other studies by other researchers show that, in all languages tested, words with pleasant connotations appear far more often in newspapers and books than their opposites.

Matlin and Stang think optimism is connected with the way we process information. We are selective in the material we choose to process from the whole mass available and not only does long term memory seem to favour pleasant information but we actually fail to process some unpleasant sensations at all. They don't even make it as far as memory.

Why? Psychoanalysts would say we operate a defence mechanism to avoid the experience of anxiety. The evolutionary explanation could be that species which don't favour pleasant information die out. Or, as **behaviourists** would have it, concentrating on pleasantness makes life more pleasant and so the behaviour is reinforced.

Oral Stage
see **Psychosexual Stages**

Orgasm

Orgasm is the sexual release that occurs at the peak of sexual excitement and arousal. Though celebrated in prose by such immortal lines as 'the earth moved', until sex researchers Masters and Johnson actually studied the physiology of the human sexual response, orgasms could not be compared or described and myths about their nature or even their existence were rife.

Masters and Johnson developed instruments that could measure everything, from colour changes in the genitals when aroused to amounts of lubrication produced. They found that there were four stages to the human sexual response cycle: the excitement phase, when arousal rapidly starts taking place; the plateau phase, during which the reactions of the previous stage are consolidated but not increased and the sexual organs are heavily congested with blood; the orgasmic phase, when all control is lost, movement becomes involuntary and muscles in the genital area contract strongly; and, finally, the resolution phase, when the blood flows back and excitement gradually decreases.

Before Masters and Johnson did their work, it was thought that in women vaginal and clitorial stimulation produced two different kind of orgasms. But now it is known that the physiological response is no different. In fact Masters and Johnson put female sexuality on the map for not only did they show that women certainly could have orgasms, they showed that they could have multiple orgasms; that the clitoris had a more important role to play in arousal than the vagina and that penetration was entirely unnecessary for female sexual satisfaction. Hence the preponderance of lesbian feminist slogans such as 'A woman needs a man like a fish needs a bicycle'.

195

But some think that Masters and Johnson and the feminists have gone too far. To Alexander Lowen, for instance, father of **bioenergetics** and follower of analyst Wilhelm Reich, the orgasm is far more than just a physiological response. He agrees that the penis is high in nerve endings and the vagina is singularly lacking in them but nerve endings, he says, are not the whole story (or why is the penis, after ejaculation, incapable of instant re-arousal: the nerve endings are still there).

Pelvic movement in sex, says Lowen, is as important as touch: and that the most intimate contact and strongest movement which can occur in a relationship between a man and a woman is that of sexual intercourse in the missionary position. The movement, and the emotions unleashed by that movement, as well as the physical arousal, all contribute towards the amazing release of orgasm.

Far from claiming that orgasm is within reach of us all, Lowen (and Reich before him) insists that very few people experience true orgasm at all. For most, it is a partial affair, an ejaculation or a climax but not an orgasm. For an orgasm, the two bodies have to be completely in tune and in rhythm, there can be no constrictions, in the form of bad blood circulation or muscle spasms or performance anxieties and each must be yielding up fully to the other. Only then can a real release, involving the whole body, occur. (Lowen is most scathing of the contorted facial expressions that usually accompany 'orgasm', the writhings and moanings and holding in of breath, all of which signify to him pain and restraint, not a healthy letting-go.)

Some might find Reichian and Lowen's views on sex a little far-fetched. But the idea that we have not fully explored our sexual potential is not to be dismissed out of hand. Eastern men and women employ in sex the easy use of muscles which many westerners don't even know exist. In the West, taboos against overt sexuality prevent most of us from freeing our pelvises even when we walk – so it's unlikely we can easily relax them in bed.

Orgone Therapy
see **Reichian Therapy**

Osteopathy
see **Manipulative Therapy**

P

Paedophilia

Paedophilia, a Greek word, literally means 'love of children' and of all the possible sexual orientations that exist, the paedophiles come under the most fire for their proclivities. For a paedophile, sexual and emotional love is directed towards children and this terrifies and reviles parents who fear that their own children could be manipulated, in all innocence, into a sexual relationship with an older man (or woman, though that is rarer).

There are many explanations for paedophilia supplied by the medical profession: the paedophile feels inadequate about his sexuality and so closeness with a sexually immature child lessens his anxiety; or the paedophile is frightened to face mature sexuality and identifies with the childishness of his love object; or he is attracted by his power or by their innocence. Paedophiles are most commonly male and may be attracted to either boys or girls.

Paedophiles, a growing number of whom now declare that they are not sick and do not wish to be 'cured', claim that theirs is a genuine affection and love for young people, which need not necessarily find sexual expression, but that all children *are* sexual beings and are capable of responding to – or initiating – a sexual advance; and that it is only adult guilt about sex which causes us to try to stamp out or ignore the sexuality of our children and their desire to express it with adults.

Certainly paedophiles, with an irrepressible pull towards young people, may be the victims of some youngsters' sudden awareness of their burgeoning sexuality and ability to command attention just as often as they are the instigators of such passion. While pederasty refers to anal intercourse with a boy, paedophilia can encompass actual sexual penetration or just fondling, mutual masturbation and general affection.

Having sexual intercourse with a child below the age of consent is an offence punishable by law and many paedophiles are so ashamed of their proclivities that they have undergone behaviour therapy in a desperate attempt to kick the habit. Others have used the current liberalizing of sexual attitudes to declare, somewhat questionably, that paedophilia is no more reprehensible than homosexuality. (But most homosexual campaigning groups are reluctant to embrace the rights of the paedophile.)

Paedophiles do quite genuinely love children and, despite parental accusations to the contrary, would rather die than do anything consciously to hurt them. However, they fail to see that their attentions may be damaging for the child psychologically and a manipulation, however unintentional, of the child's affections.

Also, paedophiles tend to love children of particular ages, rather than just particular children. So a child who receives much attention at the age of eight might find itself spurned once it has outgrown the desired age-range, and be left to cope alone with any consequences of loss.

The image of the paedophile as gentle and sensitive, which paedophile campaigners are so keen to promote, is further destroyed by the preponderance of child pornography that is now available and the salaciousness of their own campaigning literature.

Pain

The most exciting discovery in recent years of pain research has been the finding that the brain produces its own painkiller, which is between five and ten times more powerful than morphine. This natural narcotic is called *endorphin* (a running together of the words endogenous morphine, literally meaning 'morphine made from within') and was discovered during work with drug addicts.

This discovery may go some way towards explaining how certain methods of pain-suppression work. Acupuncture, for instance, may be effective because the insertion of needles in relevant body sites stimulates the brain to produce its endorphins. As with any new discovery, researchers tend to go overboard in excitement, attributing all and every as yet unexplained illness to, in this case, over- or under-production of natural endorphins. But research is in its early stages and full practical value is as yet unknown.

Meanwhile, another popular theory about the experience of pain still holds ground. This is the gate-control theory, proposed by American psychophysiologist Ronald Melzack and neuroanatomist Patrick Wall. They say that in the body's pain-signalling system there is a 'gate' which can be opened or shut according to the stimulation of certain fibres. There are large and small fibres in the sensory nerves and when the large fibres are stimulated, they effectively close the gate, so that the experience of pain is reduced. But when the small fibres are stimulated, they open the gate and increase the sensation of pain. The large fibres relay signals about heat, cold and touch, so this may explain why hot or cold compresses often relieve pain. Melzack and Wall also believe that the gate theory can explain the psychological component of pain. Positive emotions, such as joy and pleasure, close the gate while negative feelings such as fear and depression open it.

For no theory of pain can fail to take account of the psychological component. It was found in the war, for instance, that soldiers who experienced the most horrendous wounds often claimed not to feel pain while the same injuries, suffered by people in 'civvy street' induced excruciating agony. Why? Because the soldiers saw their injuries as a passport home and away from the war and the joy experienced at that overrode the experience of pain. For the non-soldiers, injury just meant an unwelcome disruption of normal life and so the pain took its full toll.

We know that anticipation of pain increases experience of pain. Physiological tests show that we expect pain to increase and so we experience that as happening, even though, there comes a point at which it peaks and reduces. Knowledge that this is the case can help us 'go over the hump' and tolerate more than we thought possible – purely by changing our expectation of pain. It has been found that patients for major surgery experience less pain and discomfort if they are told exactly what to expect in advance. Social learning is also involved in the experience of pain. Where children observe a lot of pain in their family – a parent with a chronic illness, for instance – they often develop strange pain syndromes themselves as adults. It is not uncommon for children to report recurring abdominal pain, when there is no physical basis for it, if there is a history of severe gastro/intestinal pain in their family. It is almost as if the expectation and therefore the experience of pain can be passed on within families.

So we still have much to learn about the experience of pain. But one thing is certain; it is not a simple case of the greater the injury, the greater the agony.

Paranoia

Paranoia is one of those psychiatric terms which has passed into general usage and is considerably misused as a result. We accuse other people of paranoia (being intensely distrustful and suspicious) when they are reluctant to entrust something to us or to believe us, whereas they might in fact have very good grounds for their hesitancy.

The truly paranoid person is certainly intensely distrustful and suspicious. He is also likely to be a jealous, over-sensitive, and probably highly intelligent individual, whose inability to believe that any purpose is what it purports to be leads him to suffer a persecution complex. He may believe, for instance, that innocuous passers-by are really agents from the income tax office or that a departmental meeting with which he's not involved has been called to discuss ways to get rid of him.

People who develop paranoid personalities tend to come from domineering homes, where the authoritarian demands and criticism that rain down on their heads lead them to become sullen and resentful. They feel inferior and insecure and often this manifests itself in a bad track record for keeping jobs or relationships going. They can't trust and are terrified of being manipulated, so they can't allow themselves to get really close to anyone. They justify that by finding fault with others.

Paranoia of extreme form is often an element of schizophrenia. Here accompanying delusions and hallucinations lead the sufferer to imagine he is the butt of the most bizarre plots. He may also suffer delusions of grandeur, such as thinking he is Jesus Christ or a President and this belief justifies or exacerbates the conviction that people have a reason to be out to get him. Often those who develop paranoid reactions are indeed those who have – or showed as children – some talent of which others are jealous.

It is difficult to shake paranoia because offers of help are seen as further evidence of manipulation.

Parapsychology

Parapsychology is the scientific study of paranormal phenomena. For all the advances of technology and the growth of understanding about the functioning of the human body, there is still much about our universe that defeats explanation. One such area is broadly called the paranormal and under its vast umbrella fall such phenomena as **poltergeists, UFOs**, geographical triangles and **kirlian photography**; and inexplicable mental faculties such as **telepathy, psychokinesis, clairvoyance**, precognition (**ESP**), out-of-the-body experiences, **spiritual healing, psychic surgery** and such-like.

Psychologists first became interested in trying to harness para-normal manifestations to the instruments of science at the end of the last century. Then efforts concentrated on trying to discover the causes of mental telepathy by running tests with cards in laboratory controlled experiments. Now parapsychologists have roamed further afield, investigating poltergeist phenomena and all those other intangible forces. Parapsychology is still on the fringe of psychology, for all its hundred years of existence, because of course paranormal phenomena are very difficult to control, and hard to produce to order in laboratory conditions. Investigation is made harder by the fact that individuals who manifest ESP or who can move objects and bend metal don't usually know them-selves how it's done either. The powers are not under conscious control.

But it is a fascinating field and the development of electronic hardware is making it possible to control processes which were once seen as involuntary or inexplicable (see **biofeedback**). But, for all the research, sceptics will probably still remain sceptics and some commit the cardinal sin of declaring that, if it can't be explained by known forces, it can't exist. Enthusiasts take an opposite view; that we are trapped by the limits we have set to our own consciousness and have tuned out a whole other world of sensory experience of which telepathy, etc. is only a tiny part.

Pavlov, Ivan
see **Conditioning**

Peer Counselling
see **Co-Counselling**

Penis Envy
see **Psychosexual Stages**

Perception

Every moment of the day we are bombarded with sensations: sights, sounds, tastes, smells, heat, cold, pain and texture. The term perception doesn't mean just the receipt of this sensory information. It is the ability to understand and interpret all the in-coming data and this ability is affected by individual learning and experience. Several people may see the same policeman, for instance, but the way they perceive him may vary. The upright, law-abiding citizen sees the policeman as a caretaker of society, a protector to be respected; the member of a revolutionary left-wing group sees him as a tool of the system, an authoritarian agent of the status quo. So the way we perceive the world is coloured by our own expectations and beliefs.

Perception is usually dependent on sensory information (see also ESP). Our sense organs are attuned to pick up on particular stimuli. When our eyes receive light rays, a message is sent via our nerve cells on to the brain. (See **nervous system**). Our ears respond to sound waves and chemical molecules activate the senses of smell and taste. Receptors in the skin respond to sensations of temperature, pressure and pain and muscles and body organs are also sensitive to pain, so that warning of internal illnesses and malfunction of the system can be sent to the brain. Muscles and joints also have sensory receptors which provide information about body position (kinaesthetic sense). A vestibular sense, its receptors located in the inner ear, gives us our sense of balance.

But the vast majority of sensory information that we receive comes through the visual system. The eye is a highly complex organ and the occipital lobes in the brain, which make sense of visual information, also have highly specialized cells. Some only respond to vertical slits of light, whilst others are concerned with horizontal light. This has important ramifications for the way that we code and store visual information about shapes and sizes of objects.

We have the visual equipment to differentiate between a wide variety of hues. Light is an electromagnetic energy that travels at 186,000 miles per second. Its wave-lengths contain all the colours of the spectrum and they combine to appear white. This is light in its pure form. But when light waves hit a surface, the waves break apart, giving rise to different colours according to the surface hit. For each surface absorbs chemically all of the light waves that it is capable of absorbing and throws back the reject waves. It is the rejected waves that give the appearance of colour. So buttercups absorb all light waves except yellow and send these back into the air to be picked up by our eyes. Grass absorbs all colours except green. Flowers, such as snowdrops or daisy petals, fail to absorb any light at all, so we see the whole light spectrum, i.e., white. When objects appear black, it is because all light has been absorbed. (See also **colour therapy**).

Perception is an intricate process because we do not see the individual lines or shapes that make up an object, we see the whole. We can distinguish foreground and background, even when we are looking at a picture that is two-dimensional. A building stands out against the sky, a heading stands out from the white of a page. Our inclination to see foreground and background can sometimes give rise to perceptual illusions. For instance, when we see the moon behind clouds, it appears to us as if the moon is moving instead of the clouds. This is because the moon is seen as a foreground figure against a background of clouds and we are more used to attributing movement to a figure than to background.

We also habitually 'see' more than we are presented with. If four lines are drawn to make a square but none of the lines quite join up with each other, we still 'see' a square. We close the gaps for ourselves. We also group images according to their nearness and similarity to each other. A square made up of small black squares is still seen as one large square if the spaces between the small ones are narrow and symmetrical enough.

This kind of perception seems to be innate, as studies of infant perceptions have shown. Depth perception, so vital for survival, is known to be inborn. Babies can immediately sense a drop. A very clever test of this was devised by two Cornell University researchers who placed a sheet of glass under a patterned surface in such a way that they created the illusion of the surface giving

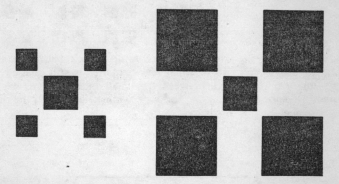

Fig 5(a). An illusion of size can be created by surrounding same-sized squares with larger or smaller squares.

Fig 5(b). We habitually 'see' more than is really there. These four lines are still seen as a square, even though they don't join up.

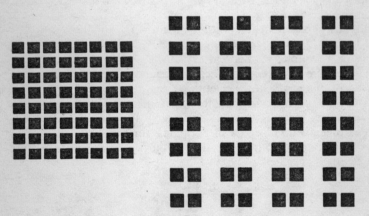

Fig 5(c). We visually group images according to their nearness to each other. A square made up of small black squares is still seen as one large square if the spaces between the small ones are narrow and symmetrical enough. If they are not quite symmetrical (as on the right) we see smaller groups of squares.

Fig 5(d). The Müller-Lyer illusion is an illusion of length.

way to a large drop. The babies placed on the 'flat' part of the surface all hesitated when they reached the part where the pattern seemed to fall away vertically, even though it was only an illusion.

However, learning also plays a part in the development of perception. Experiments on animals brought up from birth in a visually restrictive environment have shown that perceptual abilities develop according to the sensory experiences available to us. Kittens brought up in special compartments painted with all vertical lines fail to 'see' horizontal lines when brought out into a natural environment.

So visual cues are very much dependent on experience. In the West we use certain cues for recognizing faces, according to the nature of the faces we see most. This is why Westerners often say that Chinese people all look the same, and vice versa. Different visual cues are necessary which neither group have usually developed because of lack of exposure.

Similarly, a member of a small tribe in Africa, who lives within a small tree-enclosed space and is completely unaccustomed to seeing distance, will have great difficulty, when taken to a hilltop for the first time, in understanding why people far away seem the size of ants and then get bigger and bigger as they approach.

We, being used to close range and distance viewing, make the necessary adaptations for changes in size. If we see a person at the other end of a long corridor, we don't really believe that he is two feet high and that he grows as he approaches us. We know that he is six foot, despite the size of the image on the retina of our eyes. This phenomenon is called *perceptual constancy:* we perceive the environment and objects in it as unchanging, despite distortions of size or the effects of seeing objects from differing angles. We accommodate for the variations.

So much sensory data is coming in all of the time that we are attuned only to notice sudden changes. We do not hear the tick of a clock that is always in the room with us; we hear the silence, however, if it suddenly stops. We notice the look of houses and gardens and streets when we walk down the road for the first time in a new town. Once we have lived there a while, we fail to 'see' them. In other words, we see what we expect to see, instead of really 'seeing' them at all.

It is important that we become habituated to a certain amount of sensory stimuli, or else our nervous systems would be at breaking point, trying desperately to process all incoming data. But sometimes responding to expectation alone can lead to a blinkered

205

vision of the world. We often put people in mental boxes, for instance, and don't credit them with the ability for change. The man who married a timid, dependent wife continues to see and treat her as timid and dependent even if she starts to try and assert herself. Living partners become so used to each other that often they only learn to 'see' one another again once they have split up.

Seeing what we want to see can be dangerous when it results in our ignoring new information that conflicts with our perceptual set. Politicians see the world in a way that supports their own particular approach to government; trade union leaders and management see different causes for unrest at work. And personal problems can result if we insist on seeing other people as we would like them to be instead of as they are.

Perls, Fritz
see Gestalt

Personality

All the forces of heredity, biology, environment and experience combine to give each of us our own quite unique personality. The word personality comes from the Latin 'persona', meaning a mask. In Roman plays, the masks signified the characters of the actors.

Freud was the first to devise a coherent personality theory, which showed how forces of our upbringing and experience affect the way we behave and express our emotions. Neurotic personalities, he said, were caused by the repression of unmet needs. But many others besides Freud and the analysts have turned their attention to the ingredients that make up personality, and how to interpret them. Astrologers believe that certain traits are written into our stars. Early philosophers classified people according to types: the Greek doctor Hippocrates thought all temperaments were a result of excesses of certain body fluids, leading to melancholic, phlegmatic, sanguine or choleric individuals.

A more modern 'type' theory was developed by American psychologist William Sheldon, who believes that the structure of the body itself is an important factor in personality. He suggested three types: the *ectomorphs*, thin, perhaps fragile, people who are usually introverted, shy and quiet; *endomorphs* who are plump, rather soft and weak-muscled, and who like food, being mothered and are gregarious and placid; and in the middle, *mesomorphs*, strong muscular types who are active and adventurous. People, according to Sheldon, aren't necessarily spot-on to type. There are ranges within each category.

Another school of thought that links body structure with personality is **bioenergetics**. But here, it is not body that decides character, rather the other way around. People's individual ways of coping with unmet needs and tensing against pain find their expression in body posture and thwarted development. A man who is protecting himself against vulnerability may develop an extremely broad, tough chest as a defence. By getting to the core of an individual's problems and unlocking the tension, the body structure may actually be helped to change.

William Cattell was one of the first psychologists to try and group people scientifically according to personality traits. By a complex system of classification, he came up with the kinds of traits that predominate in certain types of people. Creative people, for instance, tend to be independent, don't work well in a group and are often a little tactless. Cattell developed his personality inventory into a questionnaire and it is still used to assess educational abilities, insurance risks, job compatability, etc., along with a whole battery of other personality inventories that have been developed since.

All personality tests have to be checked for reliability and objectivity. They have to produce the same result when taken several times by the same person but administered by different testers, in order to be valid; and for the score to be meaningful, there must be a large enough sample of answers against which an individual's responses can be compared.

Interest inventories concentrate on assessing people's interests, usually career-wise, as well as their personalities, and comparing them to the personalities of people who are successful in their particular chosen field.

Aptitude tests evaluate people's intellectual, creative, mechanical and physical co-ordination skills, in order to assess an individual's likely future performance at school or in a job. More general personality tests are used to diagnose personality disorders. The most widely used is the Minnesota Multiphasic Personality Inventory which consists of statements which the subject must tick as true or false. These are geared to reveal traits associated with traditional categories of mental disorder. Statements such as, 'I think people are after me' or 'I don't think about other people's feelings' may reveal whether an individual has elements of a **paranoid** or **psychopathic** personality.

The Eysenck Personality Questionnaire, based on psychologist Hans Eysenck's own theory of personality, identifies two main personality ranges: *introversion-extraversion* and *normal-neurotic*. Introversion refers to withdrawal and shyness, particularly under stress, whilst extraversion is demonstrated by a need to mix with other people, particularly when under stress. In the second range, normal means stable, balanced and calm while neurotic means unstable and anxious. We all fall somewhere within the ranges of these two scales.

Other psychologists use tests which concentrate on unstructured tasks, such as interpreting shapes or finishing sentences, in order that the tester may intuit the subject's hidden needs and motivations. Because they are based on intuition, they are the least reliable of personality testing devices (see **inkblot tests**).

However, all personality tests come under fire from critics. They are very one-dimensional and are open to misinterpretation. Much of our behaviour is learned from other people. We imitate styles and absorb others' ideas but not necessarily permanently. Superficial classification of traits does not tell the whole story. The seemingly stable individual may be a bubbling cauldron of unexpressed hostilities. New discoveries about body clocks, which have revealed that our performances may vary at different times of the day, could also affect test results. An individual who is moody in the morning may be alert and adaptable in the afternoon. But when does he take his test?

Another extremely heavy criticism of such tests is that results reinforce our own self images. If we are told we are slow learners, we may become slow learners because we believe that we are. Teachers, on the same information, may treat us as slow learners too, affecting our chances of ever proving things otherwise.

Personality is an intangible made up of intangibles. As such, it is ill-advised to rely religiously on questionnaire scores, although, individually, they may throw up some useful insights.

Personality Disorders

Not all people present psychiatrists with problems that fit neatly and conveniently into the broad categories of **neurosis** or **psy-**

chosis. Some people develop personality traits which are 'odd' or eccentric enough to cause themselves or others discomfort but their behaviour is not bizarre in the way that psychotic behaviour is bizarre, and out of touch with reality, nor is it characterized by high anxiety, as in neurosis.

Generally speaking, the term personality disorder is used to cover exaggerated manifestations of behaviour patterns which, in milder form, are common to all of us at some time. It is quite natural to be angry, anxious, shy or extravert in particular circumstances, but the person with a personality disorder may be stuck in a groove and unable to change his emotions or actions to fit changing circumstances. He may always be over-aggressive, not only when he's fighting his way through a bus queue but when he's talking to his children; he may always feel inadequate, with his friends and family as well as when in the company of more talented strangers.

Because personality disorder isn't an illness, as such, there is little psychiatrists can do except help the patient try to understand or find out why he behaves the way he does, perhaps through a course of psychotherapy. For the behaviour pattern will probably have been adopted as a way of coping with the problems of life. If someone is aggressive, it may make him feel less vulnerable, for instance. Unfortunately, the coping mechanism itself brings problems, for the individual's too rigid behaviour makes it difficult for him to deal with certain aspects of everyday life or relationships.

It is worth remembering that the term 'personality disorder' is really just a convenient pigeon-hole for doctors to slot certain behaviour patterns into, and it can accommodate just about anything. It is not some dreadful affliction from which there is no escape. Often the individual may just need to learn some new social skills.

Personality Test
see **Personality**

Phallic Stage
see **Psychosexual Stages**

Phenomenology

This tongue-twister of a word couches a very simple idea: man constructs his own reality. According to our own perspective on life, we make subjective interpretations of what we see going on around us. Unfortunately, we get so used to our own perspective, our own viewpoint on life, that we think the reality we see is the only reality. A man looks at the world not from some neutral standpoint but as a man. Being a man colours the way he interprets others' behaviour, particularly that of females. The reverse, of course, is true of women.

The phenomenological approach involves suspending one's natural standpoint and becoming conscious of *the effects of subjective reality*. Many people fail to do this when they assume that other people will react to situations in the same way that they do themselves.

The psychotherapist who takes a phenomenological approach is interested in the meaning that certain experiences or feelings have for the individual expressing them rather than interpreting them according to general values or theories.

Phobias

A phobia is an overwhelming and irrational fear of an object, situation or even a person. The most commonly known varieties are *claustrophobia* (fear of enclosed spaces, such as lifts) and *agoraphobia* (fear of public or open spaces). But some people suffer an extreme terror of cats, spiders and other animals or of inanimate objects, such as knives or pieces of dirt. There's even a variety named *parthenophobia*, which means fear of virgins.

It's often quite natural to feel a little anxiety about the sort of things that some people develop phobias about. No one would be that keen on being caught in a corner with a rattlesnake, for instance. But the phobic's anxiety reaction is excessive. He may break out in cold sweats and even faint with terror at the sight of a poodle. Phobias, of course, can be extremely crippling because the phobic person has to organize his life so that he's sure not to come in contact with the anxiety-inducing object or situation. As he can never be sure of not seeing a dog, for instance, this can be difficult. Agoraphobics are often so terrified of going out of doors that they remain housebound for years.

Freud believed that phobias were a defence against anxiety of a completely different source. The real object of fear, he said, was so anxiety-provoking that it remained unconscious and the individual transferred his fear to some external, often innocuous, object. He recommended analysis to help uncover the unconscious source of the terror.

The behaviourists think differently. They believe that phobias are created through the association of some previously unfrightening object with some particular frightening circumstance. For instance, a child walks into an empty darkened room. As he enters, a car outside the window backfires with a large bang. The child is frightened and makes the erroneous assumption that out of dark rooms come loud, frightening noises. He therefore becomes frightened of being left alone in the dark.

Behaviour therapy is certainly very effective for dealing with simple phobias of this kind or those mentioned above, and also **biofeedback**. However, even behaviour therapists admit that when a person has built up an impenetrable mass of **defence mechanisms** that surround a number of complex and unspecific fears, behaviour techniques have little to offer at all. For those, it seems, lengthy psychoanalysis or psychotherapy may be the only answer.

Photographic Memory

Photographic memory is a rather abused term. We talk of people possessing such a thing when they can 'see' where certain sentences fall on a page in a book or they can accurately recall a chart or a map. But real photographic memory is a somewhat more intricate skill.

The correct technical term is *eidetic imagery* and it is normally only found in children. But most children have lost it by the age of ten. Only about one adult in a million has the power of strong eidetic imagery.

When a picture is shown to children with eidetic imagery and then removed, they can continue to see the image as if it really is still before their eyes. If asked, they can look at the image and count the number of people in the picture or read off tiny pieces of writing that appear in the background. The image is so real that, if the original picture was shown against a background of black cardboard and then, when the picture is removed, the cardboard is folded, the image will become folded to the children too.

Unlike after-images, which we all get if we look at a strong contrast picture for a few minutes and then look at a white wall, the eidetic image can persist for days or even months. In recent years, an experiment has been developed using two separate patterns of seemingly random dots which will form a distinct image if superimposed over each other. People with eidetic imagery can be shown one pattern one day, the other the next and then mentally put them together to 'see' the shape that is formed by the two together.

It is difficult to know how many children possess such powers, as many are reluctant to admit to seeing things others can't, but some researchers claim the figure is as high as 50 per cent. So why should such an ability fade with age? One view is that our own educational system is at fault. Because we put so much emphasis on intellectual skills, such as reading and writing and arithmetic, visual skills are not encouraged. As a result, the ability starts to atrophy with disuse.

Eidetic images need not only be visual. Some people have auditory eidetic imagery, whereby they can relive certain music so intensely that they can pick out certain notes, or tactile eidetic imagery, which allows them to conjure up an image and feel its texture as if they were touching it for real.

Physiological Psychology

Physiological psychologists (sometimes called *psychobiologists*) are interested in the workings of the brain, the nervous system, hormones, genetics and all other aspects of the physical organism. But they differ from biologists because their prime interest is not to find out how the body functions but how the way the body works affects behaviour. When the physiological psychologist monitors heart rate, breathing, blood pressure, etc, he is not concerned with health but with the part physical changes play in the experience of different emotions.

Physiological psychologists have discovered, for instance, that receptors in the brain govern how much sensation we each feel, that certain sites in the brain govern the experience of certain emotions, that neural connections can be 'learned', that the two hemispheres of the brain have distinctly different functions, and that predominance of one over the other gives rise to completely different outlooks on life.

It is because of the work of these psychologists amongst others that we now have a variety of drugs that can affect mood, sex drive and activity. They have been able to identify the hormones and chemical transmitters which are responsible for certain reactions, so that people deficient in natural resources can be given artifical dosages of the necessary substance. Many physiological psychologists believe that all behaviour abnormalities and mental illnesses are the result of such biochemical imbalances, rather than the product of environmental influences and interpersonal conflicts.

This idea is dangerous; in effect it rules out the notion of 'mind', the mysterious, irreducible, self-governing element of us all that gives us our individual approach to life, our creativity and intensity of feeling. The more flexible approach is to accept that physiological and psychological factors work together to create the complex individuality of man.

Piaget, Jean
see **Developmental Psychology**

Placebos

Placebos have an important place in medicine – and psychology. They are biologically inactive substances, resembling particular drugs but containing none of that drug's properties. (Sometimes, therefore, placebos are colloquially termed 'sugar pills'.)

The purpose of these inactive drugs is in testing whether a particular, active, drug really does do what it sets out to do. People who are given the placebos should, theoretically, have no remission of symptoms.

But here human nature comes in. Many people, if they are told that the placebo is a real drug (which, of course, they are or that would defeat the object) actually recover from their illness anyway. This shows the power of belief and expectation. (Sometimes the same thing can occur when a patient unknowingly is given a drug that in fact has directly the opposite effect from that which he's been told it will have. In one case a man suffering from severe nausea was given a drug that normally induces vomiting. But he was told it would cure his problem and it did!)

Certain people who are given placebos instead of drugs not only report improvement in their condition but side effects as well. And one recent piece of research shows even more clearly the ingenuity of the human mind. People were given red, yellow and blue placebos and were told they would cure their headaches. Many patients reported back that pills of one colour worked whilst the others didn't. The most popular colour was red.

All such people are called, in the trade, placebo reactors. They are generally found to be more neurotic, suggestible and submissive than non-reactors.

Poltergeists

When the chandeliers swing, doors bang and pieces of furniture whizz across the room all by themselves, poltergeists are usually blamed for it. Poltergeists are popularly described as noisy spirits, famed for wreaking havoc through houses. It is rare for them to be linked with a particular place; more often they are linked with a particular person.

Parapsychologists think that poltergeist activity is not generated by an actual spirit, but by the unconscious efforts of certain individuals. As the focus is so often a young girl around the age of puberty it has been suggested that poltergeist activity is connected with repressed sexuality or sexual conflicts.

Though it may be simplistic to lay all the blame at the door of sex, certainly emotional conflict of one sort or another seems to be a consistent feature in the poltergeist focus. Studies show that, in the cases of all children associated with poltergeist activity, all had suffered some upheaval in the family. Most seemed to suffer from hysteria, hyperactive outbursts and anxiety.

Particularly marked in all the children – and in adult focuses too – is the craving for attention. Poltergeist activity, therefore, may be a dramatic bid to get it. (Sometimes strange phenomena surrounding a particular person cease after he or she has been paid a few visits by a psychologist/doctor/priest or whomever, indicating that attention needs certainly have something to do with it.) We do not know how poltergeist focuses actually cause remarkable effects. There are however many dramatic incidents recorded. A celebrated case was reported in Bavaria a couple of years ago where the phenomena centred on a nineteen year old secretary called Annemarie. The poltergeist effects here were electrifying – literally. Light bulbs exploded, fuses blew repeatedly and several telephones would start ringing all at once. Telephone calls were even instigated by an invisible force – on one day, 800 calls to the speaking clock were recorded! It turned out that, amongst other difficulties, the girl didn't like her job and was

214

always clockwatching. When she changed her job, the phenomena there ceased but they followed her for a while to her new one.

Poltergeist activity does seem to confirm the far-reaching and, as yet, ill-understood power of the mind, particularly the unconscious. Poltergeist focuses are as alarmed as anyone else by the strange phenomena happening all around them.

Positive Thinking

Positive thinking is a simple technique to help you make the most of your life and your abilities. It works by capitalising on a phenomenon that affects us all, called mental set (see **mental set**). Briefly, our minds become 'set' to notice things that we are expecting to see or to which we have recently had our attention drawn. For instance, if we have recently been told of a new author, we may suddenly start noticing his books in bookshops or in other peoples' homes. Of course, it can work against us too – negative set – as in cases when we read about the symptoms of some diseases and then start noticing the appropriate itches or blotches in ourselves.

Positive thinking techniques concentrate on inducing and maintaining a positive set. That means noticing and strengthening all the things which will help you to achieve a certain goal and ignoring those that will hinder it. For example, if you want to be good at changing plugs, mending fuses, etc., but you've never managed to get to grips with electrical matters, instead of thinking of electrical skills as impossibly complex – negative set, because you are reinforcing the idea that they are therefore not achievable – imagine yourself with the goal fulfilled: there you are, re-wiring complicated circuits and ably changing plugs while listening attentively to a play on the radio. Once you have developed a positive set, you will start noticing events or opportunities that will really help you achieve your goal.

It is claimed that positive thinking can work for a variety of habits or behaviour patterns you want to change: you can wake up on time by imagining, when you go to bed, that the hands of the alarm clock are saying 7.00 and you are leaping out of bed; or you can change your image by imagining yourself attractive rather than plain; if you have a knotty problem you can't solve, by imagining what it would be like if it *were* solved, you can sometimes leave the way open for your subconscious to pop up with the solution.

Belief is such a powerful force that it can make almost anything possible. American couple Carl and Stephanie Simonton encourage a positive set in their cancer patients by teaching them about the body's amazing powers of self-healing, bringing to their attention all cases of spontaneous remission and encouraging them to imagine themselves as well again. They claim that thirty per cent of their patients have recovered as a result.

So, if it works, positive thinking can be a whole lot cheaper than therapy and very self-satisfying too.

Possession
see **Exorcism**

Post-Hypnotic Suggestion

When under hypnosis, a subject can be instructed by his hypnotist to carry out a particular act at some set time in the future, be it in five minutes or six months. After the subject has been brought out of hypnosis, the message will remain implanted. Shortly before the set time comes, the individual concerned has a sense of there being something he must do; then the action takes place automatically. The person, unaware, of course, that he was 'programmed' to perform that act, usually tries to rationalize it. So, if he was instructed to rub his nose vigorously ten minutes after coming out of his hypnotic state, he would probably justify it by saying he had an itch.

The use of post-hypnotic suggestion is most commonly associated with stage hypnotists. For the amusement of the audience, the hypnotized subject will be instructed to carry out some innocuous but irrational activity (see **hypnosis**).

Post-Natal Depression

The idea that the maternal instinct is a natural part of the female make-up is deeply engrained in our society, so it is a great shock to some women who have long wanted a baby to find that their reactions after the event are any but those of great joy.

Many women experience a bout of depression, sudden changes of mood and outbursts of tearfulness for the first few days after the birth (sometimes the reaction is delayed for a few weeks). The experience may well be frightening. Some mothers believe this means that they don't want their baby and that they are incapable of motherhood.

However, post-natal depression is a well known syndrome and many doctors believe it is hormonal in origin, as there is a large change in the production of hormones during and after the birth itself. The neurosis which ensues may take the form of extreme anxiety, the development of phobias, sudden obsessions or hostility towards or fears about the baby. It is unusual, however, for mothers who have never had any emotional troubles or feelings of personal insecurity before the birth to develop them for the first time after delivery. More often the physical and mental stress of childbirth acts as a 'last straw' and brings to the surface feelings of insecurity or uncertainty which may have been hidden before.

If recognized for what it is, the depression can be quickly and easily treated. The father of the child needs to be involved in the treatment process and to be reassured that his wife's mental state is purely temporary and has nothing to do with her abilities as a mother. But, untreated, the anxiety and phobias can persist perhaps for months or even develop into a chronic pattern. In rarer cases, the mother may show signs of schizophrenia or severe manic-depression and then hospital treatment is recommended for a while.

Pre-Natal Therapy

Pre-natal therapy was developed by an Englishman, Robert St John. It is based on the ancient Chinese practice of reflexology (which works on the principle that all parts of the body find their reflection in some part of the foot). While St John was practising reflexology, he somehow discovered, he claims, that the area along the instep from the big toe to the heel corresponded with an individual's gestation period in the womb. Accordingly, by massaging this area, he claims that mental or physical faults that were laid down in the womb can be reversed.

It may sound ridiculous but he has had notable success in helping mentally handicapped children. Severely retarded youngsters, to the astonishment of their teachers or nurses, have started to open up, to respond to others, to speak and even to grow. St John says that, if reached early enough, such handicapped children can be helped back to normality. And the therapy can also work for physical disabilities, such as spasticity or paralysis. Even in adults he can effect some changes.

The massage, he claims, is easy to do and any parent can learn it. But the important part is to achieve the correct attitude towards the massage. The helper must not impose his or her own will on the patient but, instead, let the patient's own body work for him. The therapist is just a catalyst; it is the patient's own life force that is the source of the change.

Pre-natal therapy is based on the belief that consciousness is present long before birth and attitudes of mind are developed during gestation according to the ability of each individual to respond and adapt to the changes that take place in the womb. If the attitude of mind isn't right, mental or physical deficiencies result.

Postural Integration
see **Rolfing**

Premature Ejaculation
see **Sex Disorders**

Pre-Orgasmic Group
see **Sex Therapy**

Priapism

Priapism is a rare condition, fortunately, in which the penis becomes erect without there being any sexual desire. Sexual intercourse does not lead to loss of the erection. The penis becomes painful and impotence can ensue if it is not fairly rapidly drained of blood, by surgical procedures, and prevented from being re-engorged. In some medical thinking, priapism is a **psychosomatic** disorder but it is more usually known to be associated with another underlying illness, such as thrombosis or leukaemia.

Considering that impotence can be caused if the problem isn't treated quickly enough, it is strange that the condition is named after Priapos, a Greek God associated with fertility. Stone images of him straddling lichgates with his enormous member were very commonly to be found outside people's homes in Ancient Greece.

Primacy Effect

A list of adjectives which supposedly described the character of an unknown person was read out to two separate groups of students. One list started with the good attributes – intelligent, industrious, considerate, etc., and ended up with words such as envious and cynical. The other list put the less desirable traits first and followed with the good ones. Afterwards, when asked for their assessment of this unknown individual's character, the students who had heard the flattering adjectives first gave a far more favourable impression of him than their counterparts.

This experiment was carried out by Solomon Asch in 1946 and reveals what he termed the primacy effect. In other words, we tend to be influenced by whatever information we receive first and initial impressions can be extremely difficult to shift.

Other experiments in the same light have confirmed the validity of this finding. People always make judgements according to the material they read or hear first, regardless of the weight of conflicting evidence that appears later. It seems that we lay less weight on all subsequent information we hear and discount information that is not consistent with whatever we heard initially.

Primal Integration

Primal integration is a very similar technique to **primal therapy**, involving re-living of early life traumas. It was developed by analyst Bill Swarbley and he deviates from the system used by Arthur Janov in that he concentrates as much on the problems of adult life as on early childhood pains. He founded the international Primal Association, and was joined by others who had broken away from Janov's group.

He had to change the name of the therapy to primal integration because Janov had registered the name primal therapy as a service mark and so no one else is allowed to use it – a very uncommon occurrence in psychotherapy. Another similar approach is **rebirthing**.

Primal Therapy

Theories about mental illness have been founded on many things but never, before Arthur Janov, on something so simple as a scream. One scream, emitted by a patient during a session with Janov when he was working as a conventional psychotherapist, led to his formulating a dramatic new theory and a treatment which he claims is the cure for all neurosis.

The patient concerned was describing a vaudeville act in which the comedian was shuffling around the stage crying, 'Mummy, Daddy'. Janov saw that the words distressed him and asked him to repeat them. As he did so, the patient became more and more emotional until suddenly he let out the most eerie, bloodcurdling scream, the likes of which Janov had never heard before. When a similar technique in a different session induced the same response from another patient, an idea started to germinate which eventually developed as primal therapy.

The premise behind the thinking is that pain (which Janov calls Pain) is caused by traumatic experiences and, because it hurts, we devise ways of shutting the pain off, suppressing the memory of the events that caused it. But the pain has to go somewhere and it remains in the body as tension. We all tense against pain, so as not to feel it. But when the tension is long term, it starts to block all feeling and that, according to Janov, is when one becomes neurotic. Primal therapy takes the patient back to those suppressed traumatic experiences. The pain must be re-experienced and only then can the neurosis be resolved.

Janov says that there are three levels to Pain. The pains of childbirth itself are the first. The pains of childhood are the second – when the child is dependent on adults and sees all unmet needs or anger as a sign of rejection; the third line pains are those of adult life – rejection by a lover, feelings of failure, etc. The pains are usually 'resolved' in reverse, with the patient working back to re-experiencing his first trauma, that of birth itself.

Reports of primal therapy in action are quite dramatic. People are encouraged to whimper and wail like babies, thrashing limbs and drooling. In one instance, a birthmark which a woman patient had lost long ago in childhood actually came back when she relived her birth trauma. The most common pain that is relived in therapy, according to Janov, is that of rejection in childhood. Even people who remember their infancy as happy actually discover that there was much that they interpreted as rejection at the time (being left to cry alone, even just for three minutes, or being denied a treat), with resultant psychological pain.

Janov has come to believe that all forms of addiction, such as smoking, overeating, excessive drinking, and even very high sex-drives are methods people adopt to side-step their real neurosis. None of his post-primal patients drink or smoke. He also thinks homosexuality and other sexual behaviour that deviates from heterosexuality have the same root. Homosexuals who have come for primal therapy, he claims, have ceased to be homosexual after treatment.

Although he is accused of being a fraud, Janov says primal therapy is now a highly refined neuro-psychological theory. Studies undertaken at his Primal Research Laboratory in Los Angeles reveal that, after therapy, body temperature, pulse rate and blood pressure seem to drop. In some cases there have even been marked increases in the size of people's hands, feet and breasts – all proof, to Janov, that stunted growth may be due to repressed traumas about growing up.

Fears about primalling (as it is known) have been fuelled by the practices used to break down patients' prior resistance to letting go in therapy. Patients, for instance, may be kept in 'isolation' for three days, and not be allowed to smoke, drink or even eat. Then they spend three weeks during which they see only their therapist. But despite such criticism, it has caught on widely in America, where even magazines are produced about primalling experiences, and to a certain extent in England, with other therapists using similar techniques (see **primal integration**).

Problem-Solving
see **Thought**

Progesterone
see **Hormones**

Projection
see **Defence Mechanisms**

Psyche
see **Jung**

Psychedelic Drugs

Psychedelic drugs, or hallucinogens, are those which are capable of inducing dramatic neurological changes in a person who has taken them. These changes include physical reactions, such as blurred vision and profuse sweating, and mental effects, such as perceptual and time distortions, hypersensitivity to sounds, the sensation of flashing lights and extremes of emotion, such as ecstacy or deep depressions. Intellectual functioning and memory are commonly impaired during the experience.

The most common psychedelic drugs are LSD (lysergic acid diethylamide, which is a semisynthetic chemical compound and derives originally from a fungus called ergot); mescaline (or peyote) which derives from the peyote cactus; and psilocybin (known as Magic Mushroom). Because of their mind-expanding qualities, they were seized on by the sixties' youth either as an escape from reality or as a route to quick enlightenment and a more creative alternative lifestyle. Pop-culture heroes such as Timothy Leary and Ken Kesey did much to publicise the power of the psychedelics and then both did an about-face and denied that they were any answer to the ills of the world.

Although the love-and-peace era made psychedelic drugs famous as the product of an illegal high, they have a history that is far more sober and a long record as an adjunct to therapy, when used in controlled settings.

The therapeutic use of LSD has been particularly well-documented. It was discovered in 1943 by a Swiss chemist called Albert Hoffman. The fact that it had a definite effect on the nervous system led other researchers to explore its uses. It has since been used to help treat psychotic patients and alcoholics, with some success, and has even been given to people who are dying in the hopes that the experience will reduce their anxieties about death itself.

One of the most dedicated LSD researchers is Czech psychiatrist Stanislav Grof, now working in America. He was amazed to find how very differently various individuals reacted to the same dose of the same drug. Some, for instance, said they felt nothing but a slight physical discomfort; others experienced panic, hallucinations or intense sexual excitement. Grof came to the conclusion that the effects of LSD depended upon the personality of the taker and that it helped to release long-repressed feelings. This conclusion was borne out, for him, by the discovery that some of the same experiences induced by LSD occurred spontaneously, in the context of new therapies such as gestalt and bioenergetics, which concentrate on breaking down an individual's defences.

Grof maintains that LSD is a powerful catalyst of biochemical and physiological processes in the brain and helps to externalize hidden parts of the personality. The nature of one's LSD experience will therefore depend upon one's own state of mind, which explains why, in the sixties, there were many (highly publicized) 'bad trips' involving jumps from windows and attacks with knives.

LSD is a more powerful medium than mescaline or psilocybin. Aldous Huxley made mescaline famous by his own scientifically controlled experience with this mood-changing drug. But he was personally horrified by the 'turn on, tune in, drop out' era of drug experimentation and felt that an experience so 'transcendentally important' should not be entered into without proper supervision, or treated as a quick way to an entertaining high. Hallucinogens are not addictive but they do need to be treated with considerable care.

Psychiatry

Psychiatry is a branch of medicine that is specifically concerned with the diagnosis and treatment of mental disorders. Psychiatrists, in common with other specialists, are required to take further training in their chosen fields after they have been awarded their general medical degree.

Psychiatrists in hospitals tend to rely most heavily on physical treatments such as drugs or electro-convulsive therapy (ECT). But times are changing, new ideas about the nature of mental disorders are current, and psychiatrists are changing too. Many are now training in the allied skills of psychotherapy, which involves talking with a patient as a way to uncover emotional problems, instead of masking the problems temporarily with drugs.

In the psychiatric profession, there are other disciplines represented besides psychiatrists. The psychiatrist will be the leader of a team of psychiatric social workers, psychiatric nurses and clinical psychologists, all of whom are concerned with treatment and recovery from mental illness. Most work in mental hospitals but a number operate from special units concerned with drug addiction, marital problems, crisis intervention and suchlike.

Because the causes of mental illness are various and still the subject of hot debate, different practitioners take different lines. As mentioned, some believe implicitly in the power of drugs to alleviate entrenched conditions. Others claim that psychiatry is an instrument of repression, an agent of the status quo, and believe that support and understanding are the essentials for recovery from any mental breakdown. (See **anti-psychiatry**, **psychotropic drugs**, **ECT** and **psychotherapy**.)

Psychic Surgery

Psychic surgery is a form of non-medical healing. A few years ago, Western television cameras were able to capture on film in the Philippines the amazing sight of human organs being removed without any prior incision. Then screams of 'fake!' started resounding when the healer was found to be 'extracting' an organ that belonged to a pig during his operation on a human.

However, **parapsychologists** believe that it is wrong to dismiss the phenomenon just because charlatans are at it, as well as legitimate healers. Evidence, they say, is too strong for the process to be rejected out of hand.

In the 1960s a team of Western physicians went to examine the methods of a famed Brazilian healer nicknamed Arigo (good guy). He could diagnose an illness just by looking at a patient, and also demonstrated a knowledge of drugs completely incompatible with his lack of education. Films and pictures showed him using a blunt knife to cut out a boil or to make an incision in the cornea of a patient's eye while she was fully conscious. She experienced no pain and the wounds healed instantly. Arigo is famed for curing advanced cancer; on one occasion he was seen to insert his hands inside a man's stomach without making any incision and removing the cancerous growth. Arigo believes he is guided in his work by the spirit of a Dr Fritz, who gives him instructions as to what to do. Without Dr Fritz, says Arigo, he would know nothing.

This kind of curing, with the aid of a doctor spirit, is not unknown in the West. A man called George Chapman who lives in England is renowned all over the world for his healing powers. While not a doctor himself, he claims to carry out cures through the guidance of the spirit of a Dr William Lang, a surgeon eminent at the end of the last century. When Chapman is working, he speaks with the voice of Lang (recognized by Lang's own granddaughter) and uses his left hand to 'operate'. Lang was left-handed, whereas Chapman himself is right-handed.

Spiritual healing power just came upon Chapman unsought, whereas in the Philippines healers spend years perfecting the technique of invoking and harnessing the spiritual energy thought necessary for psychic surgery. The Rev Tony Agpaoa is famous

224

for his cures and has treated the most major ailments. He claims that he can open a patient's body without spilling any blood but that his patients prefer to see blood and tissue because that makes the process easier to comprehend. He has allowed himself to be subjected to rigorous scrutiny by investigators.

Certain researchers believe that psychic surgery is a form of psychokinesis, the power to move objects by mental force. If we can discover how psychokinesis occurs, they say, the bearing on all medical treatment will be tremendous.

Psychoanalysis

Psychoanalysis is based on the personality theories held by Sigmund **Freud**, father of psychoanalysis itself. But his ideas have been refined and altered by many of his successors, such as Carl **Jung**, Alfred Adler, Melanie Klein and Kevin Horney. (See **neo-Freudians** and **ego psychologists**.) It is a lengthy process aimed at bringing a patient's unconscious to his conscious awareness in therapy. Someone who undertakes psychoanalysis has to be prepared to attend sessions several times a week for a number of years. It is suitable only for highly articulate, verbal people who want to be able to express themselves fully. People who have immediate problems would be advised to choose one of the speedier therapies.

Psychoanalysts undergo special training but do not have to be qualified doctors, although many are. They have to have completed years of psychoanalysis as patients themselves before they can practise and continue it for as long as they are analysts. The method used is verbal only – there are no drugs or exercises.

The patient sits or lies on a couch whilst the therapist sits out of view. He encourages the patient to say anything that comes into his head (*free association*, see **Freud**) and may offer interpretations for what he is saying as well as for his dreams. Everything that the patient says or does is of some relevance in uncovering the unconscious. Nothing is accidental. (See **Freudian slip**). Vital to the process of psychoanalysis is **transference**, where the patient projects feelings on to the therapist, and **resistance**, where he tries to avoid facing unpleasant memories hidden in his subconscious.

A tremendous trust has to be established between therapist and patient so that the latter feels able to let go of his defences and explore his deeper motivations. When insight is achieved, the patient then applies his new knowledge about the forces or drives that motivate him to his current behaviour patterns and problems.

Because of its time-consuming nature, psychoanalysis is the least common of the psychotherapeutic approaches. Critics of psychoanalysis say that Freud's theories about the personality are totally unproven and therefore the whole process is scientifically suspect. (See **Freud** and **psychosexual stages** for details of Freud's theories.)

Psychobabble

Psychobabble is a word coined by American R. D. Rosen for what he claims is the meaningless jargon that has come into vogue with the personal **growth movement**. In the growth movement zeal to 'communicate' emotion, it has developed almost an entire language of its own, as incomprehensible to outsiders as the terms of psychoanalysis and, according to Rosen, a pure smokescreen even to insiders. Jargon such as 'exhaling negative emotions', 'coming across', 'bummed out', 'getting it', 'in a bad space', and 'living out scripts' are no more communicative of emotion than any expressions we've ever used before. Rosen thinks they block, rather than facilitate, real insight into oneself, serving merely as code words for acceptance into a group. In his book *Psychobabble*, Rosen claims that the new therapies of the growth movement are no victory over conditioning and automatized behaviour although they purport to help people 'be' what they really 'are'. They merely replace one set of patterns with another.

Psychobiology
see **Physiological Psychology**

Psychodrama

Psychodrama is an action-packed therapy. The individual acts out scenes or problems that relate to his past, his present or his future. He is known as the *protagonist*, the therapist is called the *director*, other members of the group may participate as the *cast* while the rest, who have no parts to play, make up the *audience*.

Although it is currently a popular therapeutic method within the **growth movement**, it was originally developed in the 1920s by Viennese psychiatrist Jacob Moreno, a contemporary of Freud. When he moved to America he established a centre there.

Psychodrama, say its adherents, is a way to explore the roots of past emotions. It is also a medium in which feelings may be expressed openly and new roles may be tried in an environment that is safe and also supportive. As the sessions, lasting usually between one and three hours, can be extremely highly charged with emotion, the director must be a skilled therapist, comfortable working in an explosive atmosphere.

Psychodrama has been found successful when tried with disturbed patients in hospitals, and also in private groups for the exploration of day-to-day type problems, such as difficulties in a work situation or communication problems within a family.

An example of a psychodrama scene might be the enactment of an upsetting argument a woman has had with her husband. She plays herself and gives directions to the person playing her husband about what he should say and how he should react. In recreating the scene, the woman may discover more about her own contribution to the event – that her own plea for affection was ignored because her movements and words disguised it, implying that she wanted nothing more to do with her husband at all. Or she may have the chance, by reliving the scene, to express anger that she suppressed at the time and so prevent that buried resentment from building up into a massive outburst of destructive hostility later.

Sometimes the director will suggest that the protagonist and a member of the cast change roles so that greater empathy with the other person's position is made possible.

Another possible use for psychodrama is the enactment of some future event. A person worried about his performance at a job interview, for instance, gets the chance to work out his anxieties and perceive the effects of his behaviour in advance. He can let his real anxieties show, because he is in a safe environment and perhaps be able to resolve them before the real-life event.

Other side-benefits of psychodrama are the reduction of feelings of inhibition and an increase in an individual's ability to empathize with others. By playing out his own part in a particular scene and participating in other people's, he may also learn to become more comfortable with the variety of role-switches we are all obliged to make in our lives.

Psychokinesis

Psychokinesis is the power to move objects by thought power

alone. People who are the focus for poltergeist activity seem to have the power to move furniture, swing lightshades and suchlike (see **poltergeists**), whilst Uri Geller's metal-bending feats are also a form of psychokinesis (see **metal bending**).

Scientists, of course, are not convinced unless they can replicate the activity in laboratory-controlled conditions. Their efforts seem to have concentrated on testing whether people with these purported powers can control the roll of dice. The subject concentrates his attention on the dice, trying to influence it to come to a stop showing, say, a four on the top. Many people tested have been found to score higher than chance. The problem is that it takes a lot to convince experimenters. As one psychologist has pointed out, even if the subject scored all hits, there is a tiny chance it could still be luck.

However, in the 1960s, a lady came to notice in the Soviet Union whose powers were so remarkable that researchers abandoned the doubtful dice. Madame Kulagina, as she was called, could move objects such as compasses, matchboxes and pens, even when they were placed under protective glass. She became the subject of a battery of tests carried out by excited scientists from several countries; they used sophisticated equipment to check for fraud, as well as resorting to more down to earth techniques such as passing their hands through the space between Madame Kulagina and the movable objects and crawling round the floor looking for invisible threads. Madame Kulagina could make pens and compasses jerk towards or away from her and no fraud was evident. Physiological tests in a laboratory, which had Madame Kulagina linked up with electrodes, demonstrated that, when she was exercising her amazing prowess, four times more electricity was generated from the back of her brain than was normal. Her pulse rate also rose dramatically and she could lose up to four pounds in half an hour – an effect that is reported in many cases of mind over matter.

One of the experimenters, Benson Herbert, director of the Paraphysical Laboratory in England, said he was stymied. He ruled out magnetism, electrostatics, gravity and supersonic vibration as causes and declared himself mystified by the lady's seeming powers to move matter by mental concentration alone.

Many psychologists and scientists look askance at the study of such paranormal effects, believing that they will always be inconclusive. But it is surely a mistake to imagine, because certain phenomena won't be co-operative in the laboratory (Madame

228

Kulagina's efforts apart), that those phenomena don't exist. It is after all only in recent years that we learned how to harness control of involuntary body processes to laboratory procedures (see **biofeedback**). Before that such things were dismissed in the West along with yin, yang and yogis.

Psycholinguistics

One of the most fascinating and possibly inexplicable facets of human achievement is the acquisition and use of **language**. The processes involved in learning complicated sentence structures and being able to understand and extract meaning from other people's words on the instant they are spoken are quite mind-boggling. Yet, by the age of three or four, most children have mastered it all.

The study of language, particularly the development and learning of it, forms a branch of psychology called psycholinguistics. As with most areas of psychology, there are differences of opinion about how it all works. Is it simply a behaviour that is reinforced by encouragement – children like the attention they get when they make a sound and the approval it brings? Is it all a matter of association? Or, as linguistics professor Noam Chomsky believes, is it based on mechanisms that are innate? (See **language**, but no answers promised.)

Psychology

Psychology, translating literally from the Greek, means the study of the soul. More commonly, it is described as the study of the mind or even the study of human behaviour. But none of these definitions are really correct for they are not broad enough to encompass all branches of psychology, which is really the study of man.

People very commonly confuse psychology and **psychiatry**, thinking that psychology has something to do with mental illness. Whereas psychiatry is concerned with the treatment of mental illness, psychology is the study of all behaviour, normal as well as abnormal.

Psychologists study how people behave when in groups or communities (**social psychology**); they study the way that people learn (**educational psychology**) and the factors that affect them; they study the effects of the working-place on efficiency and productivity (**industrial psychology**); they study how the memory works, how we perceive objects, how we process information (**cognitive and experimental psychology**); they study emotional, intellectual and sexual development from childhood to adulthood (**developmental psychology**); they study the body itself, to see how genes, hormones, nervous system activity, etc. affect our behaviour (**physiological psychology**); and they study what causes some people to behave abnormally and how to diagnose and treat mental illness (**clinical psychology**).

So psychologists are interested in every facet that makes human beings act and think and feel the way they do. And, of course, they all disagree amongst themselves.

Psychopath

A psychopath is a person whose behaviour is characterized by complete lack of guilt. This means that he has no conscience and suffers no anxiety feelings about anything he does, whether it causes harm to others or not.

Psychopaths are regularly manipulative, inconsiderate and out for personal gain or triumph. Because of their deceitfulness and inability to feel real affection or form attachments, they can do much emotional damage to those that get involved with them.

Psychopaths aren't necessarily unpleasant people on the surface. They are often extremely affable or give the impression of being vulnerable so that people whom they manipulate never realize what is going on.

Particularly marked characteristics of the psychopathic personality, besides lack of guilt feelings, are an inability to learn from experience and an inconsistency in what they tell different people about themselves or about supposed events. It has even been noted that many psychopaths have a tendency to leave their belongings in store with a variety of individuals who live in different areas, perhaps as an attempt to feel some kind of roots.

Little is understood about why some people have this personality. There is a theory that too early separation from the mother can lead to such emotional isolation. Or that children whose parents are inconsistent in their behaviour fail to develop a sense of right and wrong. There is now some evidence for a biochemical cause of the more violent manifestations, for some psychopaths are extremely aggressive. Recent psychopathy research indicates that a hormonal imbalance leads to the production of noradrenalin, associated with aggression, instead of **adrenalin**, associated with fear, in situations that induce stress and uncertainty (see **fight or flight reaction**). However psychopaths are not necessarily aggressive, although, when they are, their lack of conscience may enable them to perform the most barbaric of crimes without remorse.

Certainly psychopathy is very resistant to conventional psychiatric cures because it is extremely difficult to create conscience in someone who has failed to develop one. It has been noted, however, that people often 'grow out' of psychopathy as they get older and their change of behaviour is mirrored by changes in the electrical functioning of the brain. This may give weight to the view that pure psychopathy really is caused by a brain abnormality.

If this is discovered to be true, it may well have side-benefits for the numbers of people who are labelled as suffering from psychopathy when in fact they are not. Because the medical definition is so woolly, emphasising a lack of sense of responsibility and anti-social behaviour, it can apply to a great many people at some time in their lives. The stigma of the label psychopathy stays with them, preventing a normal existence and reducing job opportunities, etc. For the public associates the word with gross acts of violence or even multiple murder, as these are the cases of psychopathy that receive maximum publicity.

Psychopharmacology

Psychopharmacology, the development and study of mood-changing drugs, is a relatively new science. It has been responsible for the revolution that occurred in psychiatric treatment when drugs first became available to correct particular mental abnormalities. But it is a mixed blessing. For while drugs may alleviate symptoms, they do not correct underlying causes.

The drug LSD had much to do with this particular revolution. When it was discovered in the 1940s that LSD could bring about effects such as hallucinations, visual distortions and other strange mental states that were similar to those experienced by **psychotic** patients, the idea gelled that, if chemical substances could induce such behaviour, perhaps countering chemical remedies could prevent it. Since then we have seen massive drug trials, to find correctives for **manic-depression**, **schizophrenia**, etc., etc.

231

If the causes of psychological disturbance are often or always due to internal conflict, then these drugs will never be more than providers of relief from the most uncomfortable symptoms. If, as some people believe, some mental illnesses may actually be caused by chemical imbalances in the brain, then the right drugs could be the solution. It is an area of deep controversy and many times false hope has been raised by the seeming discovery of some bio-chemical cause for a particular illness, only to be proved ill-founded later. It is, therefore, a field that warrants considerably more research. (See **psychotropic drugs**.)

Psychosexual Stages

Freud developed a complex theory about psychosexual development and its effect on the adult personality. At the root of it is the **libido**, the sex drive which is our most powerful instinct. As we grow the libido changes its source of sexual pleasure. These sources are the **erogenous zones** – the mouth, the anus and the genitals. Each is a source of pleasure at a different time during development. The erotic stages we pass through, from infancy to adulthood, are called the psychosexual stages.

First comes the *oral stage*, in which pleasure revolves around the mouth. The baby suckles, nibbles and bites and is very dependent upon the ministrations of an adult; after the age of one, a child moves into the *anal phase*, when great pleasure is derived from the ability to produce something solid from his own body. But at this time the child also becomes faced with discipline for the first time, learning that he must temper his new fascination with faeces and undergo toilet training.

At about three, the child first becomes significantly interested in manipulating its genitals. This is the *phallic stage*, during which the child becomes consumed with love and desire for the opposite-sex parent and jealousy of the same-sex parent. Freud calls this conflict the *Oedipal complex* (*Electra complex* in girls) after Greek Oedipus who unwittingly murdered his father and married his mother, and says that, in an ideal world, the child resolves it by identifying instead of competing with the same-sex parent, and sharing the love of the opposite-sex parent. So the little boy starts to copy his father and wants to be a man like him. If this identification doesn't occur, Freud believed, the outcome is often homosexuality.

Next the child moves into what he terms the *latency* period,

232

during which time sexuality is in cold storage. But it re-emerges in adolescence, *the genital stage*. Now interest is directed towards the opposite sex and the individual is mature.

Problems start if the needs associated with each sexual stage are not properly satisfied. Then the child remains fixated at that particular phase and spends the rest of his life trying to get those needs met (see **fixation**). He achieves this either by **displacement** activity, if he changes the actual object of his natural desire (the homosexual man turns to men instead of women) or by **sublimation**, if he channels his sexual energy into a non-sexual activity, such as work.

The oral personality is one who takes to smoking, over-eating, or drinking or is excessively dependent, because his needs were not met as a baby. The anal character, thwarted in his pride at producing faeces any time and anywhere because of the rigours of his toilet training, remains fascinated with anal stimulation or tries to deny the interest by going to the other extreme and becoming excessively tidy, routine-bound and careful.

The phallic stage, with its Oedipal conflict to be resolved for the achievement of maturity, brings a variety of problems for people fixated there, characterized by numerous manifestations of unconscious anxiety. The little boy realizes what a prize his penis is and suffers *castration anxiety* – the fear that his father will castrate him because of his desire for his mother. If the Oedipal complex is not resolved by identification with the father, the castration anxiety persists, revealing itself in men, for instance, who fear intercourse with women. The castration anxiety is particularly reinforced by the knowledge that little girls do not have penises and are, according to Freud who had very sexist views, manifestly inferior beings. Boys are frightened, said Freud, that they will become like their sisters if they lose their penises. The poor unfortunate sister, however, has no hope. When she twigs that her brother has a penis, she develops a sense of inferiority (*penis envy*) and, once she realizes it is not a personal punishment but a characteristic of her gender, she comes to share male contempt for her own lesser sex. She has to seek for a penis through bearing a male child.

Freud not only had personal difficulties in relating to women, he was imbued with the social ideas of his time. He really did see women as unfinished men and presumed they could never really escape resultant psychological problems. He liked clever women but they were always objects, never equals. His views on

233

this aspect of sexuality are therefore, to put it mildly, remarkably suspect.

Despite his firm moral belief in holding sexual instincts in check, Freud was convinced that blocks in sexual development are the basis of all neurosis; that sexual energy gets dangerously dammed up inside if not expressed. He even wrote that sexuality must become acceptable, and openly discussed, instead of hidden away as a base desire. It was one of his disciples, Wilhelm **Reich**, who put actions to the words and really concentrated on unblocking sexual energy – receiving heavy censure from society as a result.

Psychosis

Psychosis is a broad psychiatric term to cover the extremely abnormal behaviour of an individual who has completely lost touch with reality. It is always difficult to say what constitutes reality or to be sure that one person's version is any more real than another's. But, in the case of truly psychotic behaviour, it is clear that the individual has retreated into a private world of fantasy and illusion and sees a totally different external environment from everyone else. In fact, the external world often seems so strange and unreal that the individual doesn't realize it is his own behaviour that is bizarre, not other people's.

The major psychosis is **schizophrenia**, which is characterized by extreme disturbances in thinking patterns and can take many forms. A **paranoid** state is one where an individual is plagued by delusions, and a **manic depressive** state is where the person suffers from very exaggerated moods of depression or elation, or swings between the two.

Psychotic behaviour can be treated, or contained, by drugs but sometimes compulsory hospitalization is necessary, when the individual is so out of touch that he may unwittingly endanger his own life or the lives of others; as in the case, for instance, of someone who is so convinced he can sway everything to his will that he jumps on to the track to stop an on-coming train.

Many people may experience what is called a psychotic episode, a brief break with reality which may well never recur. Others need the long-term control of drugs. Whilst the causes of psychotic behaviour are, of course, disputed, psychoanalysts think that underlying conflicts against which an individual has failed to build a defence lead to the complete personality breakdown, whereas some psychiatrists think the roots are organic.

Psychosomatic Illness

Illnesses where the symptoms and resultant discomfort are physical but the roots of them are thought to be psychological are called psychosomatic illnesses. Asthma and peptic ulcers have long been thought to have psychological as well as physical causes but now, with the alarming increase in prevalence of heart attacks, migraine, skin problems, back pains and arthritis, the possible emotional components of a wide range of illnesses are being taken far more seriously.

People are often very dismissive about some such complaints, saying to the sufferer disparagingly, 'Oh, it's only psychosomatic', and meaning it's all in his mind. But whether it is psychosomatic or not, the physical illness is no less real. It just means that a medical treatment alone may not have long-term effect, for the psychological causes need attention as well.

Stress is now seen as the big evil, as far as psychosomatic illnesses go. And it can often be a killer (see **stress**). It has even been suggested, though it is not a popular theory, that smoking doesn't cause death at all, it's the stress level which induces a person to smoke that is the culprit.

But why do some people get psychosomatic diseases whilst others don't? After all, modern-day life is stressful for everyone. In 1946 American researcher Raymond Cattell attempted to classify people's behaviour by their characteristics. Working with over 17,000 traits, he mathematically reduced and combined until he came up with clusters of traits that seemed to fit certain personality types. He discovered that people who suffer from psychosomatic illnesses tended to be emotionally stable and self assured, reserved and tough-minded. Neurotic personalities, on the other hand, were more often affected by feelings, apprehensive, tense and timid. He suggested that people who suffer psychosomatic illnesses are those who have the apparent psychological strength to handle stress and meet difficulties head on, but the process takes its toll internally instead.

Psychosurgery

Perhaps the most controversial treatment in all of psychiatry is psychosurgery, which involves destroying parts of the brain as a method of controlling mental illness, particularly of a violent nature.

A surgical procedure called bilateral **prefrontal lobotomy** (or **leucotomy**) was first carried out in the 1930s. This involved severing the nerve fibres that connect the pre-frontal lobes to the inner parts of the brain and, in the first apparent flushes of success, led to its use for treating countless cases of depression, schizophrenia, psychopathy and obsessionalism. In the 1950s it was discovered that such surgery wasn't all it cracked up to be and there were a great many vegetables sitting in mental hospitals who might not otherwise have been there.

With the dramatic advances that new drugs later made possible in the treatment of mental illness, surgical methods became increasingly irrelevant. However, the operations were by no means abandoned. Some neurosurgeons were still quietly working on refining the methods and, only recently, one admitted that he himself had authorized as many as 1000 pre-frontal leucotomies in recent years, for really entrenched cases of violent behaviour. Public outcry against methods which still seem barbaric despite all refinement was fuelled by the work of Boston neurosurgeon Vernon Mark who discovered that he could reduce violent behaviour by stimulating certain parts of the brain with electrodes. These electrodes and the use of radio-active substances make it possible to destroy the 'appropriate' areas while the patient is still conscious.

American psychiatrist Peter Breggin has become world-famous for the force of his protests against psychosurgery and his efforts to prevent its usage in prisons, mental hospitals and on hyperactive children. For, although we have learned a lot about the brain, much of its functioning is still a mystery, and it is impossible to know whether other vital tissues are being destroyed along with the 'diseased' tissue. Breggin maintains that this is indeed what happens and that while violent behaviour might be reduced, other emotions and also intellect are affected. Follow-up studies of cases originally claimed as successes have sometimes revealed that the desired effects of psychosurgery have not been longlasting after all.

The battle rages on. While groups in both England and America campaign for its abolition altogether, fearing its crudity and its possible abuse as a method of social control, some enthusiasts in the profession believe that refined psychosurgery has a great future as a corrective even for addictions such as gambling, obsessions and minority sexual behaviour – including homosexuality. Vernon Mark, who pioneered the electrical method, is more conservative. He believes that psychosurgery should be restricted to cases of uncontrollable aggression that is clearly caused by brain damage.

Psychosurgery is, of course, irreversible. It is therefore, in terms of human life, a very expensive method of mental illness research.

Psychosynthesis

In 1910, Roberto Assagioli went from Italy to Vienna to study a new theory, **psychoanalysis,** under an as yet unknown psychiatrist, called Sigmund Freud. But, although he took psychoanalysis back to Italy, he soon parted company with Freud's theories and developed his own approach to understanding the mind of man. He called it psychosynthesis. After years of working in the shadows, suddenly, during the last decade, his methods became popular all over the world.

He remained in the shadows so long, possibly, because his theory centres on the power of the will. The idea turns many people off at once, with thoughts of cold showers, press-ups and self-made men. But psychosynthesis is far more subtle than that. As its name suggests, it is a blending of all things: it is a method that sees man as an integral part of the universe.

Here lies the first main break with psychoanalysis. For, whereas Freud concentrates on probing the murky depths of the personality, Assagioli is equally interested in the higher unconscious, the transpersonal self (transpersonal refers to personal experiences that transcend 'ordinary' reality). It has a flavour of the mystical, although mysticism is no part of it as such.

Freud, with his theory that we are a mass of unconscious motivations, seemed to Assagioli to have destroyed the idea of individual will. The person who acknowledges this will becomes master of his destiny, make choices, changes his own personality. Will, Assagioli has said, is not the vital force but the directing agent of the personality. If we are ambivalent about anything it is not because our will is split, but because there is conflict between central will and a confusion of drives and desires. That conflict is inevitable. All human life involves choices. Neurosis is the product of trying to combine the incompatible instead of making choices.

So how does psychosynthesis actually work to blend and bind all aspects of man? There are innumerable exercises aimed at developing the personality, involving art, music, relaxation, concentration, visualisation, imagination, and meditation. Clients are asked to keep diaries, answer questionnaires and batteries of tests, as a means of uncovering elements of both the conscious and the unconscious mind.

Its critics still baulk at the idea of the will or dismiss psychosynthesis as too amorphous and too ambitious actually to achieve its end. Assagioli, who died recently, agreed it is perhaps limited by its limitlessness. But the core of it all is that we are responsible for, and have the power to effect, our own changes (instead of opting out by blaming our shortcomings on parents or society in general). And there's nothing ethereal about that.

Psychotherapy

Psychotherapy is a broad term for the treatment of mental illness or emotional disturbance without drugs or physical means such as electro-convulsive therapy (**ECT**). Technically, therefore, it covers a huge range of therapies including the following: **psychoanalysis, family therapy**, **rational-emotive therapy**, **reality therapy**, *humanistic therapies* such as **gestalt** and **Rogerian**, **behaviour therapy**, **transactional analysis** and **body therapies**, such as **bioenergetics**, **encounter groups** and **primal therapy**.

All of these are concerned with changing a person's behaviour, either directly, as in behaviour therapy, by helping him to alter undesired and inappropriate reactions (e.g. intense terror of cats) or indirectly, by encouraging him to explore his inner feelings and let go of his defences.

As a word, psychotherapy is used rather freely. Some doctors aggrandize a short chat in the surgery with the name. But in generally accepted colloquial usage, psychotherapy usually refers to treatment that takes the form of a verbal interchange between a therapist and patient (usually lasting an hour), directed at reaching the roots of a patient's problems as quickly and effectively as possible. So if a person is referred to psychotherapy by his doctor, that is what he will get, as opposed to psychoanalysis or any of the body or behaviour therapies. Psychotherapy can be given by psychiatrists, psychologists, social workers or anyone else trained to do so.

When a person undertakes a course of psychotherapy, it is important that he and the therapist agree on the goal. It may be just to get a better understanding of oneself in general or to sort out some particularly troubling problem or to improve a

238

particular relationship. Once the goal is established, the patient will probably contract to see his therapist once or twice a week and during the sessions will have the opportunity to talk through his feelings and develop self awareness.

It is not a therapeutic method that offers immediate results or instant insights and so many people now prefer to opt for body therapies such as **primal therapy** or **bioenergetics**, in which some change or insight is achieved fairly fast, even if it then takes some time to work with that new knowledge and resolve resultant conflicts.

Psychotherapy can be given on an individual basis or in groups (see **group therapy**). Psychotherapists usually prefer to speak of 'clients' rather than 'patients', in order to discourage the idea that the recipient of the therapy is in some way sick.

Psychotropic Drugs

Psychotropic drugs are mood-changing drugs that are used in psychiatry. They may be given in many forms, such as tablets, powders, liquids or injections. The amazingly rapid developments made in drug treatments (or *chemotherapy*) over the last ten years have been one of the prime causes for the discharge of large numbers of chronically ill people from mental hospitals. (See **psychopharmacology**.)

Three main groups of drugs are used in the treatment of mental illnesses: *tranquillizers*, *sedatives* and *anti-depressants*. Tranquillizers, which have the effect of calming people down, are divided into two main categories – *major tranquillizers* and minor ones. Major tranquillizers, such as Largactil, Moditen and Modecate, are a particularly important aspect of the treatment for **schizophrenia** but they are also used to alleviate **manic depression**. However, one of their major drawbacks is that they produce side effects. A person taking one of these drugs may suffer any of a range of accompanying physical effects, such as tremor of the limbs, weakness, dryness of the mouth, difficulty focusing the eyes, increased salivation and rigidity in movement. *Minor tranquillizers*, such as librium and valium, are used in the treatment of anxiety.

Sedatives also take two forms, *barbiturates* and *non-barbiturates*. Barbiturates are extremely dangerous and addictive and have no place in psychiatry. The non-barbiturates are sleeping tablets doctors prescribe.

Anti-depressant drugs, as their name implies, find their uses in the treatment of depression. There are three main varieties, *tricyclics*, *quadracyclics* and *monoaminoxidase inhibitors*. Some psychiatrists prefer the first two groups for endogenous depressions and the third for the reactive form (see **depression**). All also have possible side effects. Tricyclics and quadracyclics can cause drowsiness, skin rashes, lowering of the blood pressure and dryness of the mouth; monoaminoxidase inhibitors have similar effects but here there is the added danger of dramatic rises in blood pressure and of cerebral haemorrhage if combined with certain foods such as cheese, yeast and broad beans (patients are warned in advance).

Whilst drugs have definitely brought a revolution to psychiatry, it's a revolution that's not without its own side effects. In many cases, drugs are merely a palliative, not a cure, for the underlying emotional causes of breakdown which remain unexplored and unresolved. The illness may be contained but the circumstances that precipitated it remain unchanged. Secondly, for busy doctors for whom time is at a premium, drug prescriptions are often an expedient response to a patient's problem. The patient may find himself walking out of the surgery with a prescription for valium without even having had a chance to go into the details of what's bothering him. In many cases, a sympathetic listening ear is what's needed, not a chemical solution. Sometimes, too, drugs don't work or their effects suddenly wear off, so they can't ever be totally relied on.

Thirdly, many doctors fail to tell their patients about the possible side effects of the drug they are prescribing. So the patient starts to worry that he is even iller than he thought when he suddenly develops new symptoms such as shaking limbs or dizziness. Worse, the doctor may not even recognize the symptom as a side effect and may prescribe yet another drug to deal with it, which in turn produces its own side effects! It is always, therefore, worth demanding to know exactly what a drug is intended to achieve and what else it might give rise to en route. Some drugs have long term side effects such as sun-sensitivity.

A final problem with drugs and their all-too-easy availability from GPs is that people have the chance to become dependent on them. They imagine they can never function without their tranquillizer or that they'll never sleep without a sleeping tablet. Instead of using the drug-induced respite from emotional turmoil and a hyper-active brain as an opportunity to re-evaluate their lives and circumstances, people treat the drug itself as the solution. It is not.

Puberty

Puberty is a time of physical and psychological upheaval for both boys and girls. Occurring somewhere between the ages of ten and sixteen, it is the period when sex organs mature and young people have to come to terms with their own burgeoning sexual identity.

For girls, puberty means the onset of menstruation and the ability to conceive a child. It also involves body changes such as the development of breasts, broadening of the hips, rounding of the limbs and the growing of hair under the arm pits and around the genitals. Boys' shoulders broaden, genitals speed up growth and hair starts to appear under the arms, around the genitals and on the face. For both sexes, it is a time for rapid increase in height and weight. Around puberty, boys are capable of experiencing their first ejaculation.

The psychological effects of puberty can be far reaching if a child is not well-adjusted and secure. He or she may feel ashamed instead of proud of what is happening to his or her body and may be confused by the rise of sexual feelings. It is a time of conflict, the resolving of which can bring great 'inner turmoils' according to Freud. With support, each child will move towards independence and adulthood, seeking out peer groups and making friendships with the opposite sex. But children whose confusion over their sudden sexual identities is not acknowledged and assuaged by parents may well try to suppress the symptoms of growing up. This is commonly thought to be the basis of **anorexia nervosa**, the chronic refusal of young girls to eat, with resultant loss of weight (and shapeliness) and loss of periods, both of which signify dreaded womanhood.

Puerperal Psychosis
see **Post-Natal Depression**

Pyromania

Pyromania is an obsession with setting fire to things. Why someone should actually develop an obsession with fire is unclear but often arson is used as a way of getting attention – a pretty dramatic attempt – or a means of getting revenge for something someone else has done.

Because fires can take such a devastating toll on people's lives or property (even if that was not the original intent), people who are sent to hospitals for treatment because of arson activities and disturbed behaviour have a great deal of difficulty getting out again. They are often kept there longer than need be, as an insurance against the behaviour being repeated outside. (The longer the patient remains free of his pyromaniac tendencies while in the more controlled environment of a hospital, the happier his doctor will become about releasing him.) It's an understandable caution but in some cases it leads to an unduly lengthy loss of liberty in the wake of an isolated outbreak of arsonist activity.

R

Radical Psychology
see **Anti-Psychiatry**

Radionics

Radionics is an unusual healing method, based on the belief that the universe is made up of complicated interlocking and interacting energy fields that pervade everything. A human being, say its practitioners, is a microcosm of the universe and shares the same energy which ultimately derives from one source. (This idea is familiar in esoteric systems such as Zen and Tao, which teach that man and the universe are one.)

Radionics practitioners believe that, because we are all linked by the same energy fields, it is possible to tune into subtle energy signals which our five physical senses normally filter out. This is done by concentrating on inner powers (often known as the sixth sense) with the help of electronic equipment if necessary, and picking up signals which can then be converted into some physical form, so that the conscious mind can understand it (rather like the way a visual display screen makes 'sense' out of the pricks and dots that are fed into computer tapes).

So the radionics practitioner, when he is asked to heal a patient, concentrates his inner senses on the patient's subtle energy fields, to find out what is amiss in his body, and uses a pendulum as a physical detecting device. A very small current, which is supposedly generated in the neuro-muscular system of the patient, causes the pendulum to swing, and, by the direction of its movement, reveals the answers to questions about the patient's ailment.

The practitioner does not even have to see the patient to pinpoint the weak spot in his system. But to treat him, he needs a lock of hair or a specimen of blood via which he transmits the energy pattern necessary to correct the imbalance the patient is suffering. Weird and wonderful though all this may seem, adherents claim that radionics is no more 'mystical' than contemporary physics. An English practitioner, John Wilcox, illustrates the idea of re-aligning energy patterns with the familiar school physics experiment that involves a sheet of paper, iron filings and a magnet. When the magnet is not being used, the filings scatter everywhere, as they fall. But as soon as the magnet is placed under the paper, they line up in a symmetrical pattern.

The healing method is claimed to work for any physical or mental imbalance but it can take months or years to effect a cure for a chronic complaint, whereas a minor infection may vanish in a few days. The patient's own attitude to his health is also important. He has to be prepared to correct his own lifestyle (e.g., learn to eat correctly or take exercise) rather than expect a permanent miracle cure without any effort on his own part.

Rational-Emotive Therapy

Rational-emotive therapy is a 'reasoning' therapy which was developed in the 1960s by Albert Ellis. The aim is to help a patient change the way he *thinks* about himself. For, according to Ellis, we all grow up with false expectations, self images and other beliefs which we then vainly try to live by. We not only fail in our expectations, we become neurotic into the bargain.

We may, for instance, have been taught by our parents that, to be thought a worthwhile person, we must be good at school and excel in everything we do. By internalizing this belief, without question we may then come to spend the rest of our lives setting ourselves unrealistic goals, far out of the reach of our talents, failing to achieve them and then feeling worthless. The rational-emotive therapist would encourage us to look at that belief for the first time, realize that worth does not depend on achievement for its own sake but on, perhaps, doing one's best to the limit of one's abilities. By changing the thinking process, we may then break the neurotic pattern that we're forever repeating.

A great many of us do, without realizing it, live by assumptions that are totally irrational and which may well affect our opinion of ourselves and others. Cardinal amonst these, according to Ellis, are: the belief that we must be loved or liked by everyone; that we have no control over the miseries and unhappinesses we suffer; that it is better to avoid difficulties and opt for the easy way out of uncomfortable situations; that other people should take care of us or make sure that we are all right; that we should always take on other people's problems, regardless of our own; that certain of our behaviour patterns are the result of some past event, like an unhappy childhood, and therefore there is nothing we can do about them.

If a person can be shown that such beliefs are not unquestionable truths and can be made to see that much of his unhappiness results from his trying to live up to them as if they were, he may then come to see the world in a more realistic way, make less rigid demands of himself and others, and find his life much more easy, fun and satisfying to live.

Rats

Dogs may be man's best friends but rats are closest to the hearts and fortunes of psychologists. Since rats were introduced into the psychology laboratory in the early 1900s, primarily by the behaviourist John Watson, they have been the subject of innumerable experiments. They have been taught, amongst other things, to respond to stimulation, overcome electric shocks, redirect their blood flow and control their urinary excretions, in the process of which they may have been deprived food or water, suffered sensory isolation and given surgery and drugs.

Other animals have also been subject to testing procedures, notably monkeys in experiments on the effects of maternal deprivation.

The wide use of animals in research raises ethical issues that alarm a large number of psychologists. It is feared that psychology students may become de-sensitized to the cruelty inflicted on animals in their belief that their work is furthering the causes of science. But, in many cases, other alternatives to the use of animals may be possible and sometimes animal experiments contribute little that's useful for human knowledge at all.

Cambridge psychologist Dr Alice Heim has spoken out on this issue. She fears particularly the hardening of students' hearts against animal suffering because she herself 'had been brainwashed for some years into thinking that endless maze-running of starved, parched or mutilated rats served some justifiable scientific purpose'.

Animal experimentation in psychology is a particularly sensitive issue because, unlike medical research, the outcome is not the saving of human life but just the corroboration (or not) of theories about human behaviour.

Reality Therapy

Reality therapy was one of the first therapies to stress that responsibility for one's own actions and feelings lies with oneself – and oneself alone. It was developed by William Glasser in the early 1960s because he believed that personal satisfaction and happiness could not be experienced until one accepted full responsibility for oneself. He thought that a common feature of the disturbed personality was an unwillingness to face life for what it is.

Consequently, he was not interested in clients' pasts, the traumatic nature of their childhoods or their lack of luck in love, for which they commonly blamed their present insecurity, inadequacy, shyness or whatever. According to Glasser, it is always possible to think up reasons to explain behaviour. But that doesn't help us to change it – usually the reverse, for, if we think we are insecure because our parents didn't love us, we may see no reason to believe we can change at all.

To draw his clients away from their reliance upon rationalizations for their behaviour, Glaser concentrated on *what* they were doing, not why. He would show them the degree to which they were denying responsibility for themselves by getting them to question their behaviour. People who refused to work, or blamed their partners for a bad marriage or complained that no one loved them were righteous about their actions because they were transferring the responsibility for their own dissatisfaction on to others: why should one work when society is corrupt, etc.? But really they were making their lives miserable for themselves.

Glasser believes that people can only break their patterns by learning better ways of behaving. Only when they had accepted personal responsibility for all that had gone wrong in their lives would they be ready to learn a new, more realistic and more satisfying approach to life. The reality that Glasser pushes is the reality of living and participating in society as it is, not as it would be in an ideal world and populated with perfect people.

Rebirthing

This is **primal therapy** reincarnated and suitably altered en route. It was developed quite recently by American Leonard Orr and, whereas primal therapy involves reliving not only one's birth pains but later ones too, rebirthing concentrates on being reborn because that, in itself, according to Orr, brings bliss.

Reliving birth traumas predates even Janov's primal therapy. In the 1920s Otto Rank, a Viennese psychoanalyst, had his patients adopt a foetal position in his zeal to encourage them to re-experience their births, but he abandoned that approach later. Orr, one might say, has refined it.

The would-be rebirther attends a rebirthing seminar and a few other preliminary sessions before he relives his big day. This is done with the aid of a bathtub full of warm water, a snorkel and nose clips. The idea came to Orr when he realized that he suffered sudden anxiety whenever he had to get out of his nice warm bath. He traced this back to birth trauma. So the would-be rebirther enters the tub, heated to the temperature of amniotic fluid in the womb, and lies or is held face down in the water (using snorkel and nose clips). An experienced rebirther tells him how to breathe deeply and gradually birth memories come flooding back. Finally there is panic – supposedly the panic experienced at birth – and the individual, now reborn, is helped out, massaged and generally given comfort and attention. This process has to be repeated as often as it takes to be totally free of the birth trauma.

Breathing correctly and thinking positive thoughts are also important ingredients for future 'bliss'. Orr says rebirthers need less sleep, because sleeping in a warm bed is just a frustrated attempt to get back into the womb.

Regression

In psychoanalytic thinking, regression is a form of defence mechanism against anxiety (see **defence mechanisms**). It means resorting to childish behaviour in an unconscious ploy to deal with an uncomfortable situation by using tactics that worked as a child. But it can also be encouraged deliberately in therapy in order to take a person back into his past and re-experience some event about which he has blocked out conscious memory.

Regression as therapy is often used by hypnotists but it can also be achieved in other forms of therapy, as in the celebrated English case of Mary Barnes who was an early patient of R. D. Laing. She was encouraged to go back into her early childhood and, in her case, to feel free to play with her own excrement. Her own mother had looked extremely unfavourably on Mary's infant fascination with faeces, a response, it was thought, that had caused a number of blocks in Mary's mind about her own worth and powers of creativity.

Some psychiatrists, although admittedly few, are now starting to believe that regression can go further than childhood; they believe it can take some people back to past lives and is not only proof of reincarnation but a useful adjunct to therapy in this one.

A resurgence of interest in the possibilities of reincarnation was produced by the publication a few years ago of the Bloxham Tapes, recordings of people undergoing regression that were made by hypnotist Arnall Bloxham. Some of the accounts were truly amazing and historians confirmed the details of many of the past events that were experienced and the places that were visited. The case that made cries of fraud stick in the throats of even the most hardened sceptics was that of a woman who, during regression, became a twelfth century jewess who had been a victim of a massacre of Jews in York. She remembered a detail about a crypt in a church that just could not be verified. None of the churches there had crypts. Then a chance discovery later, during restoration of a church near York Minster, suddenly revealed a crypt that had lain hidden and unknown for centuries. That put an end to theories that the woman concerned had simply remembered, inaccurately, details of York or had seen pictures of local churches.

What has this to do with therapy? Bloxham believes that the memory of past lives helps one to live this one better. Arthur Guirdham, a retired British psychiatrist, goes further than that. He doesn't believe in regressing people through hypnotherapy but that past-life experiences should arise, spontaneously, in therapy, if the need is there. And the need often is there, he says. For he claims that some present day mental illnesses have their origins in an earlier life, and personally is convinced that several previous lives of his own explained some of the inexplicable depressions he had suffered in this one. He now links the depressions to anniversaries of violent events, including his deaths, that he experienced long ago.

Many people are troubled by vague memories of something being wrong and some have obsessions and phobias that take extremely rare forms. Guirdham thinks such neurosis has a past-life root and can be alleviated by re-experiencing and acknowledging the core of it. It is not a theory that's likely to explain most common neurosis, although it may be latched on to with false hope by a few.

Reichian Therapy

Wilhelm Reich was a disciple of **Freud** who trained many doctors in Vienna in the techniques of psychoanalysis before deciding that Freudian practice did not pay enough attention to the physical effects of repressed sexuality. He was laughed off as a madman because his ideas about sexuality were so unconventional at that time. His driving interests were analysis and Marxism and he managed to fall foul of the associations of both. He believed that repression of sexual needs and incomplete physical abandonment to orgasm led to rigidity in the individual and the establishment of authoritarian systems in society. As a result, he was thrown out of the Communist Party as well as the International Psychoanalytic Association.

But Reichian thinking is finally being taken seriously now; modern therapies, such as **primal therapy** and **bioenergetics**, and **psychosomatic medicine**, find their basis in his work.

Reich thought that energy which failed to be released through orgasm becomes dammed up in the body in muscular tensions, leading to poor posture, bad circulation and shallow breathing. He came to believe that neurosis isn't just an emotional state, it is a physical state too. He accordingly developed what he called *vegetotherapy* (the vegetative system being the entire body, unsplit between body and mind) which aimed to restore the free flow of energy by unblocking body tensions. This involved actual manipulation of the body, severe blows or direct massage, and the method caused a raising of the eye-brows amongst disdainful, traditional psychoanalysts who didn't believe in getting in close with their patients.

Reich laid great emphasis on *orgastic potency* – the capacity to surrender fully to sensation at the height of intercourse. That had nothing to do with men's ability to ejaculate or women's to achieve a climax – most people who climax are still orgastically impotent, according to Reich. Because they cannot really surrender to intimacy they suffer feelings of guilt, revulsion or hostility after sex, instead of a tremendous, all-encompassing physical and mental release of energy. Surrender can only occur if the energy is allowed to flow freely through the body to the genitals, its passage being free of blocks and neurotic tensions.

Reich thought that *character armour* and *muscular armour* were the main restrictions against orgastic potency. Character armouring resulted from years of being conditioned to be submissive in society; muscular armouring referred to inappropriate physical responses to anxiety, such as holding in breath or tightening the stomach muscles, all of which protect the body against feeling and reduce its energy flow.

His fascination with the life energy of the body (which he, like Freud, called the *libido*) led him to conclude that atmospheric energy and body energy are one – he called it *orgone energy*. His efforts to construct an orgone box designed to harness atmospheric energy for the treatment of bodily ailments brought a rain of further ridicule down on his head. But he may not have been on the wrong lines. It is now known that atmospherics *can* affect our mental states and play a part in healing (see **air ions**).

Reincarnation
see **Regression**

Relaxation

Relaxation is a state of mind which has profound effects on the body. When we are relaxed, our heart rate, blood pressure, blood flow to the muscles and muscle tension are all lowered. We use less oxygen, and blood flow to the skin and organs increases. The exact opposite is going on in our bodies when we are alert and under **stress**.

Too much stress can be physiologically damaging, so it is important to be able to relax and do so consciously, in order to give the body – and the mind – a respite. Simple relaxation techniques, such as concentrating on relaxing every part of the body in turn, can help one achieve this. More effective, and demanding more skill, is **meditation**. For those who are chronically unable to relax, **biofeedback machines**, which help to make a person aware of when he tenses his muscles and how to prevent it, have proved successful.

Repression
see **Defence Mechanism**

Resistance

Resistance is a very important feature of **psychoanalysis**. Psychoanalysis requires the patient to delve back into his past to try to uncover repressed memories of emotionally upsetting events which have, unconsciously, affected later behaviour. One of the techniques used is free association in which the patient is encouraged to say anything that comes into his head, in the hope that seeming trivia or non sequiturs might lead him to get back in touch with the painful past.

As the process is painful indeed, the patient will unconsciously do all he can to prevent uncovering those memories. After all, he will by then have spent a lifetime protecting himself against them. So, if he gets near to some insight, he will try to thwart it. This could show itself in many ways. Maybe he will start missing appointments, keep back certain thoughts because they are too 'stupid' to say, declare that he has nothing to say anyway, fall asleep on the couch, find trivial excuses to leave the room or decide the therapist is useless. This is all resistance, and the analyst's task is to show that to his patient, so that it can be overcome. Then real progress can be made with the journey back to resolve the conflicts of the past.

Rogerian Therapy

In the 1940s American psychologist Carl Rogers, influenced by the work of Freud, developed his own theories about the personality and a correspondent therapy. It is based on the idea that all human beings seek the expression of love and creativity but are thwarted by pressures to conform to the ideals of family and society. His work led to the blossoming of humanistic approaches to psychology and the **growth movement** therapies.

Rogers believes that we are almost all the product of something he termed *conditional positive regard*; that is, as children, we modify our behaviour in order to get the love and affection that comes with doing things mother's way or being what parents want us to be. We may repress feelings of fear so that our fathers will be proud of our independence and strength. We may stop ourselves from being openly critical or resentful of our parents in case that means they withdraw their love. We may pursue ballet classes or piano playing, because that is a parent's dearest wish for us, when really we have no talents in that direction and hate it. The end result is that we replace our true feelings and perceptions with false ones and this leads to later conflict with other people and our environment.

Rogers believes that the way to liberate one's true potential for feeling and creativity is to liberate one's real self. That means replacing conditional positive regard with *unconditional positive regard* – i.e., a therapist who accepts and cares for a person whatever they do. Once a person realizes he can be loved even if he reveals his fears, anger and ineptitudes, he is freed to be his real self.

To achieve this, Rogers developed *client-centred therapy*, meaning that the client directs the proceedings, decides what he wants out of it all and works through to his own solutions. The therapist doesn't interpret or criticize, he just listens or repeats the client's words and lays on the empathy with a trowel. This is often known as non-directive therapy.

But the Rogerian therapist doesn't have to sit silently or else resort to parroting his patient. He often has an active role to play in drawing attention to what might seem a particularly important statement by asking a question.

Client: But then, I suppose that nobody's parents have a particularly good relationship anyway.

Therapist: Do you think that's true of all relationships?

As Rogerian therapy is all verbal, a client has to be articulate and capable of achieving insight in order to benefit.

Rogers, Carl
see **Rogerian Therapy**

Role Playing

Life requires us to switch from one role to another according to the social setting we are in and the functions we are required to perform. In carrying out a role, we are carrying out a set of expected behaviour patterns, befitting our status in any particular group. A man plays the father role at home, the warm, dependable male head of the family; he may also play the role of the respectful, subservient employee at work and the role of the super-star in his local pub, where he's the ace member of the darts team. His behaviour is dictated by the nature of his relationship to others.

Role-playing is a facet of many therapies. It involves a client acting out either another person's role or a potential role of his own, as a means of gaining insight into the feelings and behaviour of himself and others. In **psychodrama**, a man who complains about his mother's smothering of him as a child may be asked to 'play' his mother while someone else acts out the part of him as a boy. In so doing, he may come to sympathize with the thoughts, feelings and frustrations that led his mother to cling on to him as a child. In **assertiveness training**, an individual who is terrified of speaking up for himself may be asked to act out a situation in which he expresses annoyance at someone who has barged in front of him in a bus queue. With someone else playing the part of the queue-jumper, he learns to try out a new assertive response to the situation.

Role playing enables people to explore feelings and reactions in safe, therapeutic environments.

Rolfing

As one rolfing practitioner has described it, 'our physical body is the shape of our consciousness'. A cosmic-sounding sentiment which very quickly makes down-to-earth sense on investigation of Dr Ida Rolf's techniques which now bear her name.

Dr Rolf realized that the bodies of most people are out of alignment. Poor posture brings with it a host of other ills, all of which take their mental and physical toll. Someone who leads with his chin is dragging his spine up to compensate, rounding his shoulders and pushing his stomach forwards. The effort to remain upright whilst so blatantly defying gravity not only generates back pains and shoulder tension, etc., but consumes a great deal of energy which could more fruitfully be directed elsewhere. The end product is lethargy and tension.

Dr Rolf discovered that, for correct posture, the centre of the ear, the shoulder, hip, knee and ankle all need to be in vertical alignment. She set about restoring alignment by body manipulation and deep tissue massage and found that the effects were not only better balance but generally improved state of well-being.

It takes a great deal of effort to maintain a bad posture. As the body is out of alignment, muscles tighten to keep it upright and eventually lock because of excess and incorrect pressure on them. Then other, equally inappropriate, muscles have to take over their work and in turn become hyper-active, dragging with them the immobile mass of the locked muscles. Soft tissue is made to do work it was never designed to do.

Rolfing involves working over the whole body, using the pressure of fingers, knuckles and elbows to stretch out shortened muscles and relieve pressure. In the process, the patient may experience intense pain that is not just of the physical variety. For some of his tension may be caused by the physical suppression of emotions (see **body therapies**). During the manipulation, therefore, the patient may re-experience some emotional trauma which he had locked away from memory. Not all rolfing practitioners concentrate on dealing with this emotion if it comes up. Whereas in *postural integration*, a variant of rolfing, the therapist specifically works with the patient to help him express and handle strong feelings if they emerge during the body work.

Because rolfing is painful, the patient has to learn to trust the therapist and 'go with his pain'. That means experiencing it, however intense, instead of tensing against it. By feeling the pain fully, he is eventually able to transcend it.

Rolfers are adamant that the technique is not just massage. It enables one to experience one's body as a dynamic, changing whole and the benefits attributed to it include increased sensitivity, decreased anxiety, easier breathing, more efficient use of energy, a more positive outlook on life and marked alteration in physical structure.

Rorschach Test

The Rorschach (or inkblot) test belongs to a group of what are commonly known in psychology as *projective tests*. For these the subject has to use his imagination to interpret ambiguous material, such as inkblot shapes, or to complete a story from a given opening paragraph. Because the tests are so unstructured, the psychologist hopes to learn about the subject's unconscious motivations and associations.

The inkblot test was devised by Hermann Rorschach in the early 1920s. It involves showing ten inkblots, one after another, to the person taking the test and asking him what they seem to

Fig 6. An inkblot of the type used in the Rorschach Inkblot Test.

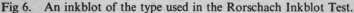

represent. The shapes are standard, not real random inkblots, and they are ambiguous enough to be widely interpreted. Rorschach testing demands skilful application by the tester as it involves not only eliciting general impressions and associations but also noting responses to individual aspects of the inkblot, such as colour, size and formation, and recording details about the subject's own behaviour during the testing – particular grimaces or sounds or tense body posture.

To be of value, test results have to be compared with those of others who have taken the same test. Then, if to most people a certain shape resembles a bus but to someone else it is definitely a grisly bear, the tester might intuit that the latter is harbouring unconscious hostility or fear. In fact, Rorschach testing can only ever be intuitive and indicative of certain possible character traits, rather than the provider of reliable data. The very ambiguity of the inkblots may lead to equally ambiguous results.

S

Sadism

Nineteenth-century psychiatrist Kraff-Ebing coined the name sadism to describe the deriving of sexual pleasure from inflicting pain on others. He took the name from the Marquis de Sade, a wealthy French aristocrat who was famed for abuses such as wounding whores with a penknife and filling the gash with hot wax for sexual kicks. But biographers claim that de Sade did not derive real joy from inflicting suffering because his own identification was always with the victim, seeing himself as a pawn of fate and wanting to show up the ugliness of an undemocratic society by exaggerating its viciousness.

And certainly, there is an element of the victim about the sadist, however much he may be seeming to seek power by hurting others. The sadist needs a **masochist** on whom to inflict pain and it is the masochist who is really calling the tune, challenging the sadist to hurt him and triumphing, orgasmically, over that hurt. (The true sadist only gets pleasure from inflicting pain in a mutually arranged situation.)

The term sadomasochism is perhaps more accurate than either sadism or masochism as few people fall exclusively into one category; there are elements of both in each, with either sadistic or masochistic tendencies predominant.

Sadists are far rarer than masochists. For whereas the masochist often uses the experience of pain to free him from deep-rooted guilt about finding sex pleasurable (if it is forced on you or it hurts, can you really be held to blame?), inflicting pain is taboo in our society. The sadist cannot play the martyr. He experiences the need to render someone else helpless, to exert a power that he fears he does not really possess. (And he does not possess it, for he is just servicing the masochist.)

Female sadists are hard to find, for the display of aggressive instincts has traditionally been far more acceptable in males than females. A connection between pain and sex is not unknown in the animal kingdom. In some species, such as the mink, sexual activity involves the infliction of numerous wounds. It is suggested that such aggression serves to reinforce the physiological conditions necessary for sexual arousal – increased blood pressure, over-breathing and muscle tension. And in human sexual relations, minor sadistic acts, such as scratching or giving love-bites, often play a part in ordinary lovemaking.

Sado-Masochism
see **Sadism**

Schizophrenia

Schizophrenia is a very disabling **mental illness**. It is described by psychiatrists as a **psychosis**, as it involves loss of touch with reality. It is thought to affect one person in every hundred in the Western world, a very high percentage, and yet there is still much misunderstanding about the nature of the disease.

Unsubtle jokes such as, 'You're never alone with schizophrenia' perpetuate the fallacy that schizophrenia is a form of split personality. In fact, it is a fragmenting of thought processes and emotions and has no Dr Jekyll and Mr Hyde element to it at all.

Key symptoms include severely disturbed thinking (which often involves the making up of words and mixing up of ideas) and strange emotional reactions (a schizophrenic may laugh at something that everyone else finds tragic). The sufferer starts to withdraw from people, makes strange faces and mutters to himself, often looks glassy-eyed and vacant and may suddenly burst into fits of inexplicable laughter. He has difficulty concentrating on any one thing for more than a moment and may forget why he's doing whatever he's in the process of: maybe he'll set off down the street, intending to go somewhere specific, then, mid-stride, turn and go somewhere else completely.

The schizophrenic fails to distinguish the real, outside world from the private world of his fantasies. External reality may become completely threatening and alien so he retires more and more into his inner world, where no one can reach him.

There are several basic categories of schizophrenia, although they are no longer used much in diagnosis: *paranoid schizophrenia* involves the individual in suffering **delusions** that people are after him. Often these are themselves a result of delusions of grandeur, where schizophrenics believe they are some famous person and so others are out for their downfall. Accompanying the delusions are auditory hallucinations, buzzing in the brain that makes the sufferer believe his thoughts are being interfered with or that he is being brainwashed by rays from the television. *Catatonic schizophrenia* is characterized by a sudden state of stupor. Such schizophrenics may spend days or weeks as if in a trance, yet they can hear and see what's going on and often later relate events that they saw happen. *Hebephrenic schizophrenia* refers to schizophrenics who resort to acting like children and suffer delusions of a mainly sexual or religious nature.

Because so little is known for sure about how and why schizophrenia is caused, instead of being referred to as one illness doctors talk of 'the schizophrenias', resulting from a variety of possible causes. Some psychiatrists believe that the disease is inherited: research with twins has shown that if one gets it, there is a higher predisposition for an identical than a non-identical twin to get it too. (See **genes**). Recent Danish research shows conclusively that the natural parents of adopted schizophrenic children had a far higher incidence of schizophrenia than did the adoptive parents.

But environmental and emotional factors also seem to play a part. There is high incidence of schizophrenia, for instance, in poverty-stricken areas. The British researcher Professor John Wing has looked at the role of the family in relapse rate and discovered that patients whose families are highly emotional and critical tend to return to hospital often, whereas patients in low-emotion homes don't even need to take their medication for long.

Another school of thought has it that schizophrenia is caused by some biochemical imbalance and the use of megavitamins enjoyed a vogue as a corrective. Although those particular results have not been stunning, brain research continues. The most controversial approach has been that of Scottish psychiatrist R. D. Laing who in the 1960s maintained that schizophrenia is a sane response to an insane society (see **anti-psychiatry**).

Fortunately, even though causes are still a mystery, the development of effective drugs, such as long-acting major tranquillizers, has provided relief for sufferers and most can lead relatively normal lives, with the aid of medication.

Scientology

Scientology has its roots in Dianetics, a form of psychotherapy devised by American writer L. Ron Hubbard, which burst upon the world in the late 1940s. Its main claim was that mental illnesses had one cause, a thing called an *engram*: an imprint in our minds of all the pain and sensory experiences associated with particular traumatic events. (The term is used in memory research to describe a memory trace.) Engrams, which kept re-imposing themselves on later, similar life-situations, could be removed by *auditing*, according to Hubbard. This involved getting the patient to relive the painful situation as often as required until it was discharged and he was *clear*. In the process, however, certain engrams kept appearing which, Hubbard presumed, could only have occurred while a person was still a foetus or in a previous life. He believed that pre-natal engrams were the most powerful influences on late psychological development.

When the 'craze' element of Dianetics had stopped drawing in crowds of would-be clears, and financial problems arose, Hubbard broke with the system, moved away and founded Scientology instead. Scientology still involves auditing and clears but it is a religion too. There is a complex philosophy involving *thetans*, all-powerful mortals who existed at the beginning of time, created games and devices to enliven their existence and then became so absorbed that they lost hold of their spiritual powers. They inhabited bodies and transmigrated to new ones when those died, but forgot that they were any more than the body they were in. Auditing, said Hubbard, could reveal the engrams of thetans going back over billions of years.

Scientology has attracted a great many truth-seekers and would-be problem-solvers. Graduates of the training can become professional auditors themselves. Many have been inspired by Scientology, despite the extensive drain on their pockets, because of the support, warmth and acceptance that is offered novices by the group. They believe they can become more competent, effective and attractive.

Scientology, however, has had a bad press, aided by stories of the lengths to which the cult will go to keep its converts and the belief systems with which members are flooded through internal newsletters and newspapers. But it still retains a strong hold, though not as high as in the sixties, and many members contract to work for the organization in return for free auditing, if they can't afford the high costs. Scientology has diversified its interests to include programmes of social reform, concerning itself with drug addiction, institutionalization in mental hospitals and learning problems, amongst others.

Some members join up for life by paying to become members of the Sea Org, the elite inner order of Scientology. The Sea Org operates from a fleet of vessels. Hubbard issues orders from the Flag Ship to the rest of the boats, from where personnel can be dispatched to carry them out.

Self Actualization

The two big names behind the flowering of the humanistic approach to psychology (the emphasis on man as an individual with free will and creative potential) were Abraham Maslow and Carl **Rogers**. While Carl Rogers concentrated on a humanistic approach to therapy, Maslow was more interested in the needs and behaviour of people who did not have 'problems'. In other words, he was concerned with the seemingly well-adjusted, rather than maladjusted personality, and how ordinary, healthy people think and feel.

This led him, in the 1950s, to develop his own theory about human needs and human potential. Only humans have a range of psychological needs as well as physical ones and, he believed, people are only freed to be concerned with higher needs if their lesser needs are satisfied. Accordingly, he presented what he called a 'hierarchy' of human needs.

At the bottom he placed physical needs such as food, sleep, sex, warmth, etc. If these vital needs are unmet, he said, an individual has no time to be concerned with any others. Someone who has no food and no roof over their head is unlikely to be concerned with philosophy. If the vital needs are met, however, the individual can then turn his attention to the next set of needs on the hierarchy, physical safety and emotional stability. Children, for instance, need to know they have a bed and a home and a link to some parent figure who is always around.

After that, an individual has to know that he is loved and wanted. He will come to value his family and his friends and gradually this need to feel important to important others will merge into a need to feel important in his own section of society; to be esteemed at work and by his peers and to earn the respect of superiors.

Only if all of these needs are met (though, maybe, in a different order) can one turn attention to self-actualization, to striving towards the fulfilment of human potential; or, as Maslow puts it, acting on 'the desire to become more and more what one is, to become everything that one is capable of becoming'. For some it might mean creating art, making music, writing lyrical prose. For others fulfilment might be achieved in motherhood, starting a successful business or being at peace with oneself.

Maslow also plotted the necessary general characteristics for genuinely self-actualized adults. They could see situations for what they were, make rational judgements, accept their own short-comings, empathize with other people, enjoy solitude as well as a few real close friendships, act independently, never fail to derive fresh joy from the wonders of life and art, experience a sense of oneness with the world while retaining a sense of detachment from all things in it and enjoy a broad sense of humour and creative thought.

Alas, later Maslow came to realize that not all people strive for self-actualization at all. Apathy and the lessons of childhood take their toll on energy and drive. The very problem which Carl Rogers was grappling with, the suppression of the real self according to the need to fit in with and be accepted by parents and society, prevents the individual from leaping up the ladder of personal growth.

Still, Maslow's work has had profound effects in industry. His theory that people can only be motivated from within, not by incentive schemes and coffee breaks, has led industrial psychologists to turn their attention to work satisfaction and self esteem as a crucial factor for productivity.

Selfish Genes

Irven De Vere is a pioneer in the new field of *sociobiology*, the understanding of human behaviour through human biology. De Vere's particular theory is that human behaviour is governed by genes. He believes that genes are basically 'selfish' and that survival of the fittest shouldn't refer to individuals and species but to individual genes. As genes perpetuate themselves through reproduction, we lay the emphasis that we do upon family ties and blood bonds. In this way, by looking after each other, we assure the continued existence not only of our own line but those of our brothers and sisters too, with whom we share genes.

In keeping with this theory, he suggests that the difference in attitude towards adultery traditionally held by men and women (men are allowed to be adulterers whilst women are not) has a genetic basis. The female's genetic investment is in bearing a child,

260

so she is more sensitive to desertion – and the withdrawal of financial support – than adultery. For, as long as she has her child, her genetic inheritance is assured. The man, however, cannot be sure that the child she bears is his, if she commits adultery, and therefore his genetic inheritance is not assured.

Sensitivity Training

Sensitivity training is a rather general term for a group approach to increasing awareness of one's relationships with others. In a group setting with or without a leader, individual members are encouraged to express their emotions freely and to learn more about how they react to similar expressions from others. Away from the office, work colleagues may decide to get together, take off their office hats and open up freely about their feelings towards each other. The hope is that, with better understanding of each other's fears, resentments and insecurities, they will learn to be more co-operative and efficient at work.

As sensitivity training is such a general term, it can be applied to **T-groups, encounter groups** or other **growth movement** approaches.

Sensory Isolation

Experiments in systematic sensory deprivation have shown quite conclusively that we need external stimulation in order to survive. Tests in America had college students spending days in special sound-proofed rooms, wearing goggles to minimize vision and gloves to reduce any sensation of touch. They lay on cots and became extremely bored. Soon they started to invent ways to stimulate themselves, such as tensing their muscles and opening and shutting their eyes, because they felt the need to feel something. After a couple of days, a great many of the students started to hallucinate – seemingly another attempt at stimulation, only unconsciously instead of consciously induced. After a few days, all students reached the point where they could stand the isolation no longer and asked to be excused.

More sophisticated experiments have been carried out with isolation tanks, which were developed by Dr John Lilly in the 1950s. Here people lie in closed tanks in water heated to a temperature at which it ceases to be discernible as water and are kept afloat by the addition of salts. In this way, they are able to lie in complete blackness, shut off from sound and all sense of touch. Again, the experience was found to produce hallucinations after a sufficiently long period.

Sensory deprivation techniques have been used for the torture of prisoners. Long term deprivation of sensory stimuli causes profound psychological impairment. However, some people believe that isolation tanks can lead them towards enlightenment. In America, tanking, as it is called, has become an expensive craze – tanks don't come cheaply – and now they are available in England too. Its defenders say that tanking doesn't cause psychological harm for it is not enforced deprivation. Freedom is just the flip of a lid away. Floating in the dark for an hour is, they say, a calming experience which enables one to get more in touch with one's self. Some users claim that tanking helps them to expand their consciousness.

For others, it is just a very pleasant way to relax and brings benefits into their everyday lives, such as heightened creativity, a clear approach to problems and a sharper awareness of people and places. Still, there are other ways to relax or find Nirvana.

Sex Differences

A major result of the women's movement has been to highlight how stereotypes of the male and female affect self-expectations, learning patterns and employment prospects for women. By the age of four, children are aware of what is seen as behaviour appropriate to their sex. The idea that males are dominant, aggressive, more intelligent, more effective and ruthless, and females are passive, accepting, loving, weak and maternal are instilled by parents and reinforced by school teachers, careers advisers and peers as well as through messages from the media. Women have learned that their primary function is to be attractive and sexy (until they become mothers, that is) and not to vie with men in male spheres such as competence at a job.

Men may grimace and say that's now old hat but, unfortunately, stereotypes are far from out the window yet. Recent surveys reveal that certain spheres, such as engineering or sciences, are still seen as essentially male preserves; students learn more if female lecturers conform to stereotypes and are soft and accepting rather than brusque and impersonal, although the latter traits go down better when shown in a male tutor. And a test given to Harvard under-graduates by researcher Matina Horner showed male students still think women aren't seriously interested in study; they're more likely, the men think, to abandon the difficult laboratory experiment and run to their boyfriend's arms. Or, if they do get down to the job, they are unthinking, unfeeling and unfeminine – or paralysed from the waist down!

Stereotypes are dangerous because they form the basis of one's self image and serve to undermine confidence if not met with conformity. Earlier research by Matina Horner proved the truism that men are unsexed by failure and women are unsexed by success. Ninety female students were given a sentence about a female who was top of her medical school class at the end of her first year. Eighty eight men saw the same sentence but with a male as the most promising student. They were asked to speculate on the student's future. Ninety-nine per cent of the men had the male student going on to a successful career in practice. The girl, however, had a bleaker destiny. In the majority of cases she later fell behind in her schooling and concentrated on helping her boyfriend through to success.

But while the sure-footed spectre of the female stereotype still impedes women's progress, another explanation for some of the differences between the sexes is starting to shape up in the physiological laboratory. For a new set of researchers, many of them women, are coming to the conclusion that a difference in brain organization makes men and women act in different ways (although learned behaviour enhances it).

It seems that, because the specialized functions of the brain (see **split brain**) are different in men and women, men have more developed spatial skills and perception of depth (which may reveal itself in mechanical tasks and mathematical subjects such as geometry) while women have superior verbal skills. According to an inventory compiled by two neuro-psychologists at Stanford University, Diane McGuinness and Karl Pribram, men also have better daylight vision, are less sensitive to extremes of temperature, are more interested in objects than people and have better body co-ordination skills; women are more sensitive to touch and temperature, process information faster (but react more slowly), have better night vision, are better able to pay attention and are generally more empathic. The researchers believe that different ratios of sex hormones acting on particular brain structures cause these variations.

Much of the research in this physiological area conflicts. American researcher Jeannette McGlone, for instance, has found that there is no real specialization in the left and right hemispheres of women's brains at all. They have their verbal and spatial centres located on both sides whereas men have speech centre on the left and spatial skills on the right.

Whatever the eventual findings and final field of agreement, sex differences in the brain are not a new justification for sexism, say the researchers. All such differences are a matter of degree. So, while women generally may be less well endowed with spatial skills, that doesn't mean that individual women cannot be far superior mathematicians to individual men. And, as McGuinness and Pribram say, 'Men and women *are* different. What needs to be made equal is the value placed upon these differences.'

Sex Disorders

Recent proliferation of information on sexual disorders might seem to imply that sexual problems are a product of the twentieth century. In fact it simply signifies the fact that both males and females have come to have higher expectations of their sex lives and to realize that underlying worries, fears and deep-seated guilt can affect sexual responses. As a result a great deal of research into sexual problems has been done. Although some sexual problems have physical causes, a great many have a psychological root.

The most common sexual disorders – or dysfunctions, as they are termed by the medical profession – are *frigidity* and *vaginismus* in women and *impotence* and *premature ejaculation* in men.

Frigidity is an unfortunately emotive word, often bandied as an insult at a woman who fails to respond to a particular male's advances. But it really describes a woman who is incapable of sexual responsiveness at any time or ever reaching orgasm. In its most severe form, the woman dislikes any kind of sexual contact; in its milder form, the woman may have once been capable of achieving orgasm and then ceases to be able to do so. Vaginismus can be one form that frigidity takes. The vaginal muscles contract so tightly that a penis cannot enter the vagina. The contractions are involuntary and may occur at the prospect of any insertion, e.g., a tampon or a speculum during a gynaecological examination. Vaginismus may be the result of dyspareunia – the experience of intercouse as painful because of internal sores or psychological factors.

Impotence is the inability in a male to sustain an erection. In some severe cases, the male may be completely unable to develop an erection at all; in other cases, he may be able to maintain an erection while masturbating but not when he is with a sexual partner. Impotence can have physical causes (such as too much alcohol in the system, or as a result of taking certain drugs), as well as psychological ones. The premature ejaculator is capable of achieving an erection but ejaculation occurs extremely quickly, sometimes before penetration or immediately afterwards. Like frigidity, it is an emotive term, for some men think they suffer from premature ejaculation if they cannot withhold orgasm until their partner is also ready to come. This is not a correct description of premature ejaculation. In fact, some sex therapists maintain there is no such thing as premature ejaculation per se. Ejaculation is only premature if it occurs too quickly for the liking of both the male and female concerned.

So what psychological factors are behind all of these sexual dysfunctions? In most cases the root is sexual anxiety, developed during childhood or fostered by bad sexual experiences. Although sexuality is acknowledged nowadays, even adults who express it freely between themselves still often find it difficult to tolerate or encourage the sexuality of their children. Some parents avoid touching or fondling their children in any way that might arouse an erotic response. Few parents touch their children's genitals or refer to them by name in the way that they refer to noses, ears, tummies and other parts of the body. The young child develops a sense of erotic pleasure very early, enjoying the sensuality of touch in a very natural and innocent way. If this is denied or called dirty, the child soon learns to feel guilty about bodily feelings and this persists into adulthood.

Women who are taught as children that it is wrong to enjoy sex may well remain uneasy about their sexuality, even though they think they have outgrown such taboos and have an enlightened approach towards sex. Unpleasant early experiences of soulless sex with inexperienced and clumsy partners may help to build up resistance against surrendering fully to the sexual expression of a loving relationship. Men, as boys, also learn that sex is dirty. They may be told not to touch themselves and to imagine, therefore, that their sexual desires are wrong. For many this may take the form of impotence with a woman they love, not wishing to inflict such evil desires upon her, while being perfectly capable of acting the stud in uninvolving one-night stands.

For men, the need to live up to the old macho image and 'perform' can cause anxiety, leading to impotence or premature ejaculation. Then the 'fear of failure' syndrome sets in. Having failed to achieve an erection once or having come too soon for comfort, he is extra concerned to 'perform' well next time. The anxiety induced causes the same thing to happen again. It is perfectly natural for erections to come and go – distraction by a sound or even a thought may cause it, for this is a natural bodily defence mechanism against possible threat. It is only anxiety about its loss that prevents the erection's return.

Psychoanalysts believe that all sexual conflicts go back to early childhood and must be unravelled before there can be change.

Whether this is the root or not, numerous situations can cause sexual unease with the result that sexual anxiety becomes a learned response. Impotence and frigidity can result from boredom with a partner, from preoccupation with other worries, from guilt about an extra-marital affair. Failure to understand the causes lead a temporary sexual dysfunction to become a long-term problem in itself.

Once little help was available for the treatment of sexual problems. But, with the work of sex therapists Masters and Johnson and the consequent development of **sex therapy** and psychosexual counselling, most people can be helped to achieve a normal sex life. Ironically, though, the more we learn about the possibilities of sexual enjoyment and surrender in our so-called enlightenment about sex, the more the pressure is on to be a fully functioning sexual being. For women, for instance, now that it is known they can not only have orgasms but multiple orgasms, there is the ever-present trap of trying too hard with the result that they fail to have an orgasm at all. Men may try too hard to be considerate partners, allowing their own needs to suffer as a result. Any form of anxiety prevents full sexual pleasure, and over-emphasis on technique or on fulfilling others' expectations is as destructive as a passionless fuck.

Sex Therapy

There are a number of methods by which sexual problems can be treated. The most longstanding is by psychoanalysis, a lengthy process whereby the analyst helps the patient delve back into his childhood to find the causes of his sexual conflicts and problems. But full analysis takes several years and this is not the approach most desired by people whose main aim is to come to terms as quickly as possible with their difficulties, and resolve them.

Less time consuming forms of counselling, often offered at psychosexual clinics attached to hospitals and by marriage guidance counsellors, concentrate on providing support for the patient and making common sense suggestions. Many such services will only see couples and the counsellor, as an outsider, will hope to offer some insight that the couple, being too involved with their problems, have failed to realize. One woman's problems were solved quite simply in this way when, in a counselling session about her lack of responsiveness to her husband, she mentioned that he never washed before coming to bed. Although she had never mentioned her dislike of this to him, she felt he was showing her disrespect; resentment built up and prevented her from responding to him sexually.

Often such counselling takes the form of *conjoint therapy*; a male and female therapist work together with the couple, talking through their problems, making suggestions about how to relax or how to extend time spent on foreplay. The therapists may suggest that the couple make a contract: the man promises to come to bed earlier and, in return, the woman to touch his genitals, and so on.

Behaviour therapy has not been without its successes in sexual therapy. Patients are taught to relax and are then asked to imagine the kinds of sexual situations that cause them most anxiety. Using their new relaxations skills, they work up through their list of qualms, imagining themselves in each situation and consciously applying relaxation techniques, so that the anxiety is reduced.

But the most dramatic advances in sex therapy have come about as a result of the work of sex therapists Masters and Johnson. William Masters and Virginia Johnson studied the sexual responses of 674 people, observing and measuring physiological changes in the genitals and elsewhere in the body during sex. Having discovered the differing needs of individuals to bring them to orgasm, they started practising sex therapy. Their second book, *Human Sexual Inadequacy*, published in 1970, described their treatment of 510 couples and 57 single people suffering various kinds of sexual problems. Their therapy was different because it concentrated on practical exercises rather than on verbal exhortations.

A male and female therapist, working with the couple or individual, would take a complete history and then embark on

267

re-educating the patients' sexual approaches. The couple contracted to abstain from intercourse and to begin at the beginning, learning how to touch each other all over the body, leaving genitals till last, and to fondle, massage and enjoy sensation without the 'threat' of performing sexually. Gradually the couple would become more at ease with each other's bodies, and gain confidence that enabled them to try intercourse again. If a man suffered from premature ejaculation, for example, the female partner was taught the squeeze technique – a method of preventing ejaculation by grasping the ridge of the penis tightly between thumb and two fingers.

These ideas have been followed and developed by other sex therapists. In some centres in America and one at least in England, surrogate therapy has also been introduced, whereby a 'partner' is provided for single people with sex problems, to help them work through a similar graduated programme. The Masters and Johnson technique is based on behaviour therapy – a learning of a new and desirable sexual response in place of an old undesired one.

Self-help discussion groups can also be helpful for dealing with sexual problems. England and America have seen the rise of *preorgasmic groups* for women who have never achieved orgasm. Here women are encouraged to talk about their sexual feelings and fears, to learn to enjoy touching their own bodies and masturbating as well as learning the basics of **assertiveness training**, to give them the ability to speak up about their sexual needs with a partner and to say no to what they do not want to do: in short, to recognize and enjoy their own sexuality.

Sex therapy is still in its early stages and new techniques for helping people overcome sexual problems are still being discovered. One such is sexual attitude re-structuring, a form of sex re-education that uses films of real-life partners making love to help people lacking in social/sexual skills to learn about the variety of possible sexual patterns. After watching films of heterosexual and homosexual couples, young and old, fit and disabled, discussion of the feelings aroused by the films take place. The aim is to counter the myths and taboos caused by ignorance and fear and to lay the foundations for a more open and accepting attitude towards sex.

Side Effects
see **Psychotropic Drugs**

Skinner, B. F.
see **Behaviourism**

Sleep

It used to be thought that someone asleep was as good as unconscious. Now we know that a great deal of brain and body activity is still going on while we are asleep, that there are different levels of sleep and that each is characterized by a specific brain wave pattern.

During the day, when we are active, our brains generate what are termed *beta rhythms* (see **brain waves**). When we are relaxed, with our eyes closed, this gives way to *alpha rhythms*, which have a slow and regular pattern when charted by an electroencephograph. It is from alpha that we move into the first stage of sleep, a drowsy half-waking, half-sleeping state during which we can be easily woken. As sleep deepens and the move into the second stage takes place, sharp points register on the EEG machine, which are called sleep spindles. And it is still relatively easy to wake the sleeper. Large, slow waves indicate stage three of sleep, which gives way to stage four, the deepest stage of sleep, during which the waves are extremely large, slow and regular. By this time, blood pressure, heart rate and temperature will have dropped considerably. The *delta rhythm* is the name given to brain wave patterns that occur during both stage three and four of sleep. (We repeat all these patterns through the night.)

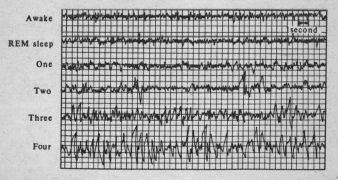

Fig 7.   Different patterns of sleep charted on an electroencephalograph machine.

It is known that stage four sleep occurs early on during sleep and that children experience more of it than adults. As we age, we have less and less really deep sleep. It is believed that this is a regenerative period for the body and it has been shown that the hormones connected with growth are most active during this time. So it makes sense that children should need the most deep sleep.

It is very difficult to rouse someone from deep sleep. It appears that it is during stage four sleep that night terrors, sleepwalking and bedwetting occur. During night terrors, people wake screaming or crying but they are unable to remember the experience in the morning. One theory is that transition between stages of sleep affects anxiety-inducing mechanisms. When a sleeper returns from deep sleep to very light sleep, the brain becomes more conscious of the carbon dioxide that has built up during deep sleep and then suddenly breathing becomes fast and deep again. This could provoke feelings of being unable to breathe and give rise to anxiety and the fear of being choked.

Nightmares, on the other hand, occur during stage one sleep and result from a slow build-up of anxiety, instead of, as in night terrors, from the sudden primitive experience of fear. Stage one sleep has aroused the most interest amongst researchers. As we drift back from stage four, through stage three and two to stage one sleep, a completely new stage seems to be entered. The sleeper seems to be sleeping so lightly that he is on the point of waking and his eyeballs move rapidly from side to side. In fact it is extremely difficult to rouse him. This period is termed, appropriately, REM (rapid eyeball movement) sleep and is considered part of stage one. The rest of the time, during stage one, there is no such movement, so that is termed non-rapid eyeball movement (NREM) sleep.

During REM sleep, brain rhythms and body activity speed up. Blood flow increases, also heart rate and breathing get faster. Because people woken during this period of sleep are usually able to report their dreams, it was thought that REM sleep must be dream sleep and that this is the time for the restoration of mental processes rather than bodily ones. People deprived of REM sleep during experiments were found to be irritable and nervous next day and, the following night, had significantly more REM stages of sleep, presumably to make up for the loss. But years of research have resulted in a mass of data not all of which by any means supports the idea that we have a strong psychological need for a specific amount of REM sleep. (It is now known that we dream at other stages during sleep as well, although dreams are not so easily recalled.) It is however agreed that sleep is the time when energy resources are focused on the human body and mind, and not on the external environment, and facilitate physical and mental repairs. Mentally, during sleep, we are not taking in new information but processing and sorting out what has been taken in during the day. (See **dreaming**.)

The knowledge that our brains are far from inactive during sleep led, some years back, to a supposition that perhaps we could even learn while asleep. But careful experiments involving rows of sleepers snoring to the accompaniment of tapes on teach-yourself French or simple mathematics resulted in zero-recall of the material in the morning. It is thought by some researchers, however, that during the drowsy state of half-wakefulness, we are more susceptible to taking in information. The theory is that, at this time, the left hemisphere of the brain, which is concerned with analytical, logical thinking, is at rest and the right side of the brain is more open to new ideas and more receptive to suggestion (see also **split brain** and **brain waves**).

Social Psychology

Social psychologists are interested in the way people are influenced by other people and to what extent society shapes our behaviour.

This encompasses a vast area of research, including studies of parental and peer-group influences on attitudes, people's need for leaders, television's role in shaping behaviour (particularly as regards sex and violence), how we come to form prejudices, our motivation to conform, the elements that attract us to other individuals and much more besides. (See **group pressure, attraction, cognitive dissonance**.)

Our behaviour in groups is particularly interesting, as it is clear that we do things then or react in ways that we never would alone. Experiments have shown, for instance, that our reactions to emergency vary according to whether we are alone or not. In one experiment, students were individually invited to fill in a questionnaire in an otherwise empty room. Then the experimenters sent smoke billowing under the door. In most cases, the student would rise and go and investigate or call for help. But when several students were in the room together, they tended to ignore the smoke. And it was not just because of embarrassment about creating a fuss in front of strangers should the smoke turn out to be harmless steam. Groups of friends were left in rooms and suddenly subjected to shouts of help from next door. Only in seventy per cent of cases did even one of them intervene.

Studies such as these are important now that it is all too common in cities for people to stand silently and watch when a stranger is attacked. The response seems to have something to do with degree of responsibility. If a person is alone in an emergency he feels all the guilt for not acting; if there is a group, the responsibility is shared, there is no direct finger of blame. Each in the crowd may assume that someone else has or should have called the police. Researchers Bibb Latane and John Darley suggest that people witnessing muggings are distressed but immobilized because they are caught up in debilitating crowd behaviour, or a state of unwilling fascination, indecision and conflict.

Conformism seems to have a more powerful hold on us than we may even realize. If asked whether they prefer a conformist or a non-conformist, people generally say the latter. But their actions show otherwise. When involved in life-situations, people tend to prefer the conformist. One of the reasons we conform is that we make social comparisons that affect our behaviour. We take cues from others about appropriate conduct. We act differently in someone else's house than we ever would at home, because the host is the barometer for conduct. In group decision-making, there is often a considerable group pressure for consensus which prevents effective argument and leads to acceptance of unsuitable lines of action. Others' enthusiasm can be a severe inhibiting factor against dissent from a more dubious party.

One of the most famous and controversial experiments in social psychology concerns obedience. In the 1960s, Stanley Milgram collected a random group of people together on the pretext that they were to take part in a study of learning methods. Each was made a 'teacher' whilst a confederate of the experimenter was the 'learner'. One by one, the teachers were seated behind a panel that had levers which, if pulled, would administer an electric shock, every time the learner gave a wrong answer. The switches were marked 'mild shock' right through to 'dangerously severe shock'. (But, of course, they were a fake.)

Milgram had thought that most people would refuse to give shocks of any real intensity. However, he found that, if people

272

were so instructed by a stranger in authority, they could even give the most severe of shocks. No subject stopped short of 300 volts and 26 out of forty administered the strongest shock, even though the 'learner' was faking groaning and pleading to be released. The 'teachers' went through severe emotional trauma about it all, sweating and trembling as they carried on, but some of them still administered the shocks even after the 'learner', having screamed and pounded on the walls of his cubicle, had long lapsed into ominous silence!

The 'teachers' had been told at the outset that they could excuse themselves from the experiment any time they wanted. But if they did demur, they were gently requested to continue. The experimenters were alarmed at how easily the teachers were persuaded to carry on. The whole study showed conclusively that people of all types and professions can be persuaded to punish or harm others if they believe it is their moral duty to obey. And, when the crunch comes, the tendency to obey, learned in childhood, can outweigh other moral stances that are learned later.

Milgram participated in another of his experiments himself. He suggested that one of his students should go up to a stranger on the subway and ask for his seat – no explanation given. Eventually one student reluctantly volunteered and found that, when he did it, people automatically gave up their seats with no questions asked. But the student didn't finish his assignment – he was meant to ask twenty people – because he found the request one of the most difficult things he'd ever had to do in his life. So Milgram tried.

As he approached a passenger, he suddenly froze and sweated. Eventually he forced himself to speak and experienced extreme panic. But the man got up. 'Taking the man's seat I was overwhelmed by the need to behave in a way that would justify my request. My head sank between my knees and I could feel my face blanching. I was not role-playing. I actually felt as if I were going to perish. As soon as I got off the train all tension disappeared.'

This personal experience revealed to Milgram just how great is the inhibitory anxiety that ordinarily prevents us from breaching social norms.

Sociopath
see **Psychopath**

Spiritual Healing
see **Faith Healing**

Split Brain

A few years ago an experimental treatment for epilepsy, devised by Roger Sperry and associates in California, accidentally opened the way to a whole new exciting field of brain research. In an effort to minimize the effects of epilepsy, they severed the *corpus callosum*, the thick cord that connects the left hemisphere of the brain to the right hemisphere. Those that underwent this operation were called split-brain patients. The epileptics seemed much improved but subtle tests revealed that the operation had separated specialized functions of the two hemispheres.

It has long been known that the left hemisphere controls the right side of the body and vice versa. The team now discovered that if, for instance, a split-brain patient touched a pencil (hidden from sight) with his right hand, he could describe it verbally. If he held it in his left, he couldn't describe it at all. However, if he were shown a selection of objects and asked to pick out with his left hand what he had been holding, he could select the pencil. In another experiment, the word 'heart' was flashed before the patient's eyes in such a way that 'he' appeared to the left eye and 'art' to the right. When asked to name the word, the patient replied 'art', as this was the part that the right eye, controlled by the left hemisphere, saw. But when asked to pick out the word from cards, the left hand (controlled by the right hemisphere) went for 'he'. In normal people, the hemispheres 'communicate' via the corpus callosum.

This was the beginning of the discovery that the left and right hemispheres have totally different specialties. A battery of experiments has shown that the left hemisphere is specially concerned with language, logic and analytical abilities, whilst the right is concerned with creativity, sense of space, musical and visual appreciation.

The left side processes information in sequences and logical patterns; the right integrates a number of inputs all at once. It is holistic and intuitive in orientation, not segmented and linear.

In the West, the left hemisphere has always been called the *major hemisphere* because damage to it causes speech and reasoning problems and we emphasize the importance of such intellectual

274

skills. But damage to the right hemisphere may be much more devastating to the artist or musician.

Professor Robert Ornstein, who has developed the study of hemisphere specialization, believes that now we have evidence that we are not intended to be totally rational, logical beings. The faculty for intuitive thought is clearly there in our brains. We have under-used it in the West, because we place less importance on it. In the East the accent is on holistic thought with a consequent under-use of left brain faculties. Now is the time, says Ornstein, to learn to synthesize the two. He and others have suggested that left and right are an analogue of Freud's conscious and unconscious. It is much easier to drown out the signals from the right side of the brain, because the 'thinking' left is so much in control.

Ornstein suggests that highest achievement is the result of integrating the two modes of consciousness of left and right brain. The brilliant Einstein was not a pure left-brain thinker. He conceived the idea central to his theory of relativity when he was imagining what it would be like to travel on a sunbeam! The artist Picasso had not only superb awareness of space and image but an almost mathematical perception.

We have laid emphasis in the West on skills such as reading, writing and arithmetic and judge intelligence and ability by prowess in those rather than in art or music or dance. But, as Ornstein says, 'evolution has given us half of the highest level of the nervous system devoted to that other mode of thought.'

We have all experienced working on a problem to no avail and then, suddenly, we have a flash of insight, a whole new approach. That, it seems, is the contribution of the right brain, unfettered by sequential and logical, often blind-alley, thought. Because it is holistic, it encompasses more possibilities simultaneously.

Our left hemispheres are in control during the day because we are 'thinking'. But, as we go towards sleep, the right hemisphere comes to the fore. Hence that drowsy between-waking-and-sleep state when we can have vivid fantasies or even hallucinatory images. It is a time when we are more in touch with our unconscious and are open to creative insights. Researcher Thomas Budzynski believes that the 'twilight zone' between waking and sleep is a pipeline to the right, non-rational side of our brain. It is marked by a theta brain rhythm (see **brain waves**), so he and co-experimenters trained subjects to maintain this state without dropping off into sleep. Then they tried to teach them things, from learning Spanish to learning not to over-eat. Effects were startlingly good, leaving the researchers to assume that the twilight state is a suggestible state during which we can assimilate much material.

All sorts of research have proliferated over recent years, concerned with the implications of hemisphere specialization. (Some sceptics say it's a fad that will come to nothing.) But amongst reports so far are claims that men and women have different brain organization. Experiments indicate that women's verbal and spatial centres are duplicated on both sides of the brain, whereas only men's are specialized. This could explain men's better ability to do two completely different activities at once and women's superior ability to integrate verbal and spatial skills into a single task. (See **sex differences**.)

But Professor Ornstein warns against going overboard with the idea that there is a 'language' hemisphere and a 'spatial' hemisphere. Both can process all information; but each is more efficient at its particular sort. And both are vitally inter-related: we need language to express intuition; we need a sense of a whole before we can analyse.

Ornstein has also found that the hemispheres are not specialized to deal with certain kinds of materials but certain types of thought. Lawyers, who are very left-brain oriented, may use left-brain skills to solve spatial puzzles (though not as effectively as people who use the right-brain). People tend to rely on the hemisphere that characterizes their customary mode of thought.

So we do not have split brain but a whole brain that encompasses two possible modes of consciousness. Perhaps by paying more attention to our under-valued right-brain qualities, we can re-train our capacities for synthesis and open ourselves to new knowledge.

Stammering

Stammering, or stuttering, is the interruption of normal speech flow by the involuntary repetition or lengthening of certain sounds. It is more common in boys than girls. Children who are going to stammer usually start before the age of five and sometimes the stutter fades out later, on its own. In other cases, speech therapy is usually successful in correcting it.

There is no clear understanding of the causes, and there is no link between stammering and the child being a thwarted left-hander (as was once thought). Psychoanalysts believe it is an expression of inner tension and conflict and may sometimes be linked with feelings of hostility; if a child feels badly towards a parent, his stammering may be an attempt to suppress such feelings and avoid their verbalization. Even if that is so, the stammer later becomes self-perpetuating. The child fails to communicate without a stutter and then, next time he is about to speak, fears he will do so again. The anxiety itself then makes him stutter.

Staplepuncture

An intriguing off-shoot from **acupuncture**, specially designed for the smoker, drinker or compulsive eater who wants to mend his ways. Staplepuncture is the brainwave of Los Angeles family doctor Lester Sacks who himself studied acupuncture. The system involves inserting a surgical staple in the ear with a special 'gun', close to the relevant acupuncture point. To stop the craving for a cigarette, a drink or a piece of bread, the staple just needs to twiddled about a bit.

Dr Sacks claims to have reduced the cigarette consumption of his patients from forty to four a day in sixty per cent of cases whilst others have given up altogether. Thirty per cent of alcoholics treated hadn't touched a drink when Sacks did a follow-up six months later and forty per cent had cut their drinking by half. He even claims a hundred drug addicts, out of two hundred treated, ceased to be dependent on drugs without suffering withdrawal symptoms. As an explanation for the failures, however, Dr Sacks says that personal motivation to succeed is absolutely essential for success.

Stereotype
see **Sex Differences**

Stress

Stress has been cited as the number one killer of the seventies. Many afflictions such as coronary thrombosis, ulcers, asthma, backache, migraine, skin problems and cancer can be **psychosomatic**, meaning that they have emotional stress as their real root. Coronary thrombosis and cancer are the killers.

The stress component of physical illnesses was first taken

seriously in the late nineteen fifties, after an experiment with monkeys. Two monkeys were given repeated electric shocks; one could do nothing about it, the other was placed near a lever which he could press each time to prevent them both getting the shock. The monkey with the responsibility developed stomach ulcers! Ulcers occur because of over-production of gastric juices, and stress can make the juices overwork. The experiment with the monkeys found that unpredictable stress (when would the next shock happen?) takes higher toll than predictable stress. Ulcers are merely one manifestation.

The link between responsibility and stress has led us to dub this special variety as executive stress, brought about by the angst of decision-making. But a recent survey by the National Institute of Occupational Safety and Health in America indicates that the most stressful jobs are those of inspectors, warehouse workers, public-relations workers, laboratory technicians, machinists, labourers, watchmen, mechanics and metal craftsmen. The tentative explanation is that jobs are particularly stressful when work objectives are unclear, when workers are torn by conflicting demands, have too little or too much to do, have little control over decisions that affect them or are responsible for other people's professional development.

But not everyone believes that stress is necessarily an evil. Research shows that it is the way we meet stress that is important. After all, not only intense strain causes stress; pleasant occasions such as going to a wedding can bring it too. Being required to adapt to personal, social and environmental influences, whether they are positive or negative, brings stress.

A recent American study looked at 161 executives who had undergone similar levels of work stress but only about half of whom had suffered illness as a result. Those that fell sick were found to have negative attitudes towards their work and tried to reduce stress by avoiding disliked activities, which in turn made them feel inadequate, angry or depressed. The healthy group had a positive self-image, were committed to their work and were adaptable to change. The researchers concluded that a positive attitude towards self and change is a key factor in dealing with stress without illness.

So one possible key to stress control seems to correspond with the goals of many humanistic therapies; to accept life the way it is, take responsibility for one's own actions, accept others as they are instead of trying to mould them into some more

278

personally pleasing image and live in the here and now instead of fantasies of the past or illusions of the future.

Real stress control is therefore more fundamental than just learning to relax at odd moments during the day, although **relaxation** techniques are important for helping us to tone down habitual hyper-responses and learning to be at ease with ourselves.

Sublimation

Sublimation is Freud's idea of a healthy way to deal with inevitable sexual conflicts. The driving sexual force, the **libido**, changes its focus from oral to anal, phallic and then genital activity, as a child grows up (see **psychosexual stages**). However, some of the libido remains fixated at the oral or anal stage, so that the individual still derives satisfaction from activities that are linked with those periods. This desire can either express itself directly (in seeking gratification of the need or in hotly opposing the need to gratify the need), or else it can be channelled into some related activity that is more socially acceptable. Freud believed, for instance, that a fixation at the anal stage might become sublimated as a love of handling money or manipulating clay.

Subnormality
see **Mental Handicap**

Sufism

Sufism can best be described by using the words of Idries Shah, its leading exponent in the West: 'Sufis claim that a certain kind of mental and other activity can produce, under special conditions and with particular effects, what is termed a higher working of the mind, leading to special perceptions whose apparatus is latent in the ordinary man. Sufism is therefore the transcending of ordinary limitations.' (*The Way Of The Sufi*, Jonathan Cape.) It is not a body of thought or a required belief system, it is an experience which has to be provoked.

Sufism is often described as a Middle East tradition, at the core of Islam. But it is not religion or culture-bound and countless people in the West are familiar with some aspects of Sufi thinking through the many books of teaching stories published by Idries Shah. These stories operate on many levels, most using humour and shock value to open the mind to a less rigid pattern of thinking.

However, Sufi development is experiential and requires a teacher who is attuned to a student's needs and particular stage of development. It cannot be 'learnt' from books alone, although they provide an important flavour and preparation for participation in authentic Sufi study. Humour and shock approaches, too, are only part of Sufi activity. It is a blend of these and other procedures which produce the Sufi school.

Sufism works through many media, not only religion, and much of its thinking has found its way into Western ideas as diverse as psychology, anthropology and physics. It does not work through empty ritual, unlike many so-called methods of enlightenment which depend upon austerities, exercises and literature appropriate only for a different time and place.

Sufism is very much grounded in the practicalities of life and there is no question of donning Eastern robes, retiring to hill tops. There are no gurus, no converts, no prizes, although of course there are imitation cults who use the same name. Its written material provides a basis for the examination and change of automatized thinking and is available for all who are capable of drawing from it.

In the language of current Western psychology, Sufism emphasizes intuitive rather than sequential thinking. This concept is becoming more familiar to us, with the recent discoveries that the left hemisphere of the brain (dominant in the West) controls logical, analytical thought, while the right is concerned with intuitive, creative, holistic thought. Sufism, in effect, taps right-brain thought, where appropriate (see also **split brain**).

Suicide

Suicide is one of the ten major causes of death; over 35,000 Americans kill themselves each year, over four people in every thousand kill themselves in London alone. American research has shown that more than twice as many men commit suicide as women (although more women attempt it), the rate is highest amongst divorced and single people, and suicide is more common over the age of forty five. Professionals resort to it more often than non-professionals, with doctors attempting it most often of all. The rate for female doctors and psychologists is three times that of the rest of the female population. Within the medical profession, more psychiatrists kill themselves than any other specialists.

Misery, loneliness, sense of helplessness and hopelessness are the commonest causes of suicide. Sometimes a sudden severe bout of **depression** can cause someone's thoughts to turn to suicide when, normally, he would have never contemplated such an act. For this reason deep depression should never be treated lightly or dismissed as a passing phase. The existence in recent years of telephone crisis services has helped to defuse, if only temporarily, the despair of being alone. But alas, overall, suicide figures are rising and there is also a marked increase in attempts made by children. More crisis intervention services are vital to deal with the alienation that is perhaps the worst by-product of our technological age.

Between 60 per cent and 80 per cent of the people who kill themselves give definite warnings of their intention prior to the act. Many suicide attempts are desperate cries for help, and do not necessarily indicate a genuine wish to die. This drastic method of bringing attention to themselves is often used by people unable to ask for help openly. They will usually make every attempt to make sure they are discovered before it is too late. But many will kill themselves in the end.

Suicide fantasies are not uncommon to a lot of people. They are indulgent fantasies of revenge – (how will they feel then!) – and as such are simply a symptom of a superficial emotional upset.

Sun Myung Moon
see **Cults**

Superego
see **Freud**

Szasz, Thomas
see **Anti-Psychiatry**

T

Tanking
see **Sensory Isolation**

Tao

Tao was one of the two mainstreams of Chinese thought (the other being Confucianism) that developed during the sixth century BC. Chinese philosophy in general differs in its approach from Western philosophy because it accents intuition rather than logic and it is concerned with the continuity of things: man and the universe are one. (See **yin/yang**.) Whereas Confucius was a humanist, whose ideal was an orderly civilized society achieved through the discipline of ceremony, Lao Tzu, the founder of Tao, believed that man's ills had occurred because he had tried to create an artificial civilization. His salvation was therefore to retreat from culture into nature.

Tao (the way) is the first principle of the universe. As man is part of the universe, his natural way is to go with it, flow with it, not to try and be separate from it and impose his own order on things. Man is part of Tao, whether he recognizes it or not. So Lao Tzu's doctrine is *wu wei* (doing nothing) expressed in the paradox: Tao invariably does nothing and yet there is nothing that is not done.

In other words, there is nothing to be achieved by striving. The way to 'be' is to go with the grain, to swim with the tide. (This idea is at the heart of aikido (see **martial arts**) where an opponent is off-balanced by the force of his own attack.) Doing nothing brings an understanding of the way of nature. Little energy need be expended, for energy is only required for going against something, not with it.

Because Tao is all of nature, it cannot really be reduced to words. ('The Tao that can be expressed in words is not the eternal Tao'.) It cannot be seen or heard but it is all-pervasive and inexhaustible. There is no divine force, only Tao.

The totality of all things is Tao. The totality, the essence, of each individual thing is called *Te. Li* is its expression in organic form – the natural asymmetrical patterns of trees, frost crystals,

282

waterfalls, etc. But man tries to impose his own laws of nature, his rigid geometry and social systems, thereby disrupting the spontaneous flow of all things. So Lao Tzu was against government and rules and believed that, if men stopped striving and went with the flow, harmony would naturally ensue.

Going back to nature is hardly practical now. But modern day exponents say Taoist attitudes still have a clear place even in a technological society. Technology is only destructive, they say, in the hands of people who try to impose their own will on the universe. Taoists do not strive to achieve. They just do whatever comes naturally and accept that whatever happens happens because it is meant to happen. Because there is a natural harmony in things, the result is order not chaos.

Tarot

Our own modern pack of playing cards is thought to have derived from the Tarot cards, an esoteric set of cards whose origins are uncertain. The Tarot, a pack made up of 78 cards instead of 52, is most commonly thought to have its origins in playing cards developed in China or Korea in the eleventh century. Another theory cites India as the source, others try to connect the Tarot with the Jewish Qabalah, or claim that the name is a corruption of Thoth, the ancient Egyptian god of magic, thereby placing its origins in the Middle East.

Many scholars claim that the Tarot cards were originally a means of disseminating secret knowledge, the key to which was held by only a handful of mystics. But the pack as it stands today, with its 22 trumps and four suits of 14 cards is more likely to be 'a conglomeration from a variety of sources, not a single compilation of ancient symbolism', according to British Tarot scholar Brian Innes.

The 22 trumps are called the Major Arcana and are all picture cards with symbolic meanings, representing the stages of life. The Fool symbolizes the innocent newborn child, the Magician symbolizes dawning self-awareness, the Lovers represent the stage in life when one leaves one's family for a mate. The Hanged Man represents the sacrifice of lower values for higher consciousness, the Death card signifies transformation, Judgement indicates the birth of the integrated self and so on.

The four suits, cups, batons, swords and discs (some historians say these suits represent the Holy Grail) also have symbolic meanings but are less significant than the major arcana. For example, the two of cups means success and good fortune; the nine of batons represents quarrels with friends and the three of swords signifies a journey.

There are many ways to read the Tarot but each depends upon intuitive skill, for readings demand interpretations. Some scholars say it is possible to make up one's own system, dealing a few cards into piles that one chooses to designate 'present predicament' or 'future possibilities' or anything that refers to a problem one wishes to resolve, and then studying the cards. Say, for instance, a woman wants to know whether she should give up her career as a singer in order to have children. If she turns up the Papess, a card that signifies creative talent, she may interpret this to mean it is the wrong time to give up her work.

The most common set systems are the Nine Card Spread, the Circular Spread and the Horseshoe Spread. The Nine Card Spread relates to past, present and future and each card has a significant meaning. The first card dealt, for instance, indicates whatever factor is most important in the inquirer's life at present; the third card reveals subconscious factors that are affecting his affairs; cards six to nine reveal the enquirer's probable actions in the near future.

Testosterone
see Hormones

T-Groups

T-Groups were the spark which ignited the whole personal **growth movement** that originated in the fifties, swept America in the sixties, and finally took hold in Britain and other countries too.

T-Groups were the brain child of American psychologist Kurt Lewin. He was worried by managers and employers' lack of training in dealing with people and so in the late 1940s, devised a method of teaching people about communication. Although T-Groups were considered a training and employers sent executives to participate in them, they were really more of an experience in relating to and understanding other people. In the groups the watchword was honesty and individuals were encouraged to open up about their feelings towards each other. The executives, it was hoped, went back to work with a heightened awareness of the way they and others ticked and the resultant confidence to take a democratic rather than an authoritarian approach to staff relations.

The results were satisfactory enough for an institution called National Training Laboratories to be set up. But during the 1950s, the accent moved from training individuals to relate to others at work to helping individuals to discover their own personal potential. As a result, encounter groups were born, although T-Groups, suitably refined and altered to fit the times, are still in existence.

Telepathy

Telepathy is the mental transmission of ideas from one person to another. It is one of four forms of extra-sensory perception (see ESP), and is the easiest to arrange laboratory tests for.

In Russia, just over a decade ago, an extremely impressive experiment took place. In Siberia a journalist called Nikolaiev went into a state of deep relaxation, watched by scientists, while in Moscow, nearly 2000 miles away, a biophysicist, Yuri Kamensky, did likewise. Then Kamensky was given six sealed envelopes, one at a time. He opened each, stared at the object inside and imagined the face of Nikolaiev as if he were behind him, peering over his shoulder at the object too. At this moment, Nikolaiev, in Siberia, was reported to feel something like a shock and then to see an object – the very same – as if it were real. All six objects were correctly 'transmitted'.

Later experiments, during which Nikolaiev was linked up to an electroencephalograph machine, showed that changes occurred in his brainwave activity at the exact moment that Kamensky concentrated on transmitting information to him.

An Astronaut, Edgar Mitchell, made an ESP experiment during the spaceflight of Apollo 14 in 1971. He had been interested in parapsychology for some years and so he arranged for four people to act as receivers on earth while he attempted to transmit the symbols on cards that he looked at on board the spacecraft. Despite a few technical hitches, the hit rate was significantly higher than chance.

Research into dream telepathy at the Dream Laboratory at Maimonides Medical Centre, in New York, seems to show that certain people can even influence the images occurring in the dreams of someone else thousands of miles away. Changes in the dreamer's brain wave activity at the time of transmission have again been monitored by EEG equipment.

Scientists are still struggling to find out how telepathy actually works.

Parapsychologists are cautious about pronouncing explanations but, as Leonid Vasilev, Chairman of Physiology at the University of Leningrad, said in 1960: 'The discovery of the energy underlying ESP will be equivalent to the discovery of atomic energy' (see **ESP**).

Therapeutic Community

The idea of the therapeutic community evolved as a reaction against the debilitating effects of institutionalization in mental hospitals (see **milieu therapy**). An environment in which a patient is not required to do anything for himself, receives no reinforcement for initiative (because no initiative is ever required) and earns praise only if he is quiet and untroublesome to the staff, in no way helps people readjust, after mental breakdowns, to life outside. Even skills which patients possessed before they came into hospital tend to be eroded once they have settled into institutional inertia.

The therapeutic community, which might be just one ward in a hospital or else a whole institution, requires the patient to take responsibility for his own life and participate in his own recovery. Staff and patients are on first name terms, to blur the distinction between helpers and helped. Patients are made responsible for the running of the place, by participation in patient committees or holding office on them, deciding the 'rules' of the establishment and taking turns in a work rota. Rules devised by patients might be that there should be a group meeting twice a week and all residents must attend; or that every person must belong to at least one workgroup or study group. Residents who break the rules have to explain themselves to the group.

In the therapeutic communities, there is great emphasis on freedom of movement and freedom of expression, either in art/music/writing/science workshops or on a more individual basis – such as painting, decorating and furnishing one's own room or sleep area. Critics question the possibly crippling effects of intense group pressure and the fact that expressiveness per se is encouraged. This could mean that a person is as emotionally rewarded for destruction or hostile behaviour as for creative and sensitive acts. Supporters of the system claim that senseless acts of destruction soon cease to have any value as an attention-getter, because no one makes a fuss about them.

Theta Waves
see **Brainwaves**

Thought

Thinking is the mental organization of ideas and concepts. Much thinking is directed towards problem-solving of one kind or another; working out plans and schedules, organizing activities, devising strategies. But we also indulge in a looser form of thought in our **fantasies** and daydreams.

Ideas and concepts arise from learning and experiences. But how do they actually get into our heads and how do we actually work with them once they are there? It is an unanswered question although countless psychologists spend their time investigating the actual processes we go through to put ideas together or to advance to the understanding of a problem. Some observe subjects solving puzzles, others use computers to simulate and analyse thinking techniques.

The psychologist Jean Piaget proposed a systematic theory of intellectual development which encompasses stages of thought (see **developmental psychology**). Others have wondered about the link between language and thought: does our knowing a word for a concept affect our ability to think about that concept? In other words, do we only think about or notice things we have language to express? (See **language**.) It seems unlikely, however, or we would never advance to new understanding in any area of science.

Other psychologists have concentrated on particular aspects of thought: how we group certain concepts in order to think about them; or the part that insight plays in thinking. Insight is that flash of understanding that seems to come on us from nowhere. It can play an important part in problem-solving. Some modern researchers think it emanates from the right hemisphere of the brain, the side that is concerned with intuition not logic (see **split brain**).

Although we tend to think in logical, sequential patterns, it isn't the only nor necessarily the most effective way. By channelling our minds in this way, we cut ourselves off from other seemingly indirect but often faster routes to solutions (see **lateral thinking**). A problem may have many solutions, not one, and the task is to be open to see them all and choose the best.

'Set' also affects our thinking. (See **mental set**.) We have certain expectations or fixed ideas which prevent us from being open to all possible information. Someone who is asked to cut into a small piece of paper a hole large enough to put his head through will never achieve it if he sticks with the idea that he must cut a simple circle.

Token Economy
see **Conditioning**

Tranquillizers
see **Psychotropic Drugs**

Transactional Analysis

Transactional analysis (TA) is the invention of American psychoanalyst Eric Berne who shot to fame with his book *Games People Play*. The nub of TA is that people interact with each other on three levels which Berne called the Child, the Parent and the Adult. The Child manifests itself in behaviour that's acceptable and expected in young children – desire for immediate gratification, resentment and moodiness if it's not forthcoming, and inability to accept responsibility. The Parent is the part of us that is entrenched with beliefs, attitude and values conferred on us by our own parents and accepted automatically. The Adult is the self-activating part of our personality, the mature part that considers each situation for itself and determines how to act appropriately.

This may seem like a layman's version of **Freud's** time-honoured id, super-ego and ego. But Freud's trinity all fight for existence at the same time, whereas Berne's are behaviour patterns that can be consciously controlled and switched in and out of at will. So a man may be the effective businessman by day, making astute decisions about his financial affairs and keeping his work-force highly motivated and satisfied (the Adult). He comes home and whimpers to his wife about his hard day as she takes off his boots and massages his ankles (the Child). Then he goes to a meeting of his local political group and holds forth about the need to impose severe penalties on kids who vandalize the telephone kiosks (the Parent).

There is nothing wrong, says Berne, with slipping from one personality part to another. But problems arise when one person in a relationship is entrenched in a particular behaviour pattern. Here the 'games' come in: Berne suggests, as common ones, 'If it weren't for you' and 'Now look what you've made me do', both child tactics for laying the responsibility for one's own actions, or lack of them, on someone else. If the person who is responding to these tactics plays the Adult, the partner may find he or she has to switch from Child to Adult too, as it is difficult to keep whining and pouting in the face of someone who is being reasonable and mature. But if the latter is stuck in Child and it has become an almost permanent behaviour pattern, conflict ensues and the other person may have to retreat to Parent.

Transactional analysis as a group therapy helps people to recognize their own chronic patterns as well as other people's. Once they have identified their behaviour traits, there is a framework from within which they can analyse and change. Unlike psychoanalysis, the individual can choose whether he wishes to root back into his deep past or just settle for dealing with the behaviour patterns of the here and now.

Transactional analysis has caught on in industry and personnel management. Airline staff, for instance, may be taught its techniques so that next time they are the butt for abuse from a passenger whose luggage is mislaid, they can identify the passenger's reactions as Child and make sure they themselves defuse the situation by responding calmly and reasonably, as an Adult.

Transcendental Meditation

Meditation has long been part of esoteric systems of the East (see **meditation**). But whereas it is there a part of a whole teaching, involving specific conditions and specific goals, transcendental meditation (TM) is an extraction specially devised for the West and to fit Western needs by the Maharishi Mahesh Yogi. It requires no special life-style, just fifteen minutes quiet meditation on a mantra (a special word given to the meditator by the TM instructor) twice a day.

The mantra is a mellifluous, smooth sound that has no meaning for the meditator, although it is supposed to have some special intrinsic powers. The meditator is told to think of his mantra in an effortless, relaxed way and, during the process, background noises start to fade from attention, leaving the individual conscious and alert, but relaxed and focused on inward sensations. Examination of the brain waves of TM meditators shows that the activity leads to the generation of alpha waves, associated with supreme calm and relaxation (see **brain waves**). Heart rate, respiration rate, oxygen consumption and skin tension all reduce, without any conscious effort. Practitioners claim they also enjoy improved memories, better co-ordination, quicker reaction times and a sense of self-fulfilment.

All these benefits attracted the attention of the medical and psychological professions in recent years. Because it is such a simple technique, cardiologist Herbert Benson recommended TM as an antidote to stress and stress-related disease, although his initial euphoria has now decreased and he suggests that any simple relaxation method will do. TM enthusiasts, however, still insist that TM methods have specially effective powers for relaxation, although this is not borne out by research. English psychologist Dr Michael West found that the effects were the same, relaxation-wise, whether people were given a real mantra to meditate by or just a word with no esoteric significance at all. It has been suggested that it is the introduction of a dominant frequency (i.e., a constantly repeated word) which works to dampen limbic activity in the brain (which is associated with emotions) so that there is a resultant quietening of that part of the brain. This would bear out the finding that one word is as good as another.

In some ways, TM is less effective as a meditation technique than others. A group of Harvard researchers monitored the brain activity of a group of TM meditators and a group who had been trained in more traditional Eastern techniques over a similar period of time. They asked the subjects to concentrate first on the sensations in their right hand and then on a certain picture. They discovered that the traditionally-trained group could use just the part of the brain required for the activity (i.e., either the motor or the visual centres) leaving the rest quiet. (Maximum effect with minimum effort is the way the brain works when we are at our most efficient.) The TM meditators had not developed this ability.

Although TM can be used just as an isolated activity to help one relax, it is also part of a more esoteric system open to those who choose to study further. TM's claims that practitioners can be taught to 'fly', become invisible and levitate have brought it a bad press in recent times, losing it the support of more orthodox adherents. And American psychologist Leon Otis recently reported that a number of long-term devotees suffered anxiety, headaches, and stomach upsets as a result of TM. He admits these symptoms were found only in a minority but a substantial enough minority to warrant taking the effects seriously.

Transexual

People who have all the physical trappings of one sex – the right hormones, chromosomes and external sex organs – but who *feel* convinced that really they belong to the other sex are called transexuals. Their sexual identity is clearly male (or female) but their own gender identity is female (or male). Whereas sexual identity is incontrovertible, gender identity is a highly personal experience, a feeling of maleness or femaleness.

This incompatibility of sex with gender may develop as a result of having been treated as a child of the opposite sex, which may occur if the parents desperately wanted their boy to be a girl or vice versa. But this isn't always the cause and some transexuals say they 'knew' they were in the wrong body from a very early age.

At one time it was common to try and 'treat' the condition but it has been found remarkably resistant to all approaches, from hypnosis and psychotherapy through to drug treatment. Now, if a person is sure that he or she really wants to live as a member of the opposite sex, and counselling shows that the desire is genuine and long-term, sex change operations are possible. Males are given hormones to stimulate breast growth, soften the skin and reduce body hair; by surgery they can have their male genitals removed and a kind of vagina provided instead, using the skin of the penis. Vocal cords can even be shortened to raise the pitch of the voice.

Females are given male hormones which increase body hair, muscle strength, etc. and terminate menstruation but, although skin can again be used to simulate a penis, it will never look very normal and, as it cannot function, the clitoris is usually left intact. But often transexuals are not particularly interested in sexual activity.

Sex change operations can have a damaging psychological effect, as they are such an assault on the body. So some transexuals prefer to 'live' as a member of the opposite sex without resorting to physical change. Transexualism is more a state of mind than the result of an operation.

Transexualism is completely different from **transvestism**. It involves an extremely deep and total sense of belonging to the wrong sex, rather than the enjoyment of play-acting the other sex.

Transference

Transference is the key to psychoanalysis. It occurs when the patient directs emotions which he really feels towards another person (usually a parent) on to the analyst. Freud believed that patients reacted to opposite-sex therapists just as they had reacted to opposite-sex parents (with seductive behaviour) and that they felt competition and rivalry with same-sex therapists, which mirrored their feelings about same-sex parents.

This transference of emotions was so common in Freud's own therapy sessions that he came to believe it to be a vital experience: all patients must repeat their early relationships with their parents until they are resolved. The lucky ones go through this process in therapy, where the analyst at least understands what is going on. Others inflict it upon their current acquaintances and intimates, who might well not understand the hostility or over-abundance of affection coming at them.

Transference is seen as such a pivot of psychoanalysis because it is only after it has been expressed that deep-seated problems can be interpreted and resolved. A man, for instance, may vie with his therapist, always claiming to know better, always wanting to do things his own way. When he comes to realize that he is acting out his early feelings of competition with his father, who constantly tried to put him down, he is on the way to resolving his present-day obsession with being one up on everyone else. Whilst Freud believed that it was only the early relationships with parents that need to be transferred, later analysts broadened the concept of transference to cover emotions felt towards other people as well.

Freud was so sure that transference was the key to the unconscious that he went to great lengths to encourage its expression. He kept his consulting room bare of anything personal, so that patients could have no idea of his likes and dislikes as an individual, refused to see patients outside of their sessions and himself sat out of view during them. In this way, he reasoned, any emotion expressed towards him couldn't have been generated by his own behaviour and had to be the projection on to him of feelings about someone else.

The creation of this artificial distance between therapist and patients also served another purpose. It prevented the analyst from becoming too involved – a phenomenon which Freud called *counter-transference*, in which the therapist's responses to the patient were the product of his own emotions and conflicts instead of a detached professionalism.

Transpersonal Psychology

Transpersonal psychology is often called the 'fourth force'. Although a rather bizarre name, it actually refers to its position as the newest development in psychological schools of thought. The first three 'forces' are **behaviourism, psychoanalysis** and **humanistic psychology**.

Abraham Maslow, one of the prime movers behind the humanistic approach which concentrates on people's need to strip off their conditioning and experience real feelings, was also the instigator of the fourth force. His theory of **self-actualization** led him to believe that people could be helped to experience their higher, creative selves and he discovered that a number of people, when freed in this way, transcended ordinary reality and experienced **mystical** states. Maslow and others similarly interested proceeded to found an association of transpersonal psychology concerned with cosmic awareness, essence and the pervading life energy at the core of being.

Transpersonal psychologists, whilst not declaring that their approach is the only approach to understanding man, are particularly interested in altered states of awareness that occur in **dreams**, during **meditation**, under drugs and in mystical experiences. They are also therefore concerned with **extra-sensory perception**.

Although transpersonal psychology, per se, has only recently emerged, its roots are in the ideas of Roberto Assagioli (see **psychosynthesis**), a contemporary of **Freud** but whose special interest was in higher consciousness, and in the work of **Jung**, who accented the collective unconscious.

Transvestite

Transvestites, most of whom are men, get sexually excited by dressing up in women's clothes. Unlike **transexuals**, they do not feel that they in fact belong to the other sex; they just enjoy being able to dress up and find it helps them relieve sexual tension.

Very many are heterosexual, married men with children. Their sex lives are on the whole conventional, but there are groups to help the wives of transvestites adapt to their husbands' strange dressing desires.

Transvestite behaviour takes many forms. Some actually derive emotional comfort from identifying with particular women during the periods that they are dressed up and may even take on feminine names for themselves. Others get a more fetishist pleasure out of the trappings of femininity, enjoying the feel of chiffon and black stockings and suspenders and the wearing of wigs and false eyelashes.

The causes of transvestism are not really known. Some believe hormone anomalies may be to blame, others credit the psychodynamic theories of a disturbed mother–child relationship, whilst behaviourists believe that dressing up as children probably brought welcome attention and reinforcement of the habit.

The ramifications of it all can get quite complex. A transexual prostitute (a man who lived as a woman and who offered a dressing up service to transvestites) once told me that he couldn't bear it if his male clients wanted sex after dressing up – because that smacked of lesbianism!

Trauma

A trauma is some painful or frightening experience which, however short-lived, has long-term ramifications. (Arthur Janov, pioneer of **primal therapy**, would say that birth trauma is a perfect example as its effects, if unresolved, last all of life.) Traumas which might lead to consequent **neurosis** include terrifying car accidents or being bitten by a wild dog. The alarm or pain caused leads to deep fear of its being re-experienced on some other occasion.

U

Unconscious
see **Freud**

V

Vaginismus
see **Sex Disorders**

Voodoo

The word voodoo popularly conjures up images of sinister black magic rites and superstition. But those who have attended and participated in voodoo ceremonies claim that it is not necessarily sinister or frightening at all.

Voodoo is the native religion of Haiti but it has spread to other parts of the West Indies and even to some Southern states in America. It is a complex belief system involving a large number of *loa*, gods and goddesses who are, for the most part, benevolent deities, willing to guide and help people if approached in the right way. If not, they can be extremely jealous and destructive, even against the priests who serve them.

Voodoo rituals involve the participants in calling down the gods, or loa, and being possessed by them. There is a strong emphasis, during the ceremonies, on drum beating and frenzied dancing, the effects of which, combined, are ecstacy and collapse of the participants. (See also **brainwashing**.)

Westerners have described the power of the ceremonies and some even claim to have been possessed themselves. It is common, they say, to feel both your feet stick to the ground while the loa possesses you. Once possessed, an individual acts as the loa acted in life (for loa are departed spirits) and, in fact, behaves perfectly rationally for the few hours that possession lasts – unless the loa is in a bad mood and the priest has to ask it to modify its behaviour!

British psychiatrist Dr William Sargant, who has attended several voodoo ceremonies, believes that voodoo gives hope and will to people who often live in the most abject and soul-destroying poverty. By becoming one with the gods, as they believe they do during the ceremonies, they are able to forget their earthly troubles and regain a sense of dignity and purpose.

Voyeurism

A voyeur is someone who gets sexual pleasure from watching the sexual activities of other people. The enjoyment that men derive from watching strip shows or sexually explicit films is essentially voyeuristic, as is the youthful practice of hiding in lovers' lanes.

But whereas we probably all have a little of the voyeuristic in us (enjoying looking at our partners' bodies for instance), the voyeur is someone whose main sexual gratification takes the form

of watching others having sex or engaged in some sexually arous-
ing activity. Usually voyeurs are men and most chronic are the
'peeping toms' who actually lurk outdoors, peering in people's
windows to get a glimpse of some sexual activity or of a female
undressing. The excitement induced by the possibility of being
caught helps to bring the voyeur to orgasm.

The voyeur is usually frightened of women, particularly of
rejection by them, and the voyeuristic fantasies tend to date back
to childhood, to childish imaginings of his own parents making
love. **Behaviour therapy** and **assertiveness training** can help such an
individual overcome his fears and learn to relate to women.

Voyeurism is not restricted to men. An American woman once
brought a case against a male neighbour, complaining that he was
creating a public nuisance by lying on his bed with his erect penis
exposed. The man admitted that he did this but denied creating a
public nuisance. For the woman had to stand on a piece of
furniture and train binoculars on him to see!

W

White Noise

White noise is a sound composed of all audible frequencies at the
same intensity, so that no one element of the sound stands out
from the rest. The sound of a waterfall or waves lapping against
the shore approximates to white noise in nature but in a laboratory
it is produced by a special generator. White noise is used in some
ESP experiments where the aim is to cut out, as far as possible,
all ordinary sensory perception so that the subject can concentrate
on senses that come from within. It is an aid to relaxation as there
is no change in the intensity of the sound that will attract the
attention.

Witchcraft
See Occult

Word Salad

A particular disturbance in thinking, associated mainly with schizophrenia, where sentences come out with all the words jumbled up, or else completely disconnected and without meaning. Sometimes the sentence may even be interspersed with words from other languages. To the person saying them, the words make perfect sense.

Workaholic

A workaholic is someone who is addicted to work. He may say he'd love to take a break but that he has to work because there is just so much to do. He can't bear leaving anything unfinished and then he has to start something new. The work-work-work-syndrome has little to do with the actual work there is to do. For, when the individual hasn't got work, he becomes agitated and anxious. He needs the work more than the work needs him. If actively prevented from working, he will probably concoct some scheme or project to do at home, just so that he can carry on keeping busy. The work syndrome is a defence-mechanism against some underlying anxiety. (See **addiction**.)

Y

Yin/Yang

In Chinese **Taoist** philosophy, yin and yang are the two elements that make up life energy. Yin is the female aspect and yang the male; both must be in balance if an individual is to be healthy and happy. Yin is associated with the moon, darkness, winter and autumn; yang with the sun, light, summer and spring. Yin is receptive and yielding; yang is aggressive and creative.

Yin and yang convey the idea that opposites are mutually supportive. For solids to exist, there must be spaces; for there to be death, there must be life.

Yin and yang are therefore not two separate forces, but two expressions of the same force. Together they are the life energy, *ch'i*. In Taoist thinking, man is one with the universe, so the elements of yin and yang are inextricably involved in all aspects of the personality (see also **I Ching**). As any blockage of the life energy causes illness, the healing art of **acupuncture** is concerned with unblocking the relevant energy pathways.

Yoga

Yoga is a Sanskrit word meaning the way in which the individual spirit merges with the universal spirit or, more simply, oneness with God. As an eastern esoteric system it involves the use of certain exercises, meditative techniques and breathing methods that enable the practitioner to screen out everyday awareness and concentrate on his inner senses. He becomes aware that his life energy is one with the energy of the universe (see also **consciousness**).

In the West it is popular, modified as a method to induce calm and maintain a fine balance of body functioning. Central to Yoga is correct breathing. Students are taught to swell out the diaphragm when breathing in and to suck it in when expelling air. (Westerners, taught to thrust their chests out and pull their stomachs in, usually do the reverse when breathing, with the result that their respiration is very shallow.) Correct breathing catalyses the whole energy system and the regulated movement, say Yoga teachers, helps the blood flow properly and keeps the muscles in tone. Poor respiration blocks energy flow and makes us feel weak and listless.

The accompanying physical movements of Yoga are called *asanas* (postures). Some are sitting positions (such as the lotus), others involve the whole body in movements that stimulate correct working of the body's organs. Shoulder stands, for instance, take the pressure off the heart, veins and arteries but stimulate activity of other organs, such as the kidneys. Movements are slow and meticulous and breathing is carefully controlled.

Practitioners claim mental and physical benefits. Few in the West, however, attain the degree of achievement of practised Yogis in the East. Yoga is so much their life that, in its induced calm and heightened awareness, they can consciously alter blood flow, digestive activity and heart rate, etc. **Biofeedback** techniques have now brought these amazing abilities within Westerners' range and the implications for health and control of illness are immense.

Z

Zen

Buddhism, brought from India to China in the seventh century, merged with Chinese **Taoist** thought to become Ch'an. Ch'an was introduced to Japan in the thirteenth century where it became known as Zen. The Zen student's goal is to realize that he is one with the universe. He can become a Buddha (an enlightened man) by seeing his own Buddha-nature: i.e. he recognizes that he always has been Buddha, because everything is one. The discovery comes through passive awareness, as in meditation, not through attempts to control or change things.

The thinking is that if we abandon all ideas of truth, we are truly open to receive truth, to experience each moment as now. Normally our minds are conditioned by our past experiences, so we are not really in the 'now' at all. Whereas, if we can weaken the hold of our egos, we can experience fully everything that happens to us at each moment in time, every thought, emotion and image as it occurs instead of as we interpret it by using experience and knowledge.

The way to do this is to do nothing. The ideal is a tranquil, open mind but it cannot be achieved if we strive for a tranquil mind. For that means doing something. Instead, the need is to experience the restlessness of one's own mind, as if a watcher, until restlessness gives way to tranquillity. The fully integrated personality belongs to a man who is no longer conscious of having a personality; he can only be free when he realizes he is already free. Thus we have the Zen paradox.

As there is nothing to do, there is nothing to teach. Zen masters are only concerned with making students aware of the obstacles they have placed in their own path. They work through the principle of no-work, another seeming paradox. The famous *Koans*, subtle Zen questions with inscrutable answers, only serve to emphasize that nothing is soluble by reason. So: 'What is the sound of one hand clapping?' asks the student. 'Listen', answers the master.

Zen tales abound of the student eager for higher truth being relegated to cleaning out the kitchens. By this, the master is showing that, as all is one, spiritual life is not separate from everyday life. Enlightenment, or realization of oneness, can come through doing ordinary, down-to-earth tasks.

Zen is concerned with concrete things, not abstracts. Nor is anything 'holy', as we learn from the monk left stranded outdoors with nothing to keep himself warm except a wooden statue of Buddha – which he burns. For that is the purpose it can best serve at that moment.

The benefits of non-attachment and living for the moment that result from ceasing to 'strive' are perhaps best expressed in this verse, from Professor R. H. Blyth's *Zen in English Literature and Oriental Classics:*

> He who bends to himself a joy
> Doth the winged life destroy,
> But he who kisses the joy as it flies
> Lives in eternity's sunrise.